Bounded Bureaucracy and the Budgetary Process in the UNITED STATES

Bounded Bureaucracy and the Budgetary Process in the UNITED STATES

JAY EUNGHA RYU

Routledge
Taylor & Francis Group
LONDON AND NEW YORK

First published 2011 by Transaction Publishers

2 Park Square, Milton Park, Abingdon, Oxfordshire OX14 4RN
711 Third Avenue, New York, NY 10017

Routledge is an imprint of the Taylor & Francis Group, an informa business

First issued in paperback 2017

Library of Congress Catalog Number: 2011008560

Library of Congress Cataloging-in-Publication Data
Ryu, Jay Eungha.
Bounded bureaucracy and the budgetary process in the United States / Jay Eungha Ryu.
p. cm.
Includes bibliographical references and index.
ISBN 978-1-4128-4289-1 (acid-free paper)
1. Budget—United States. 2. Bureaucracy—United States.
3. Centralization in government—United States. I. Title.
HJ2051.R98 2011
352.4'80973—dc22
2011008560

ISBN 13: 978-1-4128-4289-1 (hbk)
ISBN 13: 978-1-138-50776-0 (pbk)

Contents

Preface ix

1 Bureaucraticization of Budget Processes: Causing or Remedying Bounded Rationality? 1

Bounded Rationality of Decision Makers 3

Bounded Bureaucracy as a Remedy to Bounded Rationality 4

Central Budget Offices: Enhancing Information Processing and Reducing Institutional Conflicts 6

Bureaucracy to Save Bureaucratic Malfunctions 9

2 Bounded Rationality in Policy and Budget Processes 11

Bounded Rationality and Satisficing 12

Incrementalism 16

Serial Judgment 22

Disproportionate Information Processing 24

Conclusion 30

3 Bureaucratic Organizations as a Remedy to Bounded Rationality 33

Bureaucratic Organizations: Extending Human Cognitive and Analytical Capacities 36

Bureaucratic Centralization: Expediting Information Processing and Reducing Institutional Frictions 39

Bureaucratic Centralization and Moderating Impact of Organizational Strategies 49

Bureaucratic Centralization and Partisan Configurations 55

Conclusion: Bounded Bureaucracy to Bounded Rationality 60

4 Bureaucratic Centralization and the National Executive Budget Process 63

U.S. Budget Outcomes: 1961–2006 65

Bureaucratic Centralization in Presidents' Budgets 72

Institutional Frictions in the U.S. Budget Process 75

Bureaucratic Centralization and U.S. Budget Punctuations 81

Bureaucratic Centralization and U.S. Budget Stability 93

Conclusion 98

5 Bureaucratic Centralization and the Congressional Budget Process 103

Congressional Macrobudgeting: Institutions and Partisan Politics 105

The Congressional Budget Office (CBO): A Bipartisan Information Processor 113

Bureaucratic Centralization and U.S. Budget Punctuations 119

Bureaucratic Centralization and U.S. Budget Stability 129

Conclusion 133

6 Bureaucratic Centralization and the State Budget Process 135

State Budget Outcomes: 1993, 1996, 1998, and 2000 137

State Executive Budgets 141

State Legislative Budgets 148

State Budget Institutions: Item Veto and Balanced Budget Requirements 153

Bureaucratic Centralization and State Budget Punctuations 162
Bureaucratic Centralization and State Budget Stability 177
Conclusion 180
Appendix: Legislative Professionalization and State Budget Punctuations and Stability 181

7 Conclusion: Bounded Bureaucracy to Bounded Rationality 187

Bibliography 197

Index 205

Preface

Bureaucracy has been criticized from various fronts. It has been often depicted as the main source of all governmental inefficiency and ineffectiveness. Of course, we have been witnessing numerous attempts of reforming bureaucratic organizations. Ironically, this book finds that even such initiatives to reform bureaucratic malfunctions cannot be successful without utilizing a certain aspect of bureaucracy itself. It is much more ironic that I started this book project as a part of my ongoing research efforts to criticize bureaucracy and recommend alternatives to bureaucratic organizations. In my previous studies, I found that bureaucracy cannot effectively deliver public services if the services span multiple jurisdictions beyond any one bureaucratic organization. Collaborative network management can overcome the limits found in bureaucratic service delivery.

Several years ago, I started analyzing whether and how bureaucratic procedures in large government organizations delay information processing and augment organizational conflicts. Unlike my scholarly belief, empirical evidence has been indicating that a certain aspect of bureaucracy, such as bureaucratic centralization, is crucial in enhancing cognitive and analytical capacity of decision makers and reducing organizational conflicts. In addition, the functions of bureaucracy were observed to be significantly influenced by its surrounding political environments. But all in all, bureaucratic centralization significantly improves bureaucratic performance to a certain degree. So, it occurred to me that negating bureaucracy in its entirety might not be a solution to reform bureaucracy. Bureaucratic reform initiatives such as performance budgeting systems have been sweeping virtually all levels of governments. The empirical findings I have obtained over several years suggest that even such reform initiatives are not guaranteed if we completely disregard bureaucracy itself.

The financial market collapse in 2008 resulted in a sudden drop in tax revenues for governments. During the recent years, record-high deficits triggered by the market collapse have been plaguing all levels of governments and necessitating fiscal austerity. One might probably think of an adequate level of bureaucratic centralization as an add-on mechanism to control governmental waste, if not a completely stand-alone alternative to bureaucratic malfunctions. Of course, whether and how bureaucratic centralization leads to budget control is an open invitation to future rounds of research. However, the main findings in this book at least imply that expedited information processing and reduced organizational conflicts rendered by bureaucratic centralization might contain some of governmental inefficiencies. In this regard, I believe that this book will be a good start for great debates between scholars and practitioners.

Finally, I wish to thank Alex Maza for his research assistance throughout multiple phases of this book project. He made great suggestions on the general tone of this book. Brandon Lawson participated in the later phase of this project. He also made insightful comments on how to edit the entire book for lay readers. I also thank, for support for this research, the Voinovich School of Leadership and Public Affairs and Department of Political Science at Ohio University. In addition, I thank my best friend and wife, Jeongwon, and my daughters, Sueyeon and Leah, for their sustained encouragement for the completion of this book. All remaining errors in this book, of course, pertain to myself.

1

Bureaucraticization of Budget Processes: Causing or Remedying Bounded Rationality?

When policy makers make their decisions, they receive various policy inputs and process them into policy alternatives. For instance, budget decision makers receive demands from interest groups, get data on available tax revenues for upcoming fiscal years, and focus on political power transition that might affect annual budget size. However, budget decision makers, especially in governments, usually do not have enough time and resources to process all such information they obtain from their surrounding environments. In addition, they do not have cognitive and analytical capacities to review the information. This phenomenon has been described as *bounded rationality*.

Institutional procedures and limits further augment the bounded rationality. For example, there are numerous statutory provisions that control the size of revenue, spending, and budget deficits. The complicated legal, institutional, and organizational procedures limit the cognitive capacities of human decision makers. In particular, bureaucratic organizations have been specifically blamed for amplifying the bounded rationality. Bureaucracies typically have highly centralized and hierarchical structures, along with standardized procedures of operation. They have been blamed for various dysfunctions such as conformity to standard rules rather than achieving core missions, oppression of human freedom due to hierarchical control, and irresponsiveness to the public due to adhering to internal procedures of operation. In addition, bureaucratic organizations were criticized for their inability to efficiently and effectively deal with public problems beyond their organizational boundaries, which span multiple administrative jurisdictions. Strong collaboration among multiple organizations is recently suggested as a way to improve organizational performance of bureaucratic organizations (Bingham and O'Leary 2009).

However, bureaucratic organizations were originally invented to enhance information-processing capacities (i.e., cognitive and analytic capacities) of individual decision makers. In particular, bureaucratic centralization was suggested as a way to expedite information processing and reduce organizational conflicts. Central offices in bureaucratic organizations were supposed to function as a storage center for various information sources. They share the information sources with line units (e.g., departments and agencies) and also relieve their computational burden. Bureaucratic centralization was also expected to reduce tensions and conflicts among departments and agencies in bureaucratic organizations.

In the national and state budget processes, central budget coordination has been enhanced since the early twentieth century. This book finds that there are still substantial merits from bureaucratic centralization of the budget processes. Empirical findings in this book indicate that bureaucratic centralization does improve information processing and reduce organizational tensions and frictions. However, the benefits from bureaucratic centralization diminish beyond a certain threshold point. The impact of bureaucratic centralization is also tangential on whether its surrounding political environments are conducive to the functions of bureaucratic organizations. When the executive branch and legislatures are under the same party control, political conditions are highly compatible with the hierarchical settings of bureaucratic organizations in the executive branch. Bureaucratic centralization enhances information processing and reduces institutional conflicts in the executive branch. When the executive branch is confronted by the opposition party in legislatures or majority parties in two legislative chambers differ, political environments are likely to be featured by bipartisan confrontations. Ironically, evidence suggests that such bipartisan confrontations are the best conditions for central bureaucratic agencies in the legislatures, such as the Congressional Budget Office (CBO), to function as a politically neutral and efficient information processor. Therefore, bureaucratic centralization is observed to expedite information processing and reduce organizational conflicts to a certain threshold. In this book, this aspect of bureaucratic organizations is described as "*bounded bureaucracy*." The final conclusion in this book is that bounded bureaucracy can substantially improve bounded rationality.

This book investigates largely three topics. First, Chapter 2 discusses the theoretical background of the so-called bounded rationality of decision makers under institutional settings. Second, Chapter 3 indicates that organizational theorists and political scientists originally suggested bureaucratic organizations as a remedy to the bounded rationality of decision makers. Third, Chapters 4–6 explain bureaucratic centralization of the national and state budget processes in what is known as executive and Congressional budgeting systems. They also present empirical evidence from decades of national and state budget data that bureaucratic centralization of the budget processes expedite information processing and reduce organizational conflicts. The three overarching topics are briefly introduced below.

Bounded Rationality of Decision Makers

Incrementalism contends that the limits in cognitive and analytical capacities of human decision makers result in bounded rationality. The limits are augmented by prescribed legal, political, and institutional constraints. Under such restricting decision environments, decision makers are most likely to disregard informational cues such as interest group pressures, forecast revenues, and political party competition, etc., which they obtain from the decision environments. In actual decision making, they do not have enough time/resources and especially information-processing capacities to process all the information (Lindblom 1959, 1979). Instead, they focus primarily on pre-established reference points or the status quo (e.g., last year's budgets in the case of budget processes). At least, last year's budgets might have passed political consensus tests and as such, might not open up new rounds of political conflicts. Consequently, budget outcomes follow highly predictable and stabilized patterns of changes: i.e., typically 5 percent changes, seldom larger than 30 percent (Wildavsky and Caiden 2004, 46). The aspect is defined as *budget stability* in this book.

Disproportionate information-processing theory, as a more comprehensive and general theory of decision making, asserts that decision makers pay "selective" attention to a few informational cues from the decision environment. For instance, decision makers pay attention only to the demands from one specific interest group. Thus, decision making is characterized by attention-driven choice, which is also known as indicator lock. However, the disregarded facets (e.g., all factors other than the demands from one interest group) will build up pressure in the temporal policy and budget processes in the future. Decision makers will reach a point where they can no longer ignore the disregarded factors. They will give sudden attention to the facets and there will be sudden, dramatic changes in policy and budget outcomes. In addition, institutional tensions caused by institutional/legal procedures will further augment the attention-driven choice process. The result of attention-driven choice process generally leads to sudden budget changes defined as *budget punctuations* in this book. Both budget stability and punctuations are the symptoms of bounded rationality and institutional tensions (Jones and Baumgartner 2005a, 2005b). In Chapter 2, a detailed explanation will be given on how attention-driven choices will result in budget stability as well as punctuations. This is one of the reasons why disproportionate information-processing theory is treated as a comprehensive theory, which combines incrementalism and punctuated equilibrium theory. Since disproportionate information-processing theory is fairly complicated, its key points are explained in an easily understandable manner.

Bounded Bureaucracy as a Remedy to Bounded Rationality

Bureaucracy has frequently been blamed for magnifying bounded rationality of human decision makers. However, scholars have often been negligent of the fact that bureaucracy itself was invented as a mechanism to extend the limited information-processing capacity of human decision makers. Bureaucratic organizations were expected to augment human cognitive and analytical capabilities through functional specialization and coordination. In particular, bureaucratic centralization was originally suggested as a way to enhance the information-processing capacity of decision makers and reduce institutional frictions. An example of institutional frictions is conflicts among the subunits in bureaucratic organizations, which were expected to be controlled through centralized coordination (Fry and Raadschelders 2008, 85–107, 211–47).

There are some caveats on the potential benefits from bureaucratic centralization, however. First, excessive centralization might ignite resistance from line agencies. Too excessive centralization might restrict the discretion of frontline managers or street-level bureaucrats who might retain the best knowledge and skills to address specific public problems (Andrews et al. 2009). Chapter 3 provides more detailed theoretical framework and empirical evidence on how bureaucratic centralization might influence information processing of decision makers and reduce organizational conflicts. More specifically, the following two variables (e.g., for the executive branch of governments) will capture the curvilinear relationship between bureaucratic centralization and budget stability/punctuations. *Centralization* is constructed as the number of central budget office staff divided by the number of total employees in the executive branch. *Centralization*^{2} is the squared value of *Centralization*. *Centralization* will expedite information processing and reduce institutional conflicts. In contrast, excessive centralization, *Centralization*^{2}, will detract from information processing and increase institutional tension.

Second, the impacts of bureaucratic centralization on information processing and institutional conflicts will be substantially tangential on its surrounding partisan environments. In general, bureaucratic centralization will help expedite information processing and reduce institutional tensions when surrounding partisan environments are conducive to the functions of bureaucratic centralization. Under unified governments (i.e., the executive branch and legislatures under the same party control), political backdrops are highly compatible with the hierarchical settings of bureaucratic organizations in the executive branch. Bureaucratic centralization might enhance information processing and reduce institutional frictions in the executive branch. Under divided governments (i.e., the executive branch is confronted by the opposition party in legislatures or the majority parties in two legislative chambers differ), political environments are likely to be featured by bipartisan confrontations. Ironically, evidence suggests that such bipartisan confrontations are the best conditions for central bureaucratic agencies in the legislatures, such as the CBO, to function as a politically neutral and efficient information processor. In sum, bureaucratic centralization will probably reduce the frequency of budget punctuations or sudden budget changes that are symptoms of bounded rationality and institutional frictions. The function of bureaucratic centralization will substantially hinge on whether surrounding partisan configurations are favorable to their functioning.

Third, bureaucratic centralization might not augment information processing and reduce institutional frictions under routine, programmed decision-making (e.g., strongly standardized operating procedures) settings. The programmed decision-making settings have been associated with budget stability (e.g., 5–10 percent changes in annual budgets). Budget stability is characterized by stickiness and strong institutional tensions against changes in the status quo. However, numerous attempts to affect the budget stability have not been successful. Thus, bureaucratic centralization should not be blamed for what virtually nothing can achieve for budget stability. Chapter 2 gives detailed discussions of the differences between programmed vs. nonprogrammed decision-making settings and how bureaucratic centralization exerts different impacts on information processing and institutional frictions depending on such varying settings.

Figure 3.1 in Chapter 3 succinctly summarizes the key assumptions of this book. The first panel explains the core concepts of disproportionate information-processing theory introduced in Chapter 2. The lack of information-processing capacity of budget decision makers will increase indicator lock. The indicator lock will increase either budget punctuations or stability. Institutional frictions will augment the indicator lock as shown in Figure 3.1. Overall, bureaucratic centralization will reduce the probability of budget punctuations. However, it will not effectively change budget inertia or stability. In sum, bureaucratic centralization can help decision makers process informational cues flowing from the budget environments when surrounding partisan conditions are conducive to the functioning of the bureaucratic organizations. Although it is limited in enhancing information processing and reducing institutional frictions regarding budget stability, bureaucratic centralization has substantial strengths over budget punctuations. Therefore, the somewhat "bounded" bureaucracy can be a solution to bounded rationality, contrary to the common assertion in the literature.

Central Budget Offices: Enhancing Information Processing and Reducing Institutional Conflicts

Chapters 4–6 present empirical findings obtained from the national and state budget data. In Chapter 4, changes in U.S. budget authorities from 1961 to 2006 were used to test whether bureaucratic centralization reduces budget punctuations and stability. The centralization index, measured as the ratio of the Office of Management and Budget (OMB) employees to total employees in the national executive branch, was negatively correlated with the frequency of budget punctuations. Its squared value was positively associated with budget punctuations as hypothesized in Chapters 2 and 3. This implies that bureaucratic centralization might expedite information processing and reduce institutional frictions to a certain degree but beyond a certain threshold, it detracts from such benefits. However, this finding is obtained only under unified governments as also hypothesized. The political conditions under unified governments are compatible with and conducive to the hierarchical functions of bureaucracies. In contrast, bureaucratic centralization does not influence budget stability. It even increases the frequency of budget stability, especially under unified governments. Considering that virtually no attempts were successful to influence budget stability, bureaucratic centralization should not be criticized for its incapacity to process information processing and reduce budget inertia.

In sum, a moderate level of centralized budget coordination in the national executive budget process helps expedite information processing and reduce institutional frictions when the surrounding partisan configurations are similar to the hierarchical structures of bureaucratic organizations (i.e., unified governments). This observation is obtained only for budget punctuations. Bounded bureaucracy, unlike scholarly expectations, does improve bounded rationality of decision makers and reduce institutional frictions.

Using the same U.S. budget authority data, bureaucratic centralization in Congress is tested to investigate whether it affects information processing and reduce institutional frictions. In Chapter 5, bureaucratic centralization is measured as the ratio of the CBO employees to total Congressional employees. Almost the same observations reported in Chapter 4 were found for bureaucratic centralization in Congress. Adequate, not excessive, bureaucratic centralization seems to expedite information processing and reduce institutional frictions. However, this effect was found only under "divided" governments.

In Chapter 5, a lot of scholarly observations about Congressional politics are also reported. The CBO was the creation of the 1974 Congressional Budget Act that entailed numerous changes in Congress. The changes in Congressional committee systems, aspirations/behaviors of committees and their members, and budget decision processes in the 1970s are discussed in Chapter 5. This chapter also discusses what happened during the 1990s and 2000s. Congress and its committee structures are described fundamentally as fragmented and decentralized coalitions of co-equal powers. Under these conditions, the CBO has been functioning as a "bipartisan" information processor and friction reducer only when one partisan power was pitted against another. This is starkly contrasted with the OMB that has been recently criticized for its deviation from politically neutral competence. Bipartisan confrontation is the best condition for the CBO to maintain its somewhat more neutral competence by ironically taking advantage of the political cross fire. In this chapter, many anecdotal cases are introduced to show how partisan divisions can nurture the best conditions where the CBO can successfully maintain its stance as a bipartisan and neutral information processor. Bureaucratic centralization in Congress through the CBO is loosely coupled with the fragmented Congressional committee structures that are starkly contrasted with the hierarchical backdrop surrounding the OMB. Bipartisan confrontation is a better match with the fragmented nature of Congressional committee structures. Thus, when partisan configurations surrounding bureaucratic centralization are more favorable to bureaucratic functioning, bureaucratic centralization will reduce budget punctuations. Here again, bureaucratic centralization does not shake loose budget stability. Under unified governments, it even increases budget stability.

In sum, when surrounding partisan configurations (in this case, divided governments) render the condition where the CBO can maintain its neutral competence, bureaucratic centralization in Congress helps expedite information processing and reduce institutional frictions. Bounded bureaucracy can function as a solution to bounded rationality.

State government budget processes slightly differ from the national government because in most states governors retain item veto power and budgets are constrained by balanced budget requirements. Even controlling for the state-specific institutional features, bureaucratic centralization is also observed to expedite information processing and reduce institutional frictions in Chapter 6. State government subfunctional expenditures (e.g., roughly similar to agency-level spending categories) for 1993, 1996, 1998, and 2000 are used to test the same, main research question in this book. Adequate levels of bureaucratic centralization expedite information processing and reduce institutional frictions mostly under unified governments. Bureaucratic centralization even increases budget stability as well.

Bureaucratic centralization, if maintained at an adequate level, does have potential strengths. In Chapter 6, numerous state-specific cases are also introduced to show how central budget coordination relieves line agencies from excessive computational burden and reduces interagency conflicts through central coordination. This chapter ends with the same findings as in Chapters 4 and 5: i.e., *bounded bureaucracy* can serve as a mechanism to improve bounded rationality.

Bureaucracy to Save Bureaucratic Malfunctions

Bureaucratic organizations have been blamed for various kinds of malfunctions. However, they were originally invented as a way to extend cognitive and analytical capacities of individual decision makers. This book specifically investigates whether and how bureaucratic centralization in the national and state budget processes affects information processing and institutional conflicts. Surprisingly, however, there have not been sufficient empirical findings to test the main hypothesis in this book especially from the perspective of bureaucratic organizations as information-processing systems. The lack of the empirical findings is partly attributable to the lack of an adequate theoretical framework to investigate the puzzle in the literature. As shown in Chapters 2 and 3, disproportionate information-processing theory offers a pioneering model to test whether and how *bounded rationality* and *institutional conflicts* influence the changes in policy and budget outcomes.

Empirical findings using several decades of national and state budget data show that bureaucratic centralization in the national and state budget processes does expedite information processing and reduce institutional frictions, if maintained at an adequate level. Scholars of decision making, especially under institutional settings, argue that institutional settings are one of the major reasons why individual decision makers are "bounded" in their decision-making capacity. This book empirically shows that the opposite might also be true. Bureaucratic centralization can assist human decision makers as information-processing systems. In addition, it can also help reduce organizational conflicts within large bureaucratic organizations as numerous anecdotal cases evidence in the following chapters.

During the 2000s, state governments have been plagued by revenue shortages. Many state governments have attempted to develop some budget control mechanisms. One of such attempts has been performance budgeting systems. The national government has also been implementing planning-based performance budgeting systems since the early 1990s (Gilmour and Lewis 2006). One aspect of performance budgeting systems is a more enhanced role of central budget offices. For instance, the financial market crisis that swept the national economy in 2008 and 2009 also increased already record-high budget deficits for the national government. There were numerous financial regulatory reforms. In particular, the Government Performance and Results Act (GPRA) of 1993 was amended into the GPRA Modernization Act of 2010 in response to the market crisis and skyrocketing national debt. One key provision of the 2010 Act includes the renewed emphasis on the so-called cross-walking across different agencies (i.e., creating programs spanning multiple agencies) in the national government (Kamensky 2011). The role of centralized coordination across different agency programs is crucial for the success of the performance budgeting systems. In addition, implementation of the performance budgeting systems in the national government was also significantly swayed by partisan politics. The success of bureaucratic reform initiatives such as performance-based budgeting is highly tangential on its surrounding political environments (Gilmour and Lewis 2006).

The experience with the new waves of bureaucratic reform initiatives implies that reforms of bureaucratic organizations through performance budgeting systems are not guaranteed without accounting for management and implementation issues as well as their political backdrops. Efficient implementation of the reform initiatives is much more important than their creation. In particular, centralized coordination over different agency programs is a key to their success. If so, the findings in this book recommend us to have another look at the role of bureaucratic centralization in the national and state budget processes. The empirical findings in this book strongly imply that bureaucratic centralization enhances information processing and reduces organizational conflicts. Ironically, maintaining an adequate level of bureaucratic centralization is one of key aspects for successful reform initiatives for bureaucracy itself. Furthermore, the findings in this book clearly indicate that bureaucratic organizations cannot operate devoid of politics. They are exhorted to keep an eye on how their surrounding partisan configurations develop, for successful implementation of reform initiatives.

2

Bounded Rationality in Policy and Budget Processes

There are two approaches to human decision-making process. According to one approach, human beings have sufficient cognitive and analytical capacities to process the input information they obtain from the decision environment. In contrast, the other approach to human decision making asserts that there is an inherent limit in human cognitive and analytical capabilities. Although human beings intend to be rational, they instead choose decision alternatives that are minimally satisfactory with respect to their decision aspirations. This human decision-making process is well reflected in the concept of bounded rationality. Under the assumption of bounded rationality, individual human decision makers do not make comprehensive, and as such random and simultaneous searches over the continuum of decision alternatives. Instead, they make sequential searches on the spectrum of alternatives. Decision makers review alternatives one at a time. Only when the alternative is rejected do they move on the next available alternative. This is starkly contrasted with the comprehensive review where decision makers will review all alternatives all at once. In short, there is a fundamental limit in the information-processing capacity of human decision makers. This limit is further made worse by institutional settings.

Incrementalism has applied the concept of bounded rationality to explain policy and budget processes. According to incrementalism, policy or budget decision makers lack cognitive and analytical capacities to process informational cues flowing from the decision environments, such as political, fiscal, institutional, and legal factors affecting policy or budget decision making. In addition, the information they obtain is likely to be less complete. Further, the information-processing capacity of decision makers is limited by the prescribed political, legal, and institutional constraints. Typical responses to the environmental information cues are that decision makers do not pay sufficient attention to the cues. Instead, they rely on more routine approaches to process the information cues by resorting to a pre-established budget base or status quo. The result in policy or budget outcomes, therefore, will be characterized by marginal changes from the status quo or budget base. Some outlying observations of budget or policy choices will be treated as random errors.

Recently, disproportionate information-processing theory revealed that there are also more observations of sudden, dramatic policy or budget changes in addition to the marginal changes. The observations are more frequent than those that could be regarded as random errors. Disproportionate information-processing theory attributed the sudden, dramatic policy or budget changes to attention-driven choices or indicator lock. Due to the limit in the information-processing capacity of human decision makers, they are likely to disregard certain facets of informational cues flowing from decision environments. When these facets can no longer be ignored, they gain the sudden attention of decision makers. Decision makers tend to overreact to the previously unattended cues and policy or budget punctuations take place. The attention-driven choices or indicator lock is intensified by institutional frictions.

In this chapter, the main approaches explaining human decision-making processes are introduced. Human decision-making processes especially under institutional settings are featured by bounded rationality and institutional frictions. Bounded rationality and institutional frictions will lead to policy gridlock or stability according to incrementalism. The same conditions will engender policy or budget punctuations according to disproportionate information-processing theory. The clarification of these issues is the first step for introducing potential solutions to improve bounded rationality discussed in Chapter 3.

Bounded Rationality and Satisficing

Probably, one of the most influential theories of decision-making mechanisms is "the model of satisficing man" developed by Herbert Simon. Decision makers are usually bounded by the limit in their cognitive and analytical capabilities. They are likely to accept decision alternatives that are minimally satisfactory with respect to their pre-established levels of decision aspirations. There have been numerous attempts to enhance rationality in public decision making such as performance budgeting or organizational restructuring to espouse business techniques to improve efficiency and effectiveness. Despite such efforts, empirical observations of these techniques dominantly evidence that they are not successful in enhancing rationality. They were not successful mainly because cognitive capacities of decision makers were limited, especially for public policies because they are further characterized by political, legal, and institutional constraints. In terms of individual decision-making processes, Simon contended that limited cognitive and analytical capacities were the primary reasons why such rational decision processes were not successful, especially under institutional settings. Therefore, one needs to briefly review the key components of the concept of bounded rationality and satisficing. In addition, the concept provides us with groundwork for the main discussions in this chapter and Chapter 3.

According to Simon, there are several "decision maker" models. The psychological model focuses on the affective or emotional aspect of individual decision maker. The sociological model assumes that individual decision making is determined by social roles. The assumption of the economic model emphasizes the importance of cognitive and analytical processes of decision making. Simon's model of satisficing assumes that decision makers accept policy alternatives that are minimally satisfactory in terms of their decision aspirations. It is different from the psychological model in that the former focuses more on cognitive and analytical aspects of decision making. It also differs from the sociological model because human decision making is not utterly defined by individual social roles. Finally, it is also distinguished from the economic man because cognitive and analytical capacities of human beings are inherently limited (Fry and Raadschelders 2008, 221–22).

Considering that the recent debates in the field of public policy and administration have substantially focused on rational approaches to decision making, it would be worthwhile to review the fundamental assumptions and processes of economic, rational decision making first. Although it is very difficult to apply the economic model to public decision making, its logic is relatively simple, clear, and straightforward. Under the model of economic man, an individual decision maker is assumed to know all decision-relevant aspects of the surrounding decision environment. The decision maker knows all possible alternatives to achieve best results. The decision maker also knows the consequences of each alternative and furthermore, retains accurate information on the relationship between decision alternatives and their consequences. Finally, the decision maker chooses an alternative that will maximize utility and efficiency from implementing the alternative.

A fundamental limit in the rational approaches is that they did not account for uncertainty inherent in almost all phases of decision-making processes. Decision makers cannot be certain about the goals, values, and objectives of their decision making. They do not know, for certain, the range of possible alternatives. Most of all, they are uncertain about the relationship between the alternatives and their consequences. Thus, the critical limit of the rational approaches is that they did not present a generally acceptable criterion for selecting an alternative under uncertain decision environments. Although human decision makers intend to be rational, their decision strategies are significantly limited by such uncertainty (Fry and Raadschelders 2008, 222–23; Jones 2003).

Under the uncertainty in the decision environment, a satisficing man does not review all alternatives. The satisficing man ignores the complex interrelationships in the real world and makes decisions based on simple rules of thumb. In short, a satisficing man satisfices because his decision is bounded by "the limits on available information and by his own computational abilities" (Fry and Raadschelders 2008, 224). In addition, what makes Simon's model of individual decision making the most intuitive is the fact that he conceptualized a decision maker as an artificial system that adapts through his goals and values to the surrounding decision environment. More specifically, Simon regarded the decision maker as an "*information-processing system*" and contended that there are commonalities among human beings as information-processing systems. As an information-processing system, the individual decision maker can process only a few things at a time and attend to a small portion of the saved information in his or her memory, which is invoked by the decision environment at any given time in his decision-making process. Much relevant to the discussions in Chapter 3, and the empirical findings in Chapters 4–6, individual decision-making processes are composed of three stages: i.e., stimuli, memory, and a problem-solving process (Fry and Raadschelders 2008, 224–26).

The first component of individual decision-making process is a stimulus flowing from the decision environment. Unfortunately, however, individual decision makers do not pay attention to all the perceived stimuli due mainly to their limited cognitive and analytical capacities. Instead, decision makers typically pay "*selective attention to the stimuli*." The selective attention will be further reinforced by the interaction between the environmental stimuli and the information invoked from individual memory. For instance, when decision makers receive input information on budget choices regarding fiscal conditions, then they are likely to filter which part of the information will be accepted based on their past individual memories. This interaction has a couple of important implication. Environmental stimuli decide what information might be invoked but at the same time the information drawn from the individual memory also decides what environmental stimuli will be perceived and processed (Fry and Raadschelders 2008, 226). Very interestingly, the concept of selective attention is echoed by one of recent critiques of incrementalism. Disproportionate information-processing theory, introduced below, revealed that main budget actors do process environmental cues flowing from the decision environment but on the basis of selective attention or indicator lock, similar to Simon's selective attention. This is slightly different from what incrementalism generally contended. The main budget actors tend to pay virtually no attention to the stimuli. This subtle difference between information processing (albeit selective) and incrementalism will be theoretically and empirically discussed throughout this book.

The second crucial element in individual decision process is the role of individual memory. The memory contains the information that will be used as criteria to determine preferred values and goals, alternatives to achieve the values and goals, and perceptions and expectations on the relationships between the alternatives and their outcomes. There are two categories of individual memory: short-term and long-term. It is the short-term memory that decides whether information inflow from the decision environment is relevant or not. If the informational cues flowing from the environment are relevant, then individual decision makers will prioritize the cues along with all other informational stimuli. Despite the vital role of short-term memory, it is very limited and small. Therefore, individual decision makers will convert short-term memory into long-term memory. The long-term memory creates rules that specify specific responses to categorized environmental stimuli. One critical limit of the long-term memory is that it takes too long to convert short-term memory into long-term memory. Therefore, the inherent limits in individual decision-making processes are characterized by the limited capacity of the short-term memory and the time limit associated with the long-term memory (Fry and Raadschelders 2008, 226–27).

Faced with the limits, individual decision makers begin their problem-solving processes by defining a problem space. Individual decision makers define the problem space that is a subjective and simplified representation of the surrounding decision environment. They extract information from the environment and use the information to initiate a selective search for a solution to the defined problem. But a critical point is that the search activities will be continued only within the problem space based on simplified rules of thumb. In addition, the search is not comprehensive or random but sequential. Individual decision makers scan decision alternatives one at a time. When they find an alternative that minimally satisfies their decision aspirations, the alternative will be their decision choice (Fry and Raadschelders 2008, 227–28). Simon's framework of individual decision making is further elaborated by incrementalism, especially when it is applied to policy and budget decision-making processes.

Incrementalism

Lindblom (1959) argues that limits in human capacity, lack of complete information, and lack of time and resources prohibit decision makers from applying comprehensive, synoptic approaches to complex social problems. Public agencies are further constrained by political and legal limits and therefore their attention tends to be restricted to a few values and alternatives. In addition, social values or objectives are unlikely to have common relative scales and thus the comparison and relevance of the objectives differ case by case. Under this condition, incremental analysis is a better approach as a tool of analysis for decision making. Lindblom (1979) makes more detailed categorization of the incremental analysis: i.e., simple incremental analysis, disjointed incrementalism, and strategic analysis.

When decision makers confine their analysis to limited sets of policy alternatives that are marginally different from the status quo, this method of incremental analysis is called *simple incremental analysis*. This approach has been frequently employed in actual political decision making. Despite many critiques of incremental analysis, Lindblom (1979) suggests that the most frequent objection is not to this aspect of incremental analysis. Rather, it pertains to the marginal political change to which the simple incremental analysis is nicely suited. In contrast, there are many observations when analysis is further marked by an intertwining of policy goals with the empirical aspects of the policy problem. When making decisions, decision makers are more preoccupied with ills to be remedied or avoided rather than positive goals to achieve. In addition, decision makers pay more attention to a sequence of trials and errors and explore only some of the important policy consequences. More importantly, analytic work processes are fragmented to various partisan participants. Lindblom called all these aspects as *disjointed incrementalism*.

Disjointed incrementalism is a strategy practiced with various skills and is one kind of strategic analysis described below. The concept of disjointed incrementalism is similar to Simon's "satisficing." Synoptic, comprehensive, and rational decision making oftentimes results in ill-designed, accidental incompleteness. In contrast, disjointed incrementalism leads to deliberate, designed incompleteness. If disjointed incrementalism might reach a local optimum due to the satisficing approach, it is also highly likely that synoptic policy analysis and making might also return less optimal alternatives even under best conditions. Therefore, one merit from disjointed incrementalism is that it focuses more on identifiable ills to avoid rather than abstract goals to pursue. Lindblom (1979) also distinguishes the fragmentation of analysis, described as partisan mutual adjustment in disjointed incrementalism, from incremental politics. Partisan mutual adjustment includes some concept of politics. However, it should not be equated with incremental politics. It also includes a concept of analysis. For instance, interest groups try to achieve influence in partisan mutual adjustment through partisan analysis as a way to bring policy-relevant information, with which they are familiar, into policy decision making. For the case of state budget process, interest groups or lobbyists are active in providing budget-relevant information to legislatures or agency bureaucrats. In addition to their advocacy roles for vested group interests, they have been functioning as important information sources because they know what might be best budget or policy alternatives for their group interests. The alternatives are likely to be locally optimal but offer a lot of relevant information to decision makers (Ryu et al. 2007, 2008). This observation is close to Lindblom's concept of partisan analysis. Lindblom suggests, "partisan analysis is the most characteristic analytical input into politics and also the most productive" (1979, 524).

Finally, *strategic analysis* denotes an analysis limited to a thoughtfully chosen set of stratagems "to simplify complex policy problems, that is, to short-cut the conventionally comprehensive 'scientific' analysis" (Lindblom 1979, 518). Especially for complex social problems, the case for strategic analysis, rather than synopsis, as a norm is simple. Faced with too many interacting values at stake, too many alternatives, and too high uncertainty regarding the consequences of the alternatives, the best way of analysis is bounded rationality. Under the condition, decision makers rely on various simplifying strategies such as skillfully sequencing trial and errors. Lindblom takes an example. Pursuing unaided flying is a bootless, unproductive ideal. In contrast, flying turns into a productive ambition when accepting the impossibility of flying without some mechanical devices.

Two empirical studies conducted by Davis, Dempster, and Wildavsky (1966, 1974) exemplify research efforts that directly applied incremental perspectives to explaining and predicting the patterns of federal budgets. One important clue to understand governmental budgeting is the extraordinary complexity involved in budgetary calculations. By far the most influential aid to help budgetary participants deal with the overwhelming burden is the incremental method. Budgetary actors almost never review budgetary alternatives in their entirety. Instead, they review the small deviations from the previous budget level that is oftentimes described as budget base. When there is a global sharing of agreed upon expected base of organization's ongoing expenditure level, the agreement will be a powerful means of securing budgetary stability. The complicated but stabilized budgetary process can be simplified to the interaction between executive agencies, central budget offices, and legislative appropriations committees (Davis, Dempster, and Wildavsky 1966, 1974; Sharkansky 1968; Thompson 1987).

The outcome of the process was oftentimes characterized by what is labeled as *outcome* incrementalism where the results of budget change patterns follow incremental changes. In contrast, *process* incrementalism explains the process of decision making where decision makers are constrained by their limits in cognitive capacities and surrounding institutional restraints (Padgett 1980). No other theories have dominated the analysis of U.S. policy-making processes, especially public budget processes, more heavily than the incrementalist insights. Incrementalism as a model to explain budget processes, however, has been criticized for some confusing, unclear, inconsistent, and irrelevant concepts (see, among many critiques, Berry 1990; Kamlet and Mowery 1980; LeLoup 1978; Rubin 1989; Schick 1983; Wanat 1974). Incrementalism as a model of general public policy has recently been criticized by the theory of punctuated equilibrium or the theory of disproportionate information processing on how decision makers process informational clues flowing from surrounding policy environments. Before introducing the more recent critiques of incrementalism applied to policy and budget processes, it is very useful to summarize key concepts of incrementalism in formulaic forms.

The incrementalist model suggested by Davis, Dempster, and Wildavsky (1966, 1974) can easily be described in the following equation forms:

$$B_t = \alpha_i \cdot B_{t-1} + e_t. \tag{2.1}$$

$B_t(B_{t-1})$ is a budget outcome in year t ($t-1$). α_i is a parameter to be estimated and e_t is an error term that was assumed to be random and normal. By subtracting B_{t-1} from both sides in equation (2.1) and dividing them further by B_{t-1}, we have the following equation:

$$\frac{B_t - B_{t-1}}{B_{t-1}} = \alpha_i - 1 + \frac{e_t}{B_{t-1}}. \tag{2.2}$$

The left-hand side of equation (2.2) means an annual percentage change in policy or budget outcomes, which will be defined as *Increment* in this book. The increment is composed of a fixed portion of annual percentage policy change ($\alpha_i - 1$), which is seldom larger than 30 percent and often smaller than 5 percent in the case of public budgeting (Wildavsky and Caiden 2004), and a random error component. The fixed annual percentage change for typical U.S. programs has been 4 percent or so since 1947 (Jones and Baumgartner 2005b). Davis, Dempster, and Wildavsky (1974) further decomposed α_i into:

$$\alpha_i = \beta_0 + \beta_1 \cdot Z_{1t} + \beta_2 \cdot Z_{2t} + \cdots + \beta_m \cdot Z_{mt}. \tag{2.3}$$

Z_m is a set of exogenous environmental factors that budgetary decision makers account for when making budget allocation decisions. Even when various exogenous factors were controlled for, the predictive power of a more extended model did not improve over a simple model such as equation (2.1) (Davis, Dempster, and Wildavsky

1974). By further plugging equation (2.3) into equation (2.2), we can have:

$$\frac{\beta_t - \beta_{t-1}}{\beta_{t-1}} = \beta_0 - 1 + (\beta_1 \cdot Z_{1t} + \beta_2 \cdot Z_{2t} + \cdots + \beta_m \cdot Z_{mt}) + \frac{e_t}{B_{t-1}}. \quad (2.4)$$

Equation (2.4) implies that budget decision makers process informational cues flowing from the budget environments (i.e., *Z* variables) into annual percentage changes in budget outcomes. According to incrementalism, however, budget decision makers did not pay much attention to the environmental factors. Disproportionate information-processing theory suggested that incrementalism paid "proportionate" attention to the environmental factors. Thus, the *Z* variables are likely to be incorporated into budget choices in equal weights (Jones and Baumgartner 2005a, 2005b). However, some previous empirical studies indicate that under incrementalist perspectives, budget decision makers are least likely to pay attention to the environmental factors. This ignorance was criticized as one of various critiques over budgetary incrementalism (Ryu et al. 2008).

Sharkansky (1968) investigated whether there is a predictable and stabilized relationship between main budget actors envisioned in incrementalism, such as executive agencies, governors, and legislatures in state governments. Sharkansky found that agency budget requests tended to be slightly cut by governors and legislative appropriations were likely to conform to governors' budget recommendations for the agencies. In addition, agency acquisitiveness (measured as agency budget requests for the coming budget year as a percentage of current agency outlays) was negatively correlated with short-term budget success but positively related with long-term budget expansion. This means that despite short-term budget cuts more acquisitive agencies were more likely to enjoy fund increases in the long run. Sharkansky also found that budget reviewers were more likely to review budget increment (i.e., *Increment* in this book) rather than the total agency budget requests. The overall findings in the study also indicated that the influence of the budget environmental factors is weak.

Thompson (1987) also tested the same question that Sharkansky investigated. His findings are almost similar to those of Sharkansky's. One difference from Sharkansky's findings was that agencies were more acquisitive and legislatures tended to cut agency budget requests less. More importantly, in terms of long-term budget expansion, agency acquisitiveness was more critical than gubernatorial budget recommendations. Thompson further controlled for more complex changes in budget environments, such as legislative professionalism, increased professionalism in state bureaucracies, enhanced gubernatorial budget power, centralized management structures, fiscal factors, and political factors. His overall findings also indicate that budget environmental factors did not significantly influence budget choices. Sharkansky's and Thompson's findings generally note that the main budget actors, agencies, governors or central budget offices, and legislative committees or their members/staff, do not incorporate all environmental factors into budget choices. The observation is consistent with incrementalism but the role of the main budget actors needs to be further accounted for. Therefore, a more accurate depiction of budgetary incrementalism should look like equation (2.5):

$$\frac{B_t - B_{t-1}}{B_{t-1}} = (\beta_0 - 1) + M.B.A.*(\beta_1 \cdot Z_{1t} + \beta_2 \cdot Z_{2t} + \cdots \beta_m \cdot Z_{mt}) + \frac{e_t}{B_{t-1}}. \tag{2.5}$$

M.B.A. denotes the main budget actors. In fact, incrementalist insights assumed that the main budget actors paid virtually no attention to budget environmental factors. This might be due to their limited capacities and made worse by prescribed political, legal institutions. Incrementalism suggested that the main budget actors are more likely to attend to the annual, marginal budget changes instead of the *Z* variables. Disproportionate information-processing theory suggested that the main budget actors might have given equal weights to the environmental factors. However, empirical studies imply that the main budget actors are more likely to ignore the environmental factors. This is not to say that disproportionate information-processing theory made a wrong interpretation of incrementalism. Instead, much more careful discussions are warranted as elaborated below. Then, the condition is similar to the situation where the second part of the right-hand side in equation (2.5) will be zero: i.e., $M.B.A.$ * $(\beta_1 \cdot z_{1t} + \beta_2 \cdot Z_{2t} + \text{L} + \beta_m \cdot Z_{mt}) = 0$. Important enough, this condition has been at the core of controversies over incrementalism. The first line of such critiques was opened up by serial judgment.

Serial Judgment

Padgett's (1980) theory of serial judgment significantly clarified confusions over the incrementalist model, especially the second part in the right-hand side of equation (2.5). Incrementalism in the descriptive sense denotes a pattern of marginal changes in final budget choices relative to some base that is likely to be previous year's budget outcomes. Padgett labels this pattern as outcome incrementalism but that was not the focus of his study. Incrementalism in the "explanatory" sense refers to a process that underlies the process of resource allocation. Davis, Dempster, and Wildavsky (1966, 1974) presented a linear decision rule. Padgett labels this as "process incrementalism" that is the focus of his study.

According to Padgett, α_i in equation (2.2) is regarded as program shift parameters (or agency decision rule parameters). The program shift parameter illustrates how each agency[1] processes informational cues flowing from the budget environments. According to Padgett, the incrementalist model in equation (2.2) will show random and normal error terms. Then, one key question of studying incrementalism is to find out the distribution of *Increment*, the dependent variable in equation (2.2). In essence, the question is the same as finding the distribution of program shift parameters, α_i, and error terms. In equations (2.2) and (2.3), α_i is basically an additive sum of environmental factors, *Z* variables. According to a law of statistics, the distribution of α_i will be normal whether *Z*'s are nonstochastic or stochastic: i.e., whether there are systematic patterns in *Z*'s or not. Therefore, the distribution of *Increment* will also be normal.

Padgett further investigates what happens if the program shift parameters reflect heterogeneity. In other words, what happens if decision makers hold different substantive opinions about the benefits from different programs? Under the heterogeneity assumption, the distribution of *Increment* was supposed to follow *t* distributions. When the impact of *Z*'s on α_i is cumulative, instead of additive, the distribution of annual budget changes might further show what Davis, Dempster, and Wildavsky (1966) called "shift points." Although budget outcomes are incremental, budget choices respond to social, economic, and political factors. However, they do so only after sufficient pressure has been developed to cause sudden changes in budget outcomes. Padgett labeled this phenomenon observed by Davis, Dempster, and Wildavsky as a cumulative pressure theory.

Despite the elaborate discussion of process incrementalism, however, Padgett's conceptualization does not account for (β_0 – 1) in equation (2.5). Numerous studies already showed that annual budget changes, by construction and observation, include a fixed portion. Then, the distribution of annual budget changes will include a peak at the center of the distribution (denoting budget stability or inertia of ± 5 percent budget changes) combined with the normal distributions of annual budget changes. It is the concept of serial judgment that made a clear improvement over incrementalism. When Padgett develops his serial judgment theory, he clearly accounts for the peak by starting from the historical reference point that is close to the base in process incrementalism. Using the budget base as the reference point, budget decision makers open up their serial judgment and select their search direction. The key contribution of the serial judgment theory is that budget decision makers are more likely to make a bit more informed and extended search in their decision environments. This aspect of decision process is very similar to "strategic analysis" in Lindblom's incrementalism introduced earlier. Two criteria are used for decision makers' search activities. One is the probability that a certain program will be accepted on a merit basis. The other is the probability that the program will be adopted on the basis of fiscal/political climate.

Serial judgment decision makers search for and evaluate "*randomly*" discrete salient alternatives on the continuum of all possible alternatives. This aspect is starkly contrasted with the fact that under the incrementalist assumptions as well as the bounded rationality and satisficing decision makers are making *sequential* search for alternatives. Through a complicated but elaborate statistical derivation, Padgett shows that the distribution of annual budget changes will be double exponential where there is a high peak (budget inertia) and extended tails (huge budget changes), accompanied by thin shoulders (moderate budget changes). When program parameters are heterogeneous, the distribution of annual budget changes is double Paretian. The main difference between the exponential and Paretian distributions is that there is a tradeoff between the peak and tails under exponential distributions. Under Paretian distributions, there is a tradeoff between the peak and tails on the one hand and shoulders on the other (Jones, Sulkin, and Larsen 2003).

Overall, the serial judgment theory greatly elaborated incrementalism in two dimensions. One is that it showed the distribution of annual budget changes might not be normal. Second, it clarified that the main budget actors might continue their search activities slightly longer than incrementalism predicted. In other words, the second part in the right-hand side of equation (2.5) might not simply be zero: i.e., $M.B.A. * (\beta_1 \cdot Z_{1t} + \beta_2 \cdot Z_{2t} + \ldots \beta_m \cdot Z_{mt}) \neq 0$. Disproportionate information-processing theory further made a jump-improvement by substantially clearing the above scholarly confusions and establishing a more comprehensive model to explain individual and institutional decision-making processes.

Disproportionate Information Processing

Disproportionate information-processing theory can be regarded as the most comprehensive theory of decision making under institutional settings. That combines both incrementalism featured by bounded rationality and satisficing, and serial judgment into one general policy theory. Much similar to serial judgment theory, it also posits that the assumptions under incrementalism will result in normal distributions of annual policy or budget changes. For lay-readers, the awfully complicated but breaking-through model should first be interpreted in comparison with incrementalism. Jones and Baumgartner (2005b, 115–32) contend that the decision-making process depicted in incrementalism fundamentally follows "rational updating." As in the case of how the serial judgment theory interpreted incrementalism, it should also be noted that the rational updating will take place primarily over the Z variables in the second part of the right-hand side of equation (2.5). We should be cautious that what disproportionate information-processing theory as well as serial judgment theory meant by rational updating pertains to the second part of the right-hand side in equation (2.5). If one accounts for the first part of the right-hand side of equation (2.5) (i.e., fixed, marginal budget changes), then the distributions of annual budget changes might look closer to leptokurtic, rather than normal, distributions. What disproportionate information-processing theory means by rational updating is a more general condition where budget decision makers could make a bit more extended search activities over the Z variables.

Incrementalism assumed that when decision makers lack cognitive capacities to process informational cues flowing from the decision environment or the information is not complete, they will probably disregard such informational cues. Instead, they will rely more on pre-established reference points, or budget base. The flip side of this story is that when they have somewhat enhanced or the information can be more efficiently processed, this condition might be quite close to what Lindblom labeled as "strategic analysis." If they can process all the informational cues (i.e., the *Z* variables in the budget environment) with a little enhanced rationality, then the final distributions of various decision indices constructed from the cues will be normal according to the Central Limit Theorem (Jones and Baumgartner 2005b, 127–29). Thus, the outcomes of the decision indices, i.e., (α_i), which might reflect how the *Z* variables in equation (2.5) are incorporated into budget outcomes, will follow normal distributions.

Alternatively, decision makers might process the informational cues *proportionately* although Jones and Baumgartner treated this aspect almost the same as the rational updating. In real-life situations that are similar to typical conditions illustrated under incrementalism, state central budget offices oftentimes make across-the-board cuts over agency budget requests. During the recent several years, the California executive budget documents showed that agency budget requests were mandated to be cut by the same percentage amount across-the-board. This behavior of central budget coordination is more consistent with what is called, as "proportionate" information processing that is associated with incrementalism. Decision makers therefore assign equal weights onto each of all *Z* variables when they are processing the variables into decisions. Jones and Baumgartner (2005b, 129–32) show, through an elaborate computer simulation, that the distributions of proportionate information processing will be close to normal distributions.

First, they generated ten thousand random numbers, with a uniform distribution, for five variables that are supposed to be proxy factors for the *Z* variables. To make the variables more compatible with real-life informational cues, Jones and Baumgartner transformed the five random variables into nonlinear variables (all with different transformations such as cubic, exponential, etc.) so that the latter will take nonnormal shapes. The proportionate information processing implies that decision makers will sum up the five transformed variables to construct a decision index with an equal weight. The distribution of the proportional sum of the final nonlinear, nonnormal variables was almost indistinguishable from a normal distribution. Therefore, under an incrementalist insight the result of processing informational cues from the environment will be closer to normal distributions. As noted above over the theory of serial judgment, however, there is one caveat. The analysis of proportionate information processing is confined primarily to the second part of the right-hand side in equation (2.5). The analysis did not account for the fixed and marginal budget changes. When the fixed portion of the right-hand side in equation (2.5) is accounted for, the final distributions of annual budget changes, not the decision indices α_i, will look closer to a leptokurtic distribution.

In contrast to proportionate information processing, disproportionate information-processing theory clarifies the puzzles in the policy and budget literature. Instead of proportional updating, decision makers are more likely to lock onto one indicator. Thus, Jones and Baumgartner slightly modified the above simulation such that one of the five Z variables was "disproportionately" weighted by .8 and all four variables were given the weight of .05. Then, they summed up the five transformed variables with different weights. The distribution of the final summed variable is strongly leptokurtic. It was characterized by a high peak, thin shoulders, and fat tails (Jones and Baumgartner 2005b, 132–35). Jones and Baumgartner contend that any distributions of decisions, which are not normal but closer to leptokurtic, are symptomatic that decision-making processes do not follow incrementalism. As shown in Figure 4.1 in this book, the distribution of annual changes in U.S. budget authorities from 1961 to 2006 is highly leptokurtic. It is characterized by a high peak (or budget stability), thin shoulders (moderate budget changes), and fat tails (sudden, huge budget changes). Jones and Baumgartner assert that the result implies that the decision process of U.S. budget authorities might not follow incrementalism.

As in the case of serial judgment, however, some interpretation is warranted for lay-readers. In the above two simulations, the range of random numbers was contained within about ± 1. When the four variables were weighted by .05, they will surely come closer to zero. This means that most (about 80 percent of observations; i.e., four of five variables) will be close to the peak area around the mean value that will be close to zero in this case. In contrast, the variable weighted by .8 will remain in almost the same original area. These observations will be more frequently observed in the now thicker tail areas (refer to Figure 4.1 for visualization). What does this finding signify? Specifically, what is the meaning of the fact that about 80 percent of the Z variables are indexed into near zero values? This condition is almost the same as the situation where the first part of the right-hand side of equation (2.5), $(\beta_0 - 1)$, will be the modal observations. The most frequently observed result from final indexing of informational cues flowing from the budget environment will now be around the mean value closer to zero. In other words, this might take place when the main budget actors do not pay much attention to the four environmental factors. Instead, they will resort to a certain reference point that might be a pre-established budget base or an agreed-upon status quo by virtually ignoring the four factors at this point. Thus, some facets of environmental information cues are likely disregarded. However, one variable with the higher weight of .8 is more likely to be reflected into budget decisions if their now relatively larger numbers mean stronger influence onto budget choices in the simulations. Overall, most environmental factors are under-reacted to while one variable is overreacted to. Clearly, decision makers paid "disproportionate" attention to one variable. The result in policy or budget choices is that the variable with overreaction will show sudden, dramatic jump in temporal policy or budget processes.

As discussed earlier, under the standard assumptions of incrementalism such as equation (2.5), the distribution of annual budget changes is more likely to show a high peak around the so-called increment, combined with normally distributed observations of increment. The framework of disproportionate information processing implicitly assumes "the presence of the peak or budget stability" in the distribution of annual budget changes, which can be clarified from the simulations with the transformed variables with different weights. The biggest contribution of disproportionate information-processing theory, then, is that it revealed that sudden, dramatic budget changes (or budget punctuations) occur due mainly to disproportionate information processing of decision makers and that the big changes are not just random errors. Incrementalism explains well why decision makers start from the status quo and make adjustment from that point but it does not describe how decision makers reach such adjustment. In particular, the major problem of incrementalism is that it does not account for information inflow from the environment (Berry 1990; Jones and Baumgartner 2005a, 2005b; LeLoup 1978; Rubin 1989). Jones and Baumgartner thus provide a more insightful and elaborate theory detailing how decision makers process such information cues into budget choices. This aspect was lacking in incrementalist approaches to decision making (Ryu 2009).

In some cases, there is a sudden budget increase not related to disproportionate information processing. In response to the 9-11 attack or Hurricane Katrina, there were sudden increases in the homeland security function or the emergency management programs. These emergencies will be treated as random errors in incrementalism. Even in the absence of such emergencies, however, there have been sudden budget increases. In 1950, President Truman signed Social Security reforms as major amendments to the Social Security Act of 1933. The reforms expanded Old Age and Survivors Insurance benefits by about 77 percent and dramatically increased the covered population. From FY 1950 to FY 1951, the Social Security expenditures grew 25 percent and grew an additional 37 percent for the next fiscal year (Jones and Baumgartner 2005a, 145–8). The sudden changes in Social Security budgets cannot be attributable to emergency needs. In this sense, disproportionate information-processing theory creatively explains why sudden budget changes take place. Once again, the above theoretical simulations need to be further summarized in plain language for lay-readers.

Complex political systems do not automatically adapt to ever-changing environments. Rather, "new ways of thinking about public problems, rapid mobilizations of new constituencies, changes in institutional structures, and the self-reinforcing effects of these trends occasionally combine to create dramatic and unpredictable policy changes in an issue-area" (Jones, Baumgartner, and True 1998, 2). The typical pattern of policy outcomes is characterized by long periods of stability interspersed with occasional, dramatic change, or punctuated equilibrium in policy stability. Using U.S. domestic budget authorities from 1947 to 1995, Jones, Baumgartner, and True (1998) identified three distinct epochs divided by two large-scale punctuations. Their findings are starkly contrasted with what has been suggested in outcome incrementalism where policy outcomes follow stabilized, highly predictable paths of change.

In the real world of decision making, decision makers are likely to follow a decision-making path slightly different from the proportionate information processing. They are more likely to lock onto one specific indicator that serves as a heuristic for future decision making. Some aspects of environmental cues are unmonitored, unattended to. Errors in decisions due to the unattended factors will be accumulated and sudden, episodic adjustments will follow. As Jones and Baumgartner (2005a) argue, "Suddenly decision makers recognize that previously ignored facets of the environment are relevant and scramble to incorporate them. Choice is attention driven because unmonitored aspects of reality must be brought into the choice calculus as it becomes impossible to ignore them" (334). Unlike proportionate information processing in incrementalist approaches, disproportionate information processing is characterized by attention-driven choice and episodic policy adjustments.

The disproportionality in information processing will be further amplified by institutional friction. Institutional rules and procedures under collective decision-making condition incur decision costs, transaction costs, information costs, and cognitive costs. Decision costs are incurred when decision makers try to reach an agreement. They include bargaining costs between decision makers and institutionally imposed costs possibly arising from a separation-of-power governance setting. Transaction costs are incurred when decision makers try to ensure compliance to contractual agreements. Information costs are search costs. When decision makers search for relevant information for decision making, information costs are incurred. Cognitive costs are incurred for any social institutions composed of human beings due to their limited information-processing capacity. In addition to the institutional frictions that will augment disproportionate information processing, there is one more point that will further prompt budget punctuations.

As signals from environments get stronger, the institutionally incurred costs might be declining due possibly to a bandwagon effect from actions for proposed policy changes. In other words, the costs reduce actions up to some threshold but beyond the point they will amplify the reaction of the decision-making system to stronger signals. This will result in overreaction to the signals. The distribution of policy or budget outcomes due to disproportionate information processing will be the leptokurtic distributions of policy or budget outcomes, with strong stability around mean values followed by fat tails denoting sudden, episodic policy changes. Jones, Sulkin, and Larsen (2003) show that the distributions of budgetary outcomes are much more leptokurtic than other general policy or election outcomes.

In sum, incrementalism predicts that due to "lack" of efficient and complete information, decision makers do not pay attention to budget informational cues from the surrounding environments. The neglect will primarily lead to budget stability. In contrast, disproportionate information-processing theory predicts that faced with "oversupply of information" decision makers will give "selective" attention to the informational cues. The result is primarily sudden, dramatic changes in policy or budget choices. Secondarily, this will also lead to policy or budget stability (as implicitly denoted from the above computer simulations). Institutional frictions will augment the aspect of indicator lock.

The overall discussions in this chapter generally suggest that bounded rationality might be one of main reasons for disproportionate information processing or indicator lock. In most cases, human rationality is limited because his or her information-processing capacity is limited. Therefore, one can expect that when information-processing capacities of decision makers are enhanced, the possibility of disproportionate information processing will decrease and thus, the frequency of policy or budget punctuations will also decline. In addition, as institutional frictions get less intense, policy or budget punctuations are less likely to take place. Ironically, incrementalism predicts that decision makers will stick to fixed, marginal budget changes under the conditions of limited information-processing capacity and intense institutional frictions. The result is more frequent observations of policy or budget stability. As will be introduced in Chapter 3, a certain aspect of bureaucracy, bureaucratic centralization, was invented to enhance information-processing capacity of human decision makers and reduce institutional frictions. The fact is that we have long forgotten the potential function of bureaucracy. It might be interesting to investigate how bureaucratic centralization will affect budget punctuations and stability.

Conclusion

In this chapter, we have reviewed the four main approaches crucial in understanding human decision-making procedures under institutional settings. The review suggests that there are some common observations over human decision-making mechanisms and procedures. Human decision makers are bounded in their information-processing capacity. Also, institutional frictions further augment their limited capacity. Incrementalism predicts that the limited information-processing capacity of decision makers and institutional frictions are highly likely to drive main budget actors to resort to some agreed-upon reference points. The result under the incrementalist perspective is budget stability. In other words, budget outcomes will change marginally from previous ones. In stark contrast, disproportionate information-processing theory contends that decision makers will pay selective attention to a few indicators obtained from budget environments while disregarding most other facets from the decision environment. At some point in temporal policy or budget processes, the ignored facets can no longer be disregarded and will be given sudden attention. The result is sudden, dramatic changes in policy or budget outcomes. Therefore, overreaction to the ignored facets is the main reason for policy or budget punctuations. Institutional frictions augment the attention-driven choices or indicator lock, and thus policy or budget punctuations.

In sum, both policy/budget stability and punctuations are the ramifications of limited information-processing capacity and institutional frictions. Incrementalism asserts that the limited capacity and institutional frictions lead to policy or budget inertia. According to disproportionate information-processing theory, they will cause policy or budget punctuations. Overall, both budget stability and punctuations are associated with the limited capacity and frictions. Then, a crucial question is whether there might be solutions to enhance the information-processing capacity of decision makers and reduce the frictions that institutional settings surrounding decision makers generate. In this book, the answer is sought from one aspect of bureaucratic organizations, bureaucratic centralization. It is very ironic that many scholars and practitioners have contended that bureaucratic organizations were one of the main causes for bounded rationality and institutional frictions. However, bureaucratic centralization was originally suggested as a way to enhance the information-processing capacity of decision makers, and facilitate interunit communication within bureaucratic organizations, and thereby reduce institutional frictions. In various tiers of the federal system, bureaucratic centralization has been in wide operation. This has been especially the case in the budget processes. In Chapter 3, scholarly suggestions, which we have long forgotten, will be refreshed to our memory and reveal how bureaucratic centralization can extend the information-processing capacity of decision makers and reduce institutional frictions.

Note

1. The program level in Padgett's study is almost the same as the agency level in Davis, Dempster, and Wildavsky (1966, 1974).

3

Bureaucratic Organizations as a Remedy to Bounded Rationality

Bureaucracies have been frequently criticized for the seeds of their inherent incompetence and numerous cases of dysfunctions. Merton (1940, 1957) found that bureaucratic organizations are likely to be filled with their members with trained incapacity. Workers in bureaucratic organizations maintain their organizational actions based on skills that have been successfully applied to previous work settings. However, they cannot make adequate responses to the changes in surrounding organizational environments because their capabilities, which worked in the past, now cannot cope with such changes. In contrast, bureaucratic organizations pursue specialization and elaborate rules, and constantly press their members to conform to pre-established routines of obligations. Ultimately, workers in bureaucratic organizations tend to adhere to such routines or rules as an end, which are fundamentally a means to achieve organizational goals. The tendency augments mere blind conformance rather than organizational performance (Rainey 2009, 55–56; Shafritz, Russell, and Borick 2011, 270).

Bureaucracies have also been criticized in terms of behavioral consequences of bureaucratic structures. Thompson (1961) coined a familiar concept, bureaupathic official, by combining bureaucracy with pathological. Such a bureaupathic official suppresses technical and informal aspects of relationships. Instead, such a person overemphasizes the official and nontechnical aspects. Since such a person might feel insecure in his or her position, the person is likely to insist on petty prerogatives on organizational procedures or protocols. However, such procedures or protocols are least likely to help achieve organizational goals. In addition, such a person insists on his or her right to review organizational procedures and fly into a rage when he or she feels bypassed. The person usually maintains a close contact with a counterpart at a higher organizational level and takes advantage of such exclusive contact as clearance point. By controlling the communication channel, he or she protects his or her authority. Therefore, bureaucratic organizations can be inundated by bureaupathology in their members, who are overly concerned with protecting their office authority as well as too impersonal in their relations with clients and other organizational members. This type of bureaupathic officer with a concern for petty rights is everywhere in bureaucratic organizations (Rainey 2009, 56; Shafritz, Russell, and Borick 2011, 271).

In some sense, bureaucracies were suggested as a remedy to political nepotism or spoils system that prevailed throughout the nineteenth century in the United States. Recruitment and promotion of organizational members were supposed to be based on objective evaluation of their capabilities, not their tie with politicians or higher-ups in the organizations. Thus, a certain level of impersonality was believed to enhance the overall efficiency and effectiveness of the organizations. Organizational members as well as their clients were treated as impersonal cases so that organizations can continue their operations based on objective rules, which will result in speed, clarity, efficiency, and effectiveness (Rainey 2009, 28–30; Rosenbloom, Kravchuk, and Clerkin 2009, 199–208). When clients are treated as cases, however, there is a high likelihood that they might complain that they are assigned into the categories to which they feel they do not belong. Although bureaucratic organizations process the cases based on objective rules and procedures, bureaucratic decisions might fail to accurately reflect individual characteristics into case categorization. Bureaucratic impersonality can protect procedural justice but possibly at the expense of substantive or actual justice. This is another example of a bureaucratic pathology, an inversion of ends and means (Shafritz, Russell, and Borick 2011, 271–73).

Since the 1980s, bureaucracies have been heavily bashed from both practitioners and scholars. Ronald Reagan used to contend that government bureaucracy is the problem. Reagan constantly complained that government bureaucracy is like a big baby. It exemplifies an alimentary canal with a huge appetite but no sense of responsibility (Shafritz, Russell, and Borick 2011, 273–75). The recent New Public Management (NPM) movements strongly asserted that governmental agencies need to borrow management techniques and organizational structures that are similar to those used in business corporations and private market activities. The fundamental assumption behind NPM is that government and business organizations are inherently similar. Therefore, employing business management procedures into governmental organizations will improve the rigidity in governmental bureaucracies, thus enhancing governmental efficiency (Rainey 2009, 64). NPM movements have also contended that decentralized organizational structures might improve organizational performance by empowering service managers. Supporters of NPM also asserted that strategizing might make organizations more flexible and fit for purpose. Some governments have pursued such decentralized structures for improved decision making and enhanced customer orientation (Andrews et al. 2009).

In particular, Osborne and Gaebler, in their famous book *Reinventing Government* (1992), attacked the old-fashioned, centralized, bureaucratic organizations most frequently found in many government agencies. Instead, they called for enterprising government. They cited numerous governmental practices that already improved their effectiveness through decentralizing, encouraging privatization, encouraging control of public programs at the community level, customer-driven government, and making money on their operations. Enterprising government also focused on mission-driven, results-oriented government and emphasized market-oriented government. They ignited the initiative for REGO (reinventing government). The REGO movement is obviously multifaceted approaches to enhance governmental efficiency and effectiveness. However, one thing is clear that the movement demanded the drastic surgery, if not elimination, of governmental bureaucracies (Rainey 2009, 435–37). Most recently, a group of leading scholars in public management opined that bureaucratic organizations cannot address the so-called wicked public problems that span multiple jurisdictions for solution. They suggested that collaborative network management, not single bureaucratic organization, can address such issues more effectively and efficiently (Bingham and O'Leary 2008; O'Leary and Bingham 2009).

In sum, bureaucracies have been attacked from various perspectives. However, some aspects of bureaucratic organizations or arrangements still merit our further, more elaborate attention. For instance, even the scholars who emphasize the importance of collaborative network management do stress that a certain level of centralized coordination, which is one aspect of common bureaucratic organizations, is highly needed for effective management of collaborative networks (Agranoff 2007; Provan and Kenis 2008; Provan and Milward 1995). As discussed in this chapter and later chapters of this book, centralization was originally supposed to expedite information-processing capacity of human decision makers and reduce intraorganizational conflict through clear centralized coordination of functions and authorities. In fact, bureaucracy itself was the result of creative efforts by human decision makers to augment their otherwise limited information-processing capacity. The next sections will remind us that we have long been ignorant of this fundamental rationale for why such bureaucratic organizations were invented in the first place.

Bureaucratic Organizations: Extending Human Cognitive and Analytical Capacities

Weber's concept of bureaucracy best describes the general characteristics of bureaucratic organizations. His concept was based on six general principles (Mansfield 1973, 477):

> (1) there are 'fixed and official jurisdictional areas which are generally ordered by rules,' (2) organizations have a strict hierarchical system of authority, (3) administration is based on written documents, known as the files, (4) management 'presupposes thorough and expert training,' (5) bureaucratic activity is a full-time occupation, and (6) the management of the bureaucracy 'follows general rules, which are more or less stable, more or less exhaustive, and which can be learned.'

The concept of ideal-type bureaucratic organizations was further elaborated by administrative scholars like Luther Gulick. Gulick contended that what is really needed is an administrative branch capable of planning and implementing democratic policies. Gulick made various suggestions for administrative organizations. Related work should be categorized as a unit that in turn will be under the control of a single, responsible official who is selected based on technical capacity and experience. The authority of each unit head should be commensurate with his or her responsibility. All administrative work should be coordinated by a single chief executive. The chief executive should have a research staff that can assist the chief executive on the work of subunits in bureaucratic organizations and search for improved way of normal operation. In sum, Gulick's ideas can be condensed into division of work and coordination. Human beings differ in their nature, capacity, and skill. In addition, they differ in terms of their time and knowledge capacity. Therefore, division of work is highly needed. At the same time, however, integration is strongly required to coordinate the unit tasks defined in the division of work to avoid organizational confusion (Fry and Raadschelders 2008, 97–98).

Why have human decision makers pursued the creation of such bureaucratic organizations characterized by formal rules, specialization, and coordination? Decades ago, Chester Barnard offered his insightful observation to this question. According to Barnard, it is imperative to underlie the fact that human beings are under two major classes of limitations, arising from their biological faculties, or their capacities and the physical factors of their surrounding environment. As discussed in Chapter 2, Herbert Simon paid more attention to individual capacity limits when he made a comprehensive analysis of bounded rationality. In contrast, Barnard asserted that the two factors are limiting premises for individual decision making (Fry and Raadschelders 2008, 186). In Barnard's view, human beings are biologically and physically limited. However, they are still social, active, and purposeful such that they own a minimum level of free will to bypass such limitations. The limitations necessitate human beings to cooperate with other persons to achieve what they cannot achieve alone. The social and purposeful nature of human beings triggers actual cooperative behavior in organizations.

In essence, what Barnard clarifies is that "human organisms are incapable of functioning except in conjunction with other human organisms" (Fry and Raadschelders 2008, 185). Thus, cooperation is a natural result of human efforts to overcome the limitations imposed by their physical environments and biological capacity features. When the satisfaction from cooperation exceeds the cost of cooperation, the cooperative system will be maintained. Driven by their purposefulness, human beings further establish informal organizations by nurturing shared understandings, customs, habits, and institutions. Since informal organizations are passive associations, and human beings are purposeful and active, informal organizations ultimately turn into more formal organizations. The shared understandings and institutions developed in informal organizations create favorable conditions to the rise of formal organizations (Fry and Raadschelders 2008, 185–87).

Herbert Simon elaborates what Barnard assumed about human beings' decision making in an organizational environment. Simon basically viewed organizations as an environment for individual decision making. The environment is composed of a complex network of decision processes that would influence individual behavior. The organization creates stimuli that drive individuals toward specific decisions and create decision premises for their decisions. The organization also creates an organizational personality and confers this upon the persons in responsibility with the means for exerting authority. The organization takes individual decision autonomy but substitutes an organizational decision process for individual discretion in decision making. Surprisingly, this exchange system will bring about a broader context of rationality. While the organization places individual decision makers in a psychological setting that adapts individual decisions to organizational goals, the organization simultaneously provides the individuals with more abundant information for correct decision. Therefore, "the organization can overcome the computational limits of man by such devices as specialization and the division of labor, which bring expert knowledge to bear on organizational decisions and limit the required focus of attention" (Fry and Raadschelders 2008, 229).

Simon offered a more detailed analysis of the inducements-contributions exchange model than Barnard suggested. Unlike Barnard, Simon further divides the exchange system into two mechanisms; one for individual decision to participate and the other for the decision to produce. The nature of the decision to participate in the organization, especially employment contract, has particularly important connotations for both the organization and the employee. The employee is willing to sell his or her service and agrees to become a neutral instrument to perform organizational services. The willingness denotes that the employee will accept performance criteria that are not related to his or her personal values. Most importantly, from the viewpoint of the employee the cognitive demands on his or her decision-making capacity are substantially alleviated by restricting his or her attention primarily to organizational decision targets. The limited performance targets mean limited alternatives scanned and selected. In short, the organization in which individual decision makers participate significantly simplifies the decision environment for individual employees (Fry and Raadschelders 2008, 230–31).

Simon further suggested that the hierarchical system is the best decision premises for individual decision making in the organization. Complex organizations tend to be horizontally specialized. As hierarchy synchronizes parochial and disparate elements arising from the horizontal specialization, hierarchy can also heighten the level of coordination. Hierarchy can also achieve vertical specialization. The employees with greater technical expertise will be conferred greater authority. This will consequently assure that technical experts will command the organizational decision-making process. These clear assignments of authority and work responsibility will also be crucial in locating organizational accountability. In addition to the traditional justification for hierarchy, Simon further asserted that hierarchy can simplify the decision-making tasks in organizations. Complex hierarchical organizations evolve from fairly stable subsystems largely independent of the overall organization. Therefore, interdependencies are likely to be minimized and complexity will be independent of organizational size. A complex hierarchical organization will then call for reduced necessity of information transmission and ultimately decision making will be simplified (Fry and Raadschelders 2008, 233–34).

As discussed in this section, organizational scholars indicated decades ago that bureaucratic organizations, which are characterized by hierarchy, specialization, and coordination, can improve computational limits of individual decision makers. In particular, many organizational scholars have emphatically stressed that especially bureaucratic centralization can facilitate information-processing capacity of decision makers within organizations and reduce potential conflicts among organizational subunits.

Bureaucratic Centralization: Expediting Information Processing and Reducing Institutional Frictions

Unlike the recent NPM movements, organizational scholars who pioneered to establish and polish the so-called principles of public administration generally recommended that organizational activities be centrally controlled and coordinated. As discussed earlier, Barnard assumed that informal organizations are inherently passive, so they compel development of formal organizations. Barnard observes that the final stage of organizational development process is "complex" formal organizations. Complex organizations evolve from simple formal organizations because the size of the latter is constrained by limits on communication. Organizational growth demands creating new subunits but at the same time complex formal organizations also require the overall organizational goals to remain as the unifying element. To address the limits of communication, complex organizations demand that their subunits be specialized and fairly autonomous.

Most importantly, complex formal organizations require executive functions to be located in a single body. The latter will further coordinate relatively autonomous subunits by "acting as a communication center" (Fry and Raadschelder 2008, 188).

According to Barnard, organizational decisions are fundamentally dominated by organizational purposes rather than individual value preferences. As such, they are likely to be more logical, if not more correct, than individual decision making. Communication centers led by executives can best make organizational decisions because the executives are specializing in organizational decision making. This process adequately coordinates the requisite information obtained from the decision environment for organizational decisions. In this process, organizational purposes can help decision makers distinguish the relevant from irrelevant informational clues from the decision environment. Overall, Barnard's ideas boil down to the enhanced role of somewhat centralized executive functions as a communication center. In short, executives are supposed to coordinate the adjustment of cooperative systems (i.e., complex formal organizations) to environmental changes and new organizational purposes (Fry and Raadschelder 2008, 196–99). This condition can be likened to "the relationship between the brain and the rest of the body" (Fry and Raadschelder 2008, 199).

Jones and Baumgartner (2005) made a breakthrough over theoretical controversies regarding incrementalism and earlier studies on bounded rationality, as introduced in Chapter 2. Much similar to Barnard and Simon, they also suggest that organizational arrangements might function as a mechanism to augment the information-processing capacity of individual decision makers but with some caution. As individual decision makers pay selective attention to environmental stimuli, organizations might also selectively attend to policy issues because they are limited in their information-processing capacity as well. One way to augment such capacity of organizations is creating a specialized unit in bureaucratic organizations. A typical example is the Congressional committee system. Since the whole legislative body cannot process relevant policy information simultaneously, Congress also takes advantage of division of labor. Each committee develops specialized knowledge and techniques to process policy information and search for policy alternatives. This committee system substantially relieves the full legislature or central leadership of the extraordinary computational burden. Under this condition of labor division, accumulation of expertise through specialization is obtained but at the expense of incurring other transaction costs. Coordination of unrelated, disparate subunits toward the overall organizational goal incurs costs for monitoring and supervising. Thus, organizational arrangements only through creating special units cannot efficiently address the selective attention problem (Jones and Baumgartner 2005b, 38–40).

Jones and Baumgartner's theories are nicely echoing and skillfully elaborating previous theories of decision premises and behaviors. Their empirical findings are groundbreaking contributions to the theory of policy and budget processes but a significant question still remains unanswered. Why have we not paid equal attention to the role of a specialized agency, but in this case a specialized and *centralized* agency, if it is dedicated to facilitating information processing and reducing intraorganizational frictions? As detailed in Chapter 5, Congress has been characterized as the fragmented and decentralized committee system that was supposed to accelerate division of labor. It was also expected that such a decentralized system is an open invitation to institutional frictions as Jones and Baumgartner predicted. However, the Congressional Budget Office (CBO) has been deemed as a creation of a new "bureaucratic" central agency that would enhance information-processing capacity of primarily budget committees and secondarily other legislative committees (LeLoup 1977, 147). Numerous cases of the Office of Management and Budget (OMB) in the national government and equivalent central budget offices in state governments equally provide a lot of functions to relieve the computational burden of line agencies as well as chief executives. They also coordinate potential tensions among executive agencies and relieve conflicts between the executive agencies and legislative committees. While scholars have been searching for the Holy Grail to improve bounded rationality and reduce institutional frictions, they have not thought about an answer from bureaucracy itself that instead was alleged as the very source of bounded rationality.

Supporters of disproportionate information-processing theory revealed what earlier studies on bounded rationality did not find. For instance, why sudden, dramatic changes in policy or budget processes take place in the first place if they are symptomatic of reduced information-processing capacity and augmented institutional frictions. However, they did not fully account for the potential coordination of subunits in bureaucratic organizations through bureaucratic centralization. Central and specialized agencies can reduce transaction costs by minimizing intraorganizational frictions as they function as central communication centers as Barnard suggested. By way of organizational decision making based on organizational purposes, a specialized and centralized agency can also minimize information and search costs when bureaucratic organizations are discriminating the relevant from irrelevant budget information flowing from the decision environment. Herbert Simon particularly elaborated on the benefits from centralized coordination, i.e., enhancing information-processing capacity of decision makers. Surprisingly, a majority of contemporary scholars have been ignorant of how centralized coordination can enhance information-processing capacity of decision makers. Thus, Simon's old yet insightful investigation of organizational decision making is well worth another round of careful scrutiny and re-interpretation.

In Chapter 2, Simon's view of the individual decision maker as an information-processing system was introduced in detail. Individual decision makers are characterized by limited information-processing capacity. The amount of information or work that they can process or do at one time is extremely limited. This is also the reason why individuals are willing to participate in organizations. Organizations can render expert knowledge accumulated through specialization and division of labor to bear on organizational decisions. This will ultimately prevent the individuals from diffusing their limited attention to nongermane information.

Organizational decision-making process is similar to the individual decision-making process. The first step in organizational decision making is the definition of the situation. This concept is analogous to the definition of problem space for individual decision makers. Much similar to the latter, the definition of problem is a simplified model of reality that is developed to reduce the complexity of the actual decision environment. It includes "the decision maker's perception of the likelihood of future events, the range of alternatives seen as possible, expectations regarding the consequences of those alternatives, and rules for ordering the consequences according to the preferences of the decision maker" (Fry and Raadschelder 2008, 235). The decision procedure is also characterized by some form of means-ends chain where uncertainty about the relationship between alternatives and consequences increases as decision makers ascend the chain. Simon also describes the decision procedure as a loosely coupled system because decisions are divided into subunits. Under the system, organizational objectives are imperfectly reconciled with subunits. Decision criteria are driven by satisfactory alternatives, i.e., satisficing rather than optimizing (Fry and Raadschelder 2008, 235–36).

Disproportionate information-processing theory suggests almost similar explanation of how individual decision makers and organizations reach their final decisions (Jones and Baumgartner 2005a). Simon, however, further made a distinction between two basically different types of organizational decision-making procedures, programmed and nonprogrammed. Programmed decision making takes place when the stimulus from the decision environment is highly repetitive and organizations have pre-established protocols for handling such stimulus. The most frequently employed techniques under programmed decision procedures are habit, clerical routines, and organizational structure. One clear pattern of programmed decision making is that search activities for alternatives are extremely limited (Fry and Raadschelder 2008, 237–38).

This condition is very close to the situation when the second part of the right-hand side in equation (2.5) is zero: i.e., $M.B.A. * (\beta_1 \cdot Z_{1t} + \beta_2 \cdot Z_{2t} + \dots \beta_m \cdot Z_{mt}) = 0$. What does this mean? Budgetary incrementalism found that there are three main budget actors in the budget processes under typical executive budgeting systems. It also found that their interactions are highly predictable and stabilized. Executive agencies tend to pad their budget requests, central budget offices tend to cut the requests pursuant to chief executives' policy preferences and forecast revenues, and legislative committees tend to conform to gubernatorial budget recommendations. Whenever environmental stimuli show extremely repetitive patterns or are featured by intense political tensions that pit desires against desires, the main budget actors are least likely to open up previous conflicts over the fair shares of budget claimants. Typically, the fair shares are close to budget bases that are oftentimes last years' budgets for agencies. Under this condition, the protocol to process environmental stimuli, i.e., Z variables in equation (2.5), tends to be virtual ignorance of them. As in the case of programmed organizational decision making, search activities for alternatives by processing the environmental stimuli will be almost nonexistent. The result is that annual budget changes will be represented by the first part of the right-hand side in equation (2.5), $(\beta_0 - 1)$. The latter has been reported somewhere between 5–10 percent, seldom larger than 30 percent.

When we are searching for organizational and institutional arrangements that can augment information-processing capacity of human beings and thus, reduce bounded rationality, we should exert some caution about the programmed decision process. The steadfast budget stability or inertia is extremely difficult to shake loose. Human cognitive capacity limits typically lead to agreed upon levels of budget pies for all budget actors. Even when they have augmented information-processing capacity, human desires for resources cannot be self-moderated. As Wildavsky succinctly put, resources are scarce but human desires are not (Wildavsky 1997). Political features accelerate the human nature. Therefore, it is very unlikely that bureaucratic centralization might exert any significant influence on budget stability or inertia. Scholars must separate the programmed decision procedure from the nonprogrammed one when investigating the effects of organizational or institutional arrangements on budget inertia. In actuality, it has been reported that nothing can easily alter main budget actors' budget aspirations. Then, bureaucratic centralization should not be blamed for what nothing can prevent from happening.

But what happens when the second part of the right-hand side in equation (2.5) is not zero: i.e., $M.B.A. * (\beta_1 \cdot Z_{1t} + \beta_2 \cdot Z_{2t} + \cdots + \beta_m \cdot Z_{mt}) \neq 0$. As discussed in Chapter 2, one of confusions and controversies over incrementalism has been focused on whether exogenous budget environments exert significance influence on budget choices and outcomes. Previous findings are somewhat bifurcated on the impacts of exogenous factors on budget choices. One stream of budget research has consistently contended that the main budget actors have exerted dominating influence on budget outcomes, especially budget decisions at agency or department levels. The study conducted by Davis, Dempster, and Wildavsky (1974) indicated that exogenous budget environments, such as political, fiscal, and institutional factors, do not significantly affect budget choices for domestic programs in the national government. This condition is very close to the programmed decision procedures as investigated earlier: i.e., the second part of the right-hand side in equation (2.5) is zero. More recent studies emphasized that budget environments play heavier roles in budget processes (Ryu et al. 2008). Ryu et al. (2008) found that exogenous factors exert some influence on agency budget outcomes in the fifty states. However, they also showed that the aspirations and behaviors of main budget actors still dominate the state budget processes and outcomes.

In sharp contrast, disproportionate information-processing theory made a very clear and creative interpretation of whether and how exogenous environmental factors affect budget choices. Disproportionate information-processing theory offered some clues on why the findings over the impact of budget environments on budget outcomes are bifurcated. Although it did not specify who makes budget choices, it clarified at least one point. The second part of the right-hand side in equation (2.5) will not be zero. If we can assume that the main budget actors are still the most influential budget decision makers,[1] disproportionate information-processing theory explains why the empirical findings are bifurcated. The main budget actors pay attention to informational cues flowing from budget environments and process such budget information obtained from the decision environment. However, they are highly likely to selectively attend to such information. The result is, as introduced in Chapter 2, sudden, dramatic changes in budget outcomes. This implies that budget environments do influence budget choices but when and how they will do so is utterly unpredictable and random. In addition, the impact of budget environments is frequently delayed, thus resulting in no impact of budget environments on budget choices until budget punctuations take place. This clarification by disproportionate information-processing theory is no small contribution to the budgeting literature by any standards.

This condition is quite close to what Simon calls as nonprogrammed decision-making procedures. Disproportionate information-processing theory made a breakthrough in the budgeting literature by elaborating on this specific condition. Even it, however, lost sight of one important aspect to augment information-processing capacity of decision makers under nonprogrammed decision procedures as clarified in the following paragraphs. According to Simon, nonprogrammed decisions are made when decision makers face novel stimuli for which no structured responses have been developed (Fry and Raadschelder 2008, 238). In some sense, this condition might slightly differ from the situation mentioned earlier: i.e., $M.B.A. * (\beta_1 \cdot Z_{1t} + \beta_2 \cdot Z_{2t} + \cdots + \beta_m \cdot Z_{mt}) \neq 0.$. Under this situation, the main budget actors might retain some solutions to environmental stimuli. In addition, the stimuli might not be that novel. However, Simon's perception of performance gap clearly indicates that this situation strongly resembles the nonprogrammed decision-making procedures. Performance gap is detected in the face "of unsatisfactory performance in regard to previous levels of aspiration, of heightened aspirations resulting from factors such as encounters with new opportunities, or a combination of those factors" (Fry and Raadschelder 2008, 238). Decision makers open up their search activities upon finding such performance gap. More specifically, the levels of aspirations are determined by past performance levels of peer organizations or changes in the decision environment (Fry and Raadschelder 2008, 238). These factors construct a highly probable scenario in typical budget-making processes.

Can there be any measures that might help improve decision making under a condition like nonprogrammed decision procedures? Political scientists or management scholars have generally asserted that organizational or institutional arrangements cannot be solutions to nonprogrammed decision procedures. In fact as described earlier, institutional arrangements, especially bureaucratization of decision-making processes, have been blamed for multiple dysfunctions and bounded rationality. However, they have not been careful enough in indicating that earlier scholars such as Simon suggested such an organizational arrangement as a tool to improve decision making especially under *non*programmed decision procedures. According to Simon, organizations have traditionally employed judgment, rules of thumb, and training executives to cope with nonprogrammed decision premises. Simon further contended that such techniques can be improved by training in orderly thinking. Very interestingly for the main research question in this book, such techniques can be improved by "the assignment of primary responsibility for nonprogrammed decision making to top executives, and the designation of a specific unit in the organization to deal with nonprogrammed decisions" (Fry and Raadschelder 2008, 239). Various approaches of heuristic problem solving simplify informational cues or hints from the decision environment to address organizational problems. Modern techniques of heuristic problem solving are much indebted to computer simulations of actual decision making. Simulations can evaluate, systemize, and routinize the conventional skills of judgment, intuition, and creativity (Fry and Raadschelder 2008, 239). As noted in Chapter 2, Simon viewed decision making fundamentally as a process of information processing. Thus, improved decision making is strongly associated with improved, expedited information processing. Computerized simulations can help improve information processing under nonprogrammed decision procedures. More importantly, Simon contended that centralized responsibility and creation of a specific unit will probably facilitate information processing and ultimately decision-making processes.

Taking one example of public program will greatly clarify the distinction between programmed vs. nonprogrammed decision procedures. Social Security benefit programs are regarded as public programs subjected to entrenched political interests. Democrats tend to support expansion of the programs to bring about more benefits to their constituency groups, say elderly people. Even Republicans cannot propose downright cut in the benefits. They can do so but at the expense of their jobs in next elections. At best, they might propose very indirect methods to control costs for delivering the benefits, such as freezing COLA (cost of living adjustment). This is actually what Republicans pursued during the mid-1980s. With respect to core benefit provisions in Social Security benefit programs, there is virtually nothing that the main budget actors can attempt to modify unless the authorizing legislation is modified. This condition is close to the programmed decision procedure. Whatever methods are applied such as performance budget, bureaucratic centralization, NPM techniques, etc., policy or budget stability/inertia is extremely hard to review from scratch.

Except for the core benefit provisions, there have been numerous suggestions to curtail program costs or deliver better services. Partial privatization of Social Security (although this was also faced with political rallies in state capitols by elderly people) or adjusting the age of retirement was an example of cost control. There were a lot of pros and cons about the proposals. In some sense, the proposals were triggered by the recent sluggish economy and attendant revenue shortages that plagued almost all tiers of the federal system. Under this condition, it is very likely that the main budget actors selectively attend to the various informational inputs from the decision environment. In fact, selective attention is what they actually did during the recent years as disproportionate information-processing theory suggested. The informational cues might be reflected into policy or budget choices but its timing is delayed and unpredictable. Unlike disproportionate-information processing theory, however, bureaucratic centralization might help expedite processing of the information inputs under a condition similar to nonprogrammed decision procedures. This point is the key research target of this book.

In actual decision-making processes, centralization has already been at the center stage of bureaucratic systems in the national government. Around 1935, President Roosvelt realized that the federal administrative structures were deficient and exacerbated at the state and local levels. This was due to numerous categorical grants, administrative supervision of relief and economic rehabilitation. In 1935, he appointed his Committee on Administrative Management, consisting of Louis Brownlow as chairman, and Luther Gulick and Charles Merriam. The committee recommendations have been criticized by new public administration but continue to occupy the center stage of the discourses on public administration. In actuality, it was the Brownlow Committee on Administrative Management that ignited the debate on centralization and decentralization. A key summary of Brownlow's memorandum for the committee best describes the main suggestions for administrative reform in the national government. The committee should recommend (Egger 1990, 71):

> That the President establish a White House secretariat who under an executive secretariat will develop the direct lines of communications with all staff agencies except the Budget (this agency will directly report to the President).
>
> That through the establishment of the White House secretariat, the President coordinate the work of multiple line and operating agencies regarding information and recommendations.
>
> That the President be given continuing power to regroup, consolidate, and reorganize the departments, agencies and bureaus in the national government; and that to facilitate President's work in this respect the research function in the Bureau of the Budget be developed.
>
> That for effective coordination of executive agency programs, Congress also needs to be somehow coordinated. Congress needs to create its own agent to review and audit the activities of the executive branch and to report to Congress through the committees set up by the two Congressional houses.

The committee report submitted in 1937 was ultimately enacted into the Reorganization Act of 1939. The White House Office was expanded and the Executive Office was created. The Bureau of Budget (BOB) was transferred to it. The net effect was substantially reinforcing the role and administrative authority of the President as chief administrator. One of the key suggestions in the Brownlow Committee was to enhance the coordination power of the President over line agencies regarding information and programmatic recommendations. Gulick, one of the committee's core members, made a case for centralized coordination on various grounds. Centralization would expedite planning processes. It would achieve economies of scale, reduce conflict, and eliminate overlapping among various executive units. Centralization would also help increase specialization, higher levels of expertise, and career opportunities. Finally, centralization would provide focus for the citizen's attention and reduce the citizen's task to manageable proportions (Egger 1990, 78).

Gulick's practical suggestions are also closely related to his scholarly positions about division of work and coordination. Division of work and grouping unit tasks according to the principle of homogeneity is what Gulick labels as a bottom-up perspective. However, the bottom-up view ignores the need for coordination in the bureaucratic organization. Thus, Gulick proposed a top-down view such that if functional specialization is inevitable, coordination is a necessity (Fry and Raadschelders 2008, 99). Therefore, bureaucratic centralization was already in operation in the national government. Bureaucratic centralization as applied to the national government was supposed to primarily expedite communications among different subunits in bureaucratic organizations, which might reduce intraorganizational tensions and conflicts. This aspect might be slightly contrasted with the scholarly positions discussed earlier. Simon also finds the increased information-processing capacity of decision makers as the primary merit of bureaucratic centralization.

In sum, bureaucratic centralization is hypothesized to expedite information-processing capacity of decision makers and reduce conflicts among sub-decision units in bureaucratic organizations. However, this expectation might not be realized for a decision condition similar to programmed decision procedures that have been characterized by extreme levels of bounded rationality and political, institutional stickiness.

Bureaucratic Centralization and Moderating Impact of Organizational Strategies

Budget processes in various levels of governments in the United States have been substantially centralized beginning from the executive budgeting systems in the early part of the twentieth century, which were featured by strong central coordination functions by central budget offices on behalf of chief executives. The 1974 Congressional Budget and Impoundment Control Act ignited the development of Congressional macro-budgeting as well. As detailed in Chapters 4–6, bureaucratic centralization was supposed to expedite information processing and reduce institutional frictions in budget processes. Despite the insightful scholarly assumptions about how bureaucratic centralization might affect information processing and institutional frictions, there have been virtually no empirical studies that illuminate the impact of bureaucratic centralization. The lack of such empirical studies is substantially attributable to the difficulty developing measures of the outcomes associated with information processing and institutional frictions. Instead, some of the existing empirical studies tested whether centralization affects organizational performance. In some sense, one can expect that expedited information processing and reduced organizational conflicts within bureaucratic organizations can enhance organizational performance. Therefore, the studies on organizational performance can help develop our expectations of how bureaucratic centralization can affect information processing and friction reducing as well.

Andrews et al.'s recent study (2009) provides succinct summaries of past empirical findings. Most of all, they present very useful categories of organizational strategies, which can be juxtaposed to equation (2.5). It can also be contrasted with the distinction between programmed vs. nonprogrammed decision procedures. Based on Miles and Snow (1978), the authors test whether organizations perform better when structures match well their strategies. In particular, they investigate under what organizational strategies centralization can enhance organizational performance.

Centralization typically covers two meanings in organization studies. Hierarchy of authority denotes the extent to which organizational decisions are made at the upper levels of organizational hierarchies. Participation in decision making refers to the degree to which organizational staff can participate in organizational decision making. According to classical theorists of bureaucracy, there is no doubt that centralization will be reasonably related to organizational performance. It is asserted that centralized decision making is essential for effectiveness and efficiency of large bureaucratic organizations. Taylor's ideas contended that scientific management is possible only when decision making is confined to a small cadre of management planners. Overall, bureaucratic centralization might speed up decision processes, provide firm direction and goals, and develop clear lines of hierarchical authority. The centralized coordination will thus minimize the potential for damaging internal conflict (Andrews et al. 2009).

On the other hand, others posit that centralization causes a lot of bureaucratic dysfunctions such as rigidity, red tape, and abuses of monopoly power. Bureaucratic controls might lead frontline staff to spend disproportionate time searching for ways to bypass established rules. This will ultimately detract from external and internal accountability. According to supporters of participative decision making, centralization deprives middle managers and street-level bureaucrats of the chances to make independent decisions, modify inflexible rules and procedures, and their responsiveness to changing environmental circumstances. In fact, previous studies conducted since the early 1970s show that empirical findings are strictly bifurcated (Andrews et al. 2009, Table 1).

A study on thirty organizations in one U.S. city reported that hierarchy of authority increased productivity. At the same time, however, participation in decision making also boosted efficiency of operation (Glisson and Martin 1980). In two community correctional facilities in Oregon and Colorado, participation in decision making decreased perceptions of implementation success (Maynard-Moody, Musheno, and Palumbo 1990). The study conducted by Moynihan and Pandey (2005) showed that hierarchy of authority decreased staff perceptions of effectiveness in eighty-three U.S. state-level health and human service agencies. In sixty-seven New York manpower agencies, participation in decision making increased output but decreased staff perceptions of effectiveness (Whetten 1978). According to Andrews et al. (2009), one potential reason for the bifurcated relationship between centralization and organizational performance might be due to some missing links. The authors assert that the missing links might be the role of strategic choice.

The authors use four ideal types of strategic stance of organizations to conceptualize strategy, based on Miles and Snow (1978). Prospectors almost continually search for new market opportunities. These types of organizations experiment with potential responses to the emerging trends in their surrounding environments. They often develop new products and services. Defenders maintain a conservative stance with respect to new product development. They are mostly devoted to improving the efficiency of their current operations and focus on price and quality rather than new services or markets. Analyzers share characteristics of both prospector and defender. They are rarely first movers. Instead, they look for competitors' new ideas and make a quick decision to adopt most promising ideas. Top managers in reactor-type organizations do not have a consistent and stable strategy for responding to the changes and uncertainty in their surrounding environments. Reactors seldom make any environmental adjustments until they are forced to do so. Most organizations share multiple characteristics and analyzers are redundant with other types of organizations. So, the authors categorize organizational strategies into prospecting, defending, and reacting. Successful pursuit of organizational strategies highly hinges on adopting the most appropriate internal structure and processes. A fit between the pursued strategy and internal organizational structures is the necessary condition for successful organizational performance (Andrews et al. 2009; Rainey 2009, 192–96).

Therefore, prospectors and defenders have distinctive internal structures while reactors do not have consistent internal arrangements. Central management needs to be allowed the ability to control organizational operations in defender-type organizations. Defenders are observed to maximize the efficiency of internal procedures. A classic bureaucracy exemplifies defender-type organizations. In bureaucratic organizations, top-level executives retain the necessary information for organizational operation and the proper vantage point for controlling operations across several organizational subunits. In contrast, the administrative system in prospector-type organizations needs to deploy and coordinate resources across the subunits rather than centrally plan and control organizational operations. Middle managers and frontline staff can apply their expertise in various areas to decision making without being constrained by centralized managerial control. Finally, reactors lack any specific organizational arrangements to respond consistently to their surrounding environments. When the relationships between strategies and structures are obtained, organizations might improve their performance.

Their empirical findings show that hierarchy of authority (centralization) improves public service performance in defender-type organizations. Inverted measure of participation (i.e., weak participation) also increased performance in defender-type organizations. Participation was positively correlated with public service performance in prospector-type organizations as expected. However, weaker hierarchical authority (inverted hierarchy of authority) is not significantly correlated. This denotes that participation in prospector-type organizations improves performance but low level of hierarchical authority does not guarantee enhanced organizational performance. Finally, neither centralization nor participation was significantly related with public service performance in reactor-type organizations.

Defender-type organizations pick up in performance through enhanced centralization and reduced decision participation. Some studies suggest that centralized decision making might increase goal ambiguity but it might also help maintain stable service priorities when top managers are pursuing a strategy of making operations more efficient. An earlier study also indicates that centralization expedites production-oriented goals by reducing environmental uncertainty and clearly indicating the service mission to middle managers and frontline staff. According to the interview conducted by the authors, managerial decision making became more centralized as the top management sought to respond to a hostile operating environment. "This had increased efficiency by reducing the 'inconsistencies' sometimes associated with decentralized decision making, especially intraorganizational communication and office administration costs" (Andrews et al. 2009, 71). When goals and objectives are stable over time, defending strategies are more likely to improve performance.

For prospector-type organizations, staff involvement in decision making improves service performance but delegating the authority to staff does not improve it. In particular, enhanced participation may enable senior managers to identify opportunities for service improvement. Participatory decision making leads to more responsive service development by maximizing the points of contact between service managers and users. Evidence from the mental healthcare sector shows that decentralized decision making produces clients with more individual-oriented attention. Another study indicates that street-level bureaucrats should participate in decision making because they know what works best as a result of their daily interactions with clients. An interview conducted by the authors revealed that a prospector-type education service organization performed better through increased involvement of school head teachers in developing strategic decision making. In contrast, delegating authority does not improve performance for prospector-type organizations.

For reactor-type organizations, the degree of hierarchy of authority and participation did not make any difference. For them, strategy is typically imposed by surrounding external conditions. Relative degree of centralization does not have influence on the content of their decisions. A manager in a reactor-type organization responded that their decisions were fundamentally directed by a national strategic framework and local political agenda. Under such conditions, senior and middle managers were unable to affect service delivery decisions (Andrews et al. 2009).

The findings offer intuitive clues on how centralization might affect information-processing capacity of decision makers and institutional frictions within bureaucratic organizations. First of all, the reactor-type strategies are closely associated with the programmed decision procedures. As noted earlier, the programmed decision procedures are common patterns of search strategy when the main budget actors do primarily rely on pre-established routines. Policy or budget inertia or stability is the most salient feature of this type of decision procedures. Therefore, one might expect that centralization might not exert any significant influence on budget stability under programmed decision procedures or in reactor-type organizations.

In contrast, the nonprogrammed decision procedures are likely to be found under defender-type strategies. Defenders, for instance, bureaucratic organizations as noted earlier, are not pursuing creation of new products or markets. Instead, they are focused on improving current operation. In the case of Social Security benefit programs, fundamental provisions in the programs are extremely hard to modify or thoroughly review. This condition pertains to the programmed decision procedures or reactor-type strategies. With respect to efficiency improvement, however, budget decision makers might pursue some new techniques (e.g., cost control through partial privatization that is suggested from the decision environment). This situation is closer to defender-type strategies that can be easily associated with the nonprogrammed decision procedures. Therefore, bureaucratic centralization can expedite information processing over such efficiency measures or reduce institutional frictions as Andrews et al. (2009) observed.

There is still one caveat regarding Andrews et al.'s findings. Under some conditions, bureaucratic centralization might enhance information-processing capacity of decision makers and reduce institutional frictions. However, when bureaucratic centralization is excessive, i.e., too strong central control over subunits in bureaucratic organizations, might detract from its benefits. In particular, excessive centralization might ignite tensions and conflicts between subunits and central agencies. In actuality, this is what critiques of bureaucracies defined as the bureaucratic dysfunctions. Lindblom's (1979) concept of the so-called "partisan analysis" is fundamentally consistent with the notion that fragmented systems are sometimes more efficient in processing informational cues flowing from the decision environment. Therefore, there is a high likelihood of "non-linear" relationship between bureaucratic centralization and the key target in this book. In other words, bureaucratic centralization might enhance information-processing capacity of decision makers and reduce institutional frictions. However, excessive centralization might hamper the information-processing capacity and especially, increase institutional frictions.

Finally, Gulick warned that the span of control for managers and supervisors at each level within bureaucratic organizations, including central agency management, should be constrained by the expertise, time, and energy of managers and supervisors. Originally, the concept of span of control pertains to the number of subordinates under the control of superiors (Fry and Raasschelder 2008, 99; Rainey 2009, 30–31). However, one can also interpret the concept in a more general term of managerial work capacity. This means that managers and supervisors need to be assigned adequate workload that they can manage with their knowledge and energy. If too heavy workload is placed on managers and supervisors, their productivity might ultimately decline. Therefore, one can also expect a curvilinear relationship between the workload of the central office staff and the target variable in this book.

Meier and Bohte (2000) investigated whether span of control is correlated with organizational performance in Texas school districts during the 1990s. They developed four measures of span of control. One of them, which is relevant for this book, is the ratio of students to teacher. Thus, students are regarded as subordinates under supervision of superior. This measure is a surrogate for an adequate number of students that a teacher can instruct and supervise (Meier and Bohte 2000). Then, this measure of span of control is fairly similar to the concept of workload in this book, which will be defined in the next chapters. Meier and Bohte (2000) found, as expected in this book, a curvilinear relationship between the ratio of students to teacher and school performance. A similar observation is expected for this book. Within their capacity limit, as workload expands workers in central offices can expedite the information-processing capacity and mediate conflicts among subunits. However, beyond their capacity limits such benefits might be diluted.

Bureaucratic Centralization and Partisan Configurations

By now, we all know that virtually every public issue ultimately reaches Congressional Hill. Politics permeates nearly all stages of policy and budget decision processes. Bureaucratic organizational structures are found in the national and state executive branches, and even under the Congressional committee structures. Bureaucracies are operating their programmatic imperatives under the backdrop of politics. In this sense, it is necessary to investigate whether and how politics moderates the impacts of bureaucratic centralization on information processing and institutional frictions. In particular, with respect to fiscal decision making, partisan configurations were observed to exert significant impacts on how governments can react to external revenue shocks.

Alt and Lowry (1994, 2004) conducted empirical tests that are useful for investigating whether and how the impact of bureaucratic centralization on information processing and institutional frictions is moderated by partisan configurations. Nothing can prevent unified governments from moving toward preferred governmental budget levels, namely, the "fiscal scale" or the proportion of income collected as public revenue. Fiscal transitions might be somewhat slowed by budgetary inertia or some other institutional friction such as entitlements and entrenched constituencies. However, new budget levels tend to reflect the fiscal scale pursued by the new majority party. Since most politicians are implicitly assumed to pursue fiscal balance, unified governments are likely to make quick adjustments to unplanned revenue shocks (Alt and Lowry 1994, 2000).

Under split branch governments where the executive branches face both houses dominated by different parties, one can expect a similar observation to unified governments, i.e., budget levels are likely to reflect the fiscal scales preferred by new majority parties in legislatures. The literature suggests that voters generally punish the governor's party in legislatures for being out of fiscal balance. Faced with veto-induced deficits or unpopular surpluses, governors will make efforts to achieve fiscal balance. This tendency is also enhanced because especially veto-induced imbalances will strengthen the position of opposing legislative parties. Then, the opposing parties might be able to impose their fiscal preferences "unilaterally" (Alt and Lowry 2000, 1041). Since legislators in governors' parties are likely to pursue budget balance to avoid voters' punishment, therefore, they press governors to accept the opposing parties' unilateral fiscal preferences in legislatures. When the overall legislatures are strong enough to override gubernatorial vetoes, they can impose their own budget preferences on governors subject to the preference of last votes needed to override executive vetoes. Even when legislatures are less powerful, they can impose their preferences by virtue of their appropriation powers subject to previous year's budget conditions (Alt and Lowry 1994, 2000). In sum, split branch governments are also highly likely to make quicker fiscal adjustments to external revenue shocks. This might be possible because policy gridlock under split branch governments, which is likely to be primarily caused by the opposing parties in the legislatures, might not be significant enough to block majority parties' (in this case, legislative) fiscal preferences.

In split legislature governments each house is under different partisan control; therefore, interbranch veto bargaining problems will be replaced by interchamber coordination issues (Alt and Lowry 1994, 2000). Two different observations might apply to budget outcomes under split legislature governments. One approach suggests that policy gridlock is more likely under split legislature governments. Partisan actors advantaged might be those whose preferences are closer to reversion budgets adopted when budget decisions are not made. Another approach suggests that chambers whose ideals are closer to governors might be more advantaged. Typically, governors' parties will have more leveraging power in conference committees. Presumably, results of bargaining would be closer to governors' preferences. Alt and Lowry (2000) contend that at least one thing is clear. Any budgets that satisfy the governors' legislative parties also satisfy governors and are less likely to be vetoed.

Clarke (1998) suggests similar observations but with slightly different connotation. Under split legislature governments, governors usually have one partisan chamber ally in state legislatures. During conference committee sessions, governors' partisans are likely to support governors' positions because they politically agree with governors. "They may also use the threat of the governor's veto, which they can help sustain, to gain concessions they personally desire from the opposition members of the committee" (Clarke 1998, 10). This will result in weaker conflict between branches by "forcing the both sides to adopt the governor's position" (Clarke 1998, 10). In addition, governors attempt to let legislative leaders and legislators know that if they change some items in governor's budget recommendations, item-vetoes might be invoked over specific projects in legislators' districts. The threats of item-veto powers might contain potential conflict over problematic pork projects in advance. Rosenthal (2004) similarly indicated that legislators under split legislature governments tend to conform to gubernatorial policy stance. Therefore, one might assume that split legislature governments might be characterized by lower levels of institutional frictions. It should be noted that this scenario might be observed when partisan contingencies are moderated by other institutions, such as item-veto powers.

Thus, one question remains ambiguous whether or not policy gridlock and institutional frictions are more intense under split branch governments than under split legislature governments. As Coleman (1999) suggests, however, it is likely that interparty transaction costs are higher than intraparty transaction costs. In addition, Alt and Lowry (1994, 2000) found that the speed of fiscal adjustment was fastest under unified governments. Under split branch governments the speed was also fairly fast, although it was not as fast as that under unified governments. The speed was slowest under split legislature governments. Partisan configurations can, therefore, render decision environments that are either hostile or conducive to bureaucratic centralization. If so, we can develop some expectations on the contingencies under which bureaucratic centralization might exert different impacts on information processing and institutional frictions. The decision environment under unified governments primarily and split branch governments secondarily might produce conditions close to the hierarchical structures of bureaucratic organizations where uniform partisan preferences dominate. Under split legislature governments that are likely characterized by heightened institutional frictions, the benefits from bureaucratic centralization might be less salient.

However, there is one caveat over the impact of bureaucratic centralization on information processing and institutional frictions in the legislative branch. In particular, the CBO has been observed to function as a bipartisan neutral information processor (and thus an efficient information processor) only when one partisan power is pitted against another. Congress is characterized by fundamentally fragmented and decentralized committee structures. Political environments surrounding the CBO, which are created by divided partisan control, will best match the fragmented and decentralized Congressional structures. Then, the CBO will function best under divided governments where surrounding political environments will render the most favorable conditions for their functions. Overall, it is hypothesized in this chapter that when partisan configurations surrounding bureaucratic centralization are conducive to its functioning, it will enhance information processing and reduce institutional frictions. The moderating impacts of partisan configurations will be empirically tested in Chapters 4–6.

Figure 3.1 succinctly summarizes the key assumptions of this book. The first panel explains the core concepts of disproportionate information-processing theory introduced in Chapter 2. The lack of information-processing capacity of budget decision makers will increase indicator lock. As also detailed in Chapter 2, the indicator lock will increase either budget punctuations or stability. Institutional frictions will augment the indicator lock as shown in Figure 3.1. According to incrementalism, the lack of information-processing capacity and prescribed institutions will directly increase the probability of budget stability. Bureaucratic centralization will enhance the information-processing capacity of budget decision makers and reduce institutional frictions up to an adequate level of centralization. The hypothesized impact of bureaucratic centralization will be moderated by partisan configurations. Overall, bureaucratic centralization will further reduce the probability of budget punctuations. In contrast, it will not effectively affect budget inertia.

Figure 3.1 Information-Processing Capacity, Institutional Frictions, and Bureaucratic Centralization

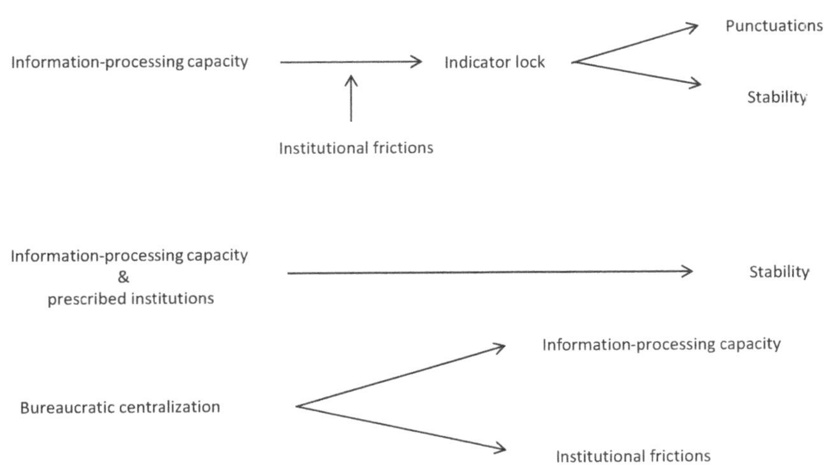

Conclusion: Bounded Bureaucracy to Bounded Rationality

Bureaucracy has frequently been criticized from various fronts such as trained incapacity, bureaupathology, and goal displacement. Bureaucracy has also been regarded as one of main reasons for bounded rationality of human decision makers. However, scholars have been negligent of the fact that bureaucracy itself was invented as a way to extend the limited information-processing capacity of human decision makers. Bureaucratic organizations augment human cognitive and analytical capabilities through functional specialization and coordination. Otherwise, bureaucratic organizations can reduce cognitive demands on individual decision makers by restricting individual attention only to organizationally imposed goals and aspirations. In addition, even scholars who developed alternative theories of policy and budget processes, for instance, disproportionate information-processing theory, did not pay attention to potential benefits from bureaucracy. In particular, bureaucratic centralization was originally suggested as a way to enhance the information-processing capacity of decision makers. It was also supposed to reduce institutional frictions such as conflicts among bureaucratic subunits.

In this chapter, three main expectations are developed on whether and how bureaucratic centralization can render such benefits. First, bureaucratic centralization is expected to facilitate information processing and reduce institutional frictions under decision environments that are similar to what Simon defined as nonprogrammed decision procedures. However, its impact on information processing and institutional frictions will be curvilinear: i.e., bureaucratic centralization will realize such benefits but excessive centralization might detract from them. Second, the impacts of bureaucratic centralization on information processing and institutional frictions will be substantially tangential on its surrounding partisan configurations. In general, bureaucratic centralization is the most likely to engender the benefits under unified governments. Third, bureaucratic centralization might not exert any significant influence under decision environments that are similar to what Simon labeled as programmed decision environments. In fact, the conditions are strictly associated with budget inertia or stability that has been the main target of incrementalism. It is well known that no policy or administrative measures have successfully modified budget inertia yet. Thus, bureaucratic centralization is not alone in failing to improve decision processes under budget inertia.

In sum, bureaucracy can merit some further scrutiny on how it can enhance information processing and reduce institutional frictions. Bureaucratic centralization is expected to achieve such benefits but under some specified conditions. Therefore, "*bounded bureaucracy*" is suggested as a tool to address bounded rationality that has featured decision processes under institutional settings. Chapters 4–6 make strong cases for bounded bureaucracy.

Note

1. Considering the recent rapid changes in budget environments, investigating who the main budget actors are will be another significant future research agenda.

4

Bureaucratic Centralization and the National Executive Budget Process

Bureaucratic organizations have been criticized for various bureaucratic malfunctions, as discussed in Chapter 3. Public-choice economists have identified the absence of a market for products and services that governmental agencies render as the most critical reason for unlimited budgetary expansion. Thus, bureaucratic agencies tend to act as a sole supplier of public goods to appropriators. Based on their almost monopolistic control over the true costs of service delivery, bureaucrats have been viewed to maximize their bureau budgets that are larger than socially efficient budget amounts (Niskanen 1971).

From a perspective of sociology, bureaucratic hierarchies detract from effective communications between organizational members. Where the Weberian ideal type of bureaucratic organizations anticipated more efficient execution of organizational goals and targets through systematic procedures, organizational members have shown obsessive conformity to rules or standardized operating procedures, in what is known as goal displacement. Furthermore, "bureaucracy is said to treat human beings callously at the minimum and, at the maximum, crushingly" (Goodsell 2004, 15). In addition, bureaucracy is notoriously biased for an elitist domination within a society. This perspective depicts bureaucratic organizations fundamentally as instruments to serve oligarchic and conservative organizations (Goodsell 2004, 14). Well, it sounds like, bureaucracy contains all evils and we should have already abandoned all forms of bureaucratic organizations and procedures. The mandate to bash, if not abolish, bureaucracy seems to be way overdue.

Despite the critiques of bureaucracies, a group of management scholars have vigorously worked on and are working on developing organizational and managerial innovations that can overcome some of the critiques of bureaucracies. Current social problems and public agenda that bureaucratic agencies, especially governmental agencies, tackle get wicked. They defy the capacity of a single bureaucratic organization in terms of geographic coverage, resource availability, and most of all information-processing capacity. Management scholars diagnose the current public agenda to be basically different in their nature: i.e., they are intertwined across different jurisdictions and organizations. What they suggest as potential solutions is collaborative network management across various public and private entities (O'Leary and Bingham 2009).

However, even the scholars who have been in search of the more innovative management techniques acknowledge the essential necessity for efficient management skills and organizational structures within a single bureaucratic entity (Ingraham and Lynn 2004; Rainey and Ryu 2004). In particular, organizational structures that were re-engineered to be streamlined in accordance with organizational strategic goals and plans did make substantial improvement in organizational performance for bureaucratic organizations. Therefore, an extended analysis of advantages from bureaucratic organizations is warranted. Management and policy scholars throughout the 1980s and the 1990s have much more emphatically evidenced this aspect. In essence, what they contend is that we should not blame bureaucracies for what no other entities can do. For what most private and public organizations can do, bureaucracies have also been reporting excellent, frequently more excellent, performance results. Even public-choice economists have recently declared that there is no sufficient evidence for bureaucratic budget maximization (Goodsell 2004). In addition, when bureaucratic organizations operate their missions, they function much faster than we simply imagine (Rainey and Steinbauer 1999).

In particular, many scholars acknowledged that merits from bureaucratic centralization were inherently assumed in the development of the Weberian sense of large but more efficient human organizations. As discussed in Chapter 3, the specific dimension of bureaucracy is still under-investigated. Management and policy scholars have not paid full empirical attention to the potential benefits from bureaucratic centralization. There are not sufficient empirical studies investigating how to improve information-processing capacity of policy and budget decision makers and reduce institutional frictions. In the real-world case, budget preparation and approval processes in the national government have been highly institutionalized and featured by the bureaucratic centralization during the twentieth century. This chapter empirically investigates whether bureaucratic centralization enhances information-processing capacity of budget decision makers and reduces institutional frictions in the process of preparing President's budgets in the national government.

U.S. Budget Outcomes: 1961–2006

Under the executive budgeting system, agencies in the executive branch usually initiate their budget proposals, although legislatures retain the ultimate power of the purse. In the process of agency budget proposal, budget aspirations (for instance, agency's attitude for budget expansion) and behaviors (for example, agency's actual budget padding) of agency bureaucrats heavily influence and form the content of agency budget requests. This aspect of budget preparations has been the single-most frequently studied topic in the budgeting literature. Agency bureaucrats collect relevant pieces of budget information from a variety of sources such as interest groups, lobbyists, previous legislative committee hearings, and their institutional memories (i.e., what they hear and learn from their predecessors) (Rubin 2003; Wildavsky and Caiden 2004).

As noted in the incrementalist perspective of budget processes, the starting point of understanding public budgeting is the extraordinary complexity involved in the computations of budget numbers. Constrained by their cognitive as well as resource capacity limits for achieving computational rationality, agency bureaucrats rely more on their political experience. They learned that requesting overly excessive increases in their agency budgets over last year's might invite an extra round of investigation from legislators. If they request decreased budgets, then legislators might approve the self-moderated budget amounts. Thus, agency bureaucrats tend to pursue a bit of budget padding but avoid excessively increased budget requests. If agency bureaucrats request unusually high increases in their requests, this might entail a loss of confidence from legislators and invite extra rounds of budget scrutiny (Davis, Dempster, and Wildavsky 1966; Wildavsky and Caiden 2004). Empirical studies show that despite the risk of being caught on budget padding more assertive agencies (i.e., those who request budgets more than needed) were likely to receive larger budgets (Sharkansky 1968; Thompson 1987). This pattern of the political maneuver typically shows that the practical change in agency budgets is seldom larger than 30 percent, most frequently smaller than 5 percent as discussed in Chapter 2.

What about annual changes in U.S. budget authorities that closely match budget outcomes at the agency level? To answer this question, U.S. budget data according to OMB's subfunctional budget categories were obtained. The OMB issues the Budget of the United States Government. The U.S. Budget contains the president's budget message, analytical and economic information about president's budget proposals, and other budgetary publications such as historical budget tables on outlays and budget authorities by function, subfunctions, and agencies. One note is that the categorization of agencies is closer to the level of departments under the OMB categorization. Budget authority refers to legal authority to incur financial obligations. When specific amounts of dollars approved in each authority are actually executed, they will result in actual budget outlays. Thus, when Congress approves agencies to spend budgets, it gives budget authority to the agencies. Budget authority includes new budget authority in a certain year's budget, which is mostly the same as annual appropriations. It also includes permanent budget authority, which makes a certain obligation, such as the Social Security fund, without needing annual congressional action. All money in the Social Security fund is available without obligation but only the portion of the fund obligated for a certain year is counted as a new budget authority (Schick 2007, 40–42). Budget authority further includes legal authority to borrow and contract. Budget authorities tend to be close to actual outlays (Schick 2007, 40–42; True 2007, 46).

In this chapter, data on U.S. budget authority from Fiscal Year (FY) 1947 to FY 2006 collected by True (2007) will be used for empirical analysis. One of many advantages in the data set is that historical budget records, i.e., contemporary budget authorities, were converted to present functional or subfunctional categorizations, i.e., current budget authorities. This enables researchers to test what happened to the same budget functional or subfunctional categories, either incremental budget changes or sudden, dramatic budget changes. This is a very important feature especially for testing the main research question in this book. When previous subfunctional budget categories are moved to new budget categories, the previous categories might show sudden, dramatic budget cuts while the new budget categories might report new, sudden budget increases. Both of the changes will be registered as sudden, episodic budget punctuations. In fact, those cases might not be a correct observation of budget punctuation. By carefully re-categorizing the movements across different subfunctional categories, the data set gives a more accurate count of budget punctuations.

The U.S. budget authorities are first reported based on the OMB functional budget classification. The OMB functions are constructed according to the purposes or programmatic goals the U.S. Government tries to achieve, rather than objects of expenditures (i.e., line items), clienteles, or geographical areas served. For instance, the OMB functional code 350 (the agriculture function) provides federal assistance primarily to food producers. It further includes two subfunctional categories: the farm income stabilization subfunction (the OMB functional code 351) and the agricultural research and services subfunction (the OMB functional code 352). The main advantages from the functional and subfunctional classification are: first, the categories are exhaustive and mutually exclusive and second, the classification is supported by a detailed accounting system. As such, double counting across programs and subfunctions is minimized (True 2007, 49).

The U.S. budget data set is further categorized into four macrofunctions, domestic discretionary subfunctions, financial subfunctions, mandatory subfunctions, and national security subfunctions. Domestic discretionary subfunctions include mostly annual appropriations for domestic programs such as energy, transportation, education, and various social services. There were forty such subfunctions. Financial subfunctions include budget categories, such as credit activity, offsetting receipts, and government-wide contra-accounts, which are likely to be the result of business-like activities. For example, mortgage credit, postal service, interest earned on trust funds, and asset sales are typically operated on a fee-for-service basis. Many of these categories will be recorded as offsetting receipts and appear as negative numbers for budget authorities because the latter typically defines spending authorities. There were sixteen such functions. Mandatory subfunctions, mostly based on permanent budget authorities, are provided for entitlement authorities other than annual appropriations. Medicare, food and nutrition assistance, Social Security, and various other income security programs are the examples of entitlement authorities. In addition, interest on public debt is also a mandatory subfunction because the national government is obligated to pay interest based on its full faith and creditworthiness. There were thirteen mandatory subfunctions. Finally, national security subfunctions related to national defense or international programs related to national security included seven such subfunctions.

These OMB *sub*functions, not OMB functions, were the main target of this research because they were closer to agency-level budget outcomes that have long been the core target of the budgeting literature. One caveat with the OMB subfunctional categories in the data set used in this chapter is that they include some kinds of inter-fund or -program transactions such as trust fund and offsetting receipts among governmental funds. Since they are more likely to be transactions between the programs in the national government, they were excluded from the analysis. Therefore, except for offsetting receipts that result from typical business-like activities such as Postal Service included in financial subfunctions,[1] the trust fund and offsetting receipts between governmental funds included in each of OMB "functions" were deleted from the analysis.

Later in this chapter, statistical analysis was conducted to find out whether bureaucratic centralization actually enhances information-processing capacity of budget decision makers and reduces institutional frictions. The variables to construct bureaucratic centralization and other control factors were available only for the period from 1961 to 2006. For this reason, the data set used for this chapter covers data from FY 1961 to FY 2006. Altogether, seventy-six subfunctional budget authorities for forty-six years were first analyzed to see whether governmental budgets are reflecting bounded rationality and institutional frictions that might be caused by political and institutional prescriptions. National security subfunctional authorities were converted into year 2000 constant dollar by using the price deflator for federal defense programs. Also, all other subfunctional authorities were also converted into year 2000 constant dollar by using the price deflator for federal nondefense programs.

Do changes in U.S. budget authorities follow incremental growth patterns or sudden, dramatic lurches as suggested by supporters of disproportionate information-processing theory? The main target variable is $\frac{B_t - B_{t-1}}{B_{t-1}}$ that was defined as *Increment* in Chapter 2, which are annual changes in OMB subfunctional budget authorities. For a computational purpose, observations of budgets that were missing or just zeroes, in the previous and current years, were deleted from analysis. For a visual purpose, values of *Increment* larger than +1 or smaller than −1 were further eliminated and their distribution is depicted in Figure 4.1.

Figure 4.1 indicates that changes in U.S. budget authorities strongly follow a leptokurtic distribution as discussed in Chapter 2. The mean value of *Increment* is about 1.25 percent. According to the incrementalist perspective, the value of annual budget changes is often smaller than 5 percent. Jones and Baumgartner (2005a, 2005b), using the same data used in this chapter, reported that annual changes in U.S. budget authorities were about 4 percent from 1947 to 2003. However, their cutoff points were wider than those in Figure 4.1. When the range of observations was expanded to ± 5 (i.e., 500 percent) and observations of budget authorities before 1961 were added, the mean value of *Increment* was about 4.5 percent. Therefore, the result introduced in Figure 4.1 is not substantial deviation from the findings in the budgeting literature. Figure 4.1 also includes a normal approximation curve over the histograms of actual frequency distributions of *Increment*.

Figure 4.1 Distributions of *Increment* in U.S. Budget Authority: 1961 to 2006

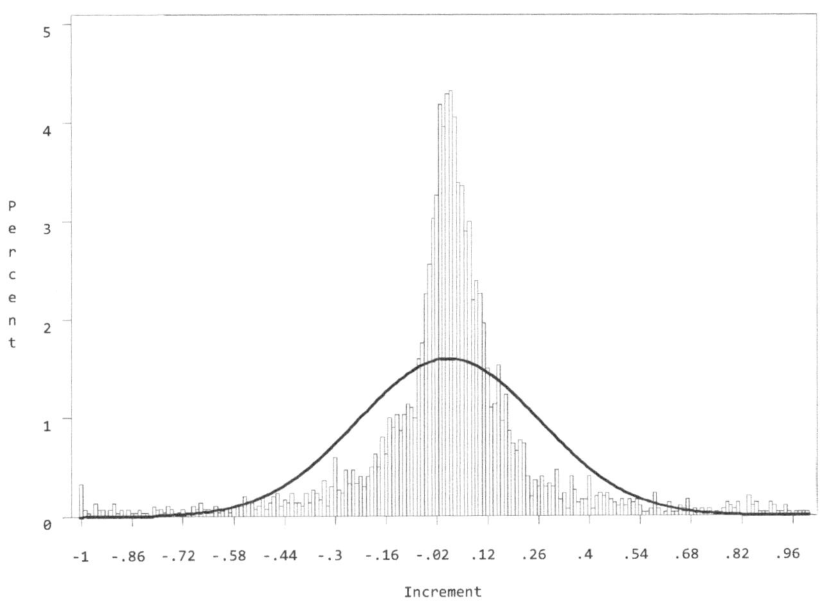

Notes: 3,052, Mean (1.25 percent); Std. Dev. (25.0 percent); Kurtosis (4.35).

Compared to the normal approximation curve, actual frequency distributions of *Increment* have an abnormally high peak. The range of observations that belong to the area of high peak is between –.08 (i.e., –8 percent) and .13 (13 percent). The range was visually and statistically identified. Approximately 55.9 percent of all observations belong to this high peak area. [2] According to budgetary incrementalism, bounded rationality and political/institutional prescriptions force budget decision makers revert to some manageable (in terms of information-processing capacity) and agreeable (in terms of minimizing the possibility of re-surfacing previous political tensions and subsequent institutional frictions) reference points. The reference points are often called budget base and is likely to be the previous year's budget amounts. Given their capacity limits and potential conflicts, budget participants tend not to touch the budget base. Instead, they tend to make marginal adjustment from the budget base and typical results are marginal budget changes, often smaller than 5 percent, which they typically review. About 56 percent of observations of *Increment* fall within this range that can be labeled as the zone of budgetary incrementalism or budget stability. Therefore, budgetary incrementalism still explains a substantial portion of U.S. budget changes.

Figure 4.1 also shows that approximately 32.4 percent of all observations of *Increment* fall within the range of moderate budget changes. Moderate budget changes differ from budget moderation. Budget scholars use budget moderation almost the same as the budget stability, where governmental budgets change annually by a small margin as shown in Figure 4.1. Due to capacity limits and institutional frictions or implicit consent on fair shares of all budget participants, budget decision makers exert caution in proposing their agency budgets. This phenomenon is known as budget moderation. In actuality, earlier critiques of budgetary incrementalism already reported that annual budget changes in federal agencies did show patterns of budget changes much larger than those observed in the zone of budget stability or moderation (LeLoup and Moreland 1978). The changes are larger, in absolute terms, than the cutoff points for the budget stability in Figure 4.1, for instance. Thus, observations of *Increment* outside of the cutoff points, but smaller than extreme values discussed shortly, will be defined as moderate budget changes in this book. Then, earlier critiques over budgetary incrementalism are also substantially supported. As much as about 32 percent of changes in

U.S. budget authorities show budget change patterns much larger than those depicted in budgetary incrementalism.

Most importantly, about 11.8 percent of observations of *Increment* fall into the range of sudden, dramatic budget changes. The range is known as the zone of budget punctuations. Moderate budget changes implied the presence of budget changes larger than those in the zone of budget stability. However, we need to pay extra attention to those observations within the zone of budget punctuations especially because disproportionate information-processing theory provided different theoretical interpretations over the budget lurch. Since standard deviation of the distributions of *Increment* in Figure 4.1 is about 25 percent, most observations of *Increment* will taper off beyond ± .75 (75 percent) that is three standard deviations away from the mean value under normal distributions. However, there are about 11.8 percent of observations with budget punctuations: observations of histograms crossing over the normal approximation curve in Figure 4.1.

Why do these budget punctuations, with more frequent observations than expected under normal distributions, occur? Disproportionate information-processing theory suggested, as discussed in Chapter 2, that almost the same reasons that caused budget stability might induce such dramatic budget changes. In other words, due to bounded rationality of budget decision makers and institutional frictions, budget decision makers tend to disregard information cues flowing from budget environments. Faced with oversupply of budget information, they are likely to anchor on what they believe to be the norms of budget processes and outcomes. Therefore, they tend to disproportionately lock onto some indicators when they are processing such budget information. At some point in the temporal budget processes, they can no longer ignore the previously disregarded facets of budget information inputs. This will result in sudden budget changes when decision makers give disproportionately stronger attention now to the previously ignored factors. Such attention-driven choices will be augmented by institutional frictions. The final result of attention-driven budget choices will be sudden, dramatic budget changes.

Overall, empirical analysis of changes in U.S. budget authorities from 1961 to 2006 evidences that budgetary incrementalism is still fairly alive and well but at the same time there are more frequent observations of budget changes larger than those depicted in incrementalism, especially budget punctuations. Then, the key question is whether bureaucratic centralization can function as a tool to augment budget decision makers' information-processing capacity and reduce institutional frictions. For this purpose, one needs to investigate first whether and how bureaucratic centralization affects budget punctuations primarily and budget stability secondarily.

Bureaucratic Centralization in Presidents' Budgets

At the national level, the executive budget movement was critically spurred by a strong need for enhancing efficiency in governments. When budgets are prepared by agency bureaucrats, they are highly likely to pursue maximization of their parochial agency budgets. This was especially the case whenever there was no central locus of budget control over agency budget proposals. Even when representatives of the general public heavily direct budget preparation, they are trying to bring benefits to their constituency groups or regions. Probably, political representatives might increase effectiveness of governmental programs by offering some programmatic benefits to their constituency groups, albeit at the expense of the whole society. In this sense, even Progressive reformers were deemed to have favored expansionary, activist governments, not necessarily governmental efficiency. According to Rubin (1994), it was Taft conservatives who focused more on cost saving and efficiency. Partly in response to the Progressive reformers, Taft conservatives opted for a strong chief executive who can control agency requests, cut spending, and give tax relief to business rather than public involvement as reflected in the Progressive spirit. The Taft conservatives were regarded as a more pivotal factor that put momentum on the executive budget reform initiatives.

As discussed in Chapter 3, then, the most fundamental assumption behind the executive budget reforms was that central budget control center, especially chief executives in the executive branch, had superior informational advantages over agency budget proposals than their legislative counterparts. In the provisions prepared in the Budget and Accounting Act of 1921, the central budget office, the Bureau of Budget (BOB, now OMB), was supposed to do what chief executives were expected to do over agency budget requests. Armed with their expert techniques and executive supervisory authorities, central budget office staffs would review agency budget proposals for unnecessary budget padding and streamlined agency budget proposals pursuant to available budget resources and chief executive's political and policy preferences. However, central budget office staffs were also expected to reconcile organizational conflicts between various agency programs and served as intermediaries to mediate such interdepartmental conflicts. In addition, central budget offices could assist line agencies while processing extraordinarily burdensome layers of budget information flowing into the agencies from budget environments. This illustrates how bureaucratic organizations can extend the information-processing capacity of budget decision makers as discussed in Chapter 3. So, we need to test whether bureaucratic centralization in the executive branch can enhance information-processing capacity of budget decision makers and reduce institutional frictions. The key question and the definition of bureaucratic centralization seem fairly clear. However, measuring and operationalizing bureaucratic centralization is quite a challenge.

The first challenge is that since the target variable in this chapter is changes in U.S. budget authorities, it is highly legitimate to develop indices that tap bureaucratic centralization directly associated with *budget* preparation and outcomes. In the 1921 Budget and Accounting Act, the central budget office was BOB. As the name implies, BOB was primarily focused on budget issues. However, throughout the reorganization initiative in the early 1970s BOB was renamed into OMB but the change was not merely confined to the change in the title of the central budget office. The "M" function, that is management function, has been much more enhanced (Mosher and Stephenson 1982). In addition, policy functions have been gradually embedded in OMB functions, with a more recent example being OMB's supervisory role over the Program Assessment Rating Tool (PART) implementation (Gilmour and Lewis 2006). A fundamental problem is that indices that measure only the budget analysis function of central budget offices, as was done for state executive budget models in Chapter 6, are currently unavailable. Despite the limits, it has been reported that OMB still exerts tight control over budget proposals made by executive agencies (LeLoup 1977; Schick 2007). For this reason, OMB staff will be used as the primary part to construct bureaucratic centralization.

The second challenge is that one needs to investigate how bureaucratic centralization influences agency-level budget preparation and outcome. In other words, for the case in this chapter we need to measure the level of bureaucratic centralization that was linked *separately* to the preparation and finalization of each of the seventy-six OMB subfunctional budget authorities. Each of central budget office staffs might be assigned to one agency or part of agencies. Unfortunately, however, data to tap that kind of separate roles of the central budget office staffs are virtually nonexistent and do not seem to be available in the future as well. Instead, the most viable option that can measure bureaucratic centralization and is still fairly acceptable for tapping the centralization tied to budget preparation and finalization is developing a somewhat aggregate index of bureaucratic centralization.

As described in Table 4A.1, bureaucratic centralization in the executive budget process is measured as the number of OMB staff divided by the number of total employees in the national executive branch in a certain year. On average, there were about 575 staffs in the OMB and about 2,823,296 employees in the national executive branch in a given year. Thus, there were approximately two OMB staffs per ten thousand executive employees. The centralization measure, *Centralization*, was standardized for a better comparison with other control variables in the final regression analyses. All variables in Table 4A.1 were standardized, except for election dummies explained later. In addition, all variables used as control variables to explain budget punctuations and stability are one year lagged because under the executive budget system, budget preparation starts about eighteen months before the final budget appropriations. Thus, most control variables, especially executive centralization variables, constructed for about one year before the appropriation of budget authorities seem to be better measures that affect budget appropriations.[3] Robinson et al. (2007) developed an index of bureaucratic centralization as the percentage of spending on central administration, which represents resources allocated to central managerial activities. However, central managerial activities seem rather too broad to be a measure of bureaucratic centralization linked to budget outcomes and will pose another challenge to developing a measure of bureaucratic centralization. More specific measures such as the number of OMB staff might tap bureaucratic centralization associated with budget outcomes more accurately.

One caveat is that bureaucratic centralization does not augment budget decision maker's information-processing capacity without limits. Bureaucratic centralization will facilitate organizational information-processing capacity of bureaucratic organizations that were supposed to facilitate human information-processing capacity. However, too tight central control will detract from the advantages from bureaucratic centralization. This implies that there will be a curvilinear relationship between bureaucratic centralization and information-processing capacity of budget decision makers. At some unknown yet efficient point of bureaucratic centralization, bureaucratic centralization will expedite information-processing capacity of decision makers. Beyond the efficient threshold, however, bureaucratic centralization might detract from such a capacity. The curvilinear relationship was tapped by creating a squared measure of centralization, *Centralization*^{2}. Robinson et al. (2007) report somewhat ambivalent findings that bureaucratic centralization increases large budget changes (i.e., budget punctuations in this chapter) but decreases small budget changes (i.e., budget stability in this chapter). If budget punctuations are symptomatic for bounded rationality and institutional frictions, and bureaucratic centralization can help augment information-processing capacity of budget decision makers, then it would probably decrease budget punctuations at the least. One potential reason for the ambivalent influence of bureaucratic centralization in Robinson et al. might be the hidden curvilinear relationship between bureaucratic centralization and information-processing capacity.

Assumptions in ideal-type bureaucratic organizations suggest that each organizational member should be familiar with their job responsibilities and be assigned what they can successfully implement probably through adequate job training. In actuality, Gulick's concept, span of control, is nothing but a reiteration of this original assumption in bureaucratic organizations. Staffs in central budget offices, therefore, should also be assigned an adequate workload. General expectation is that central budget office staffs might be able to process budget-related information up to a certain point but beyond the capacity limit they cannot process such information as efficiently as they did previously. *Central Capacity Load* is a measure constructed as the budget authority of each of OMB subfunctional categories divided by the number of OMB staffs. This index measures the load of work that OMB staffs are to fulfill. *Central Capacity Load*^{2} is the squared value of *Central Capacity Load*. If the assumptions on the impact of central capacity load on information-processing capacity are accurate, *Central Capacity Load* will reduce budget punctuations but *Central Capacity Load*^{2} will increase the frequency of budget punctuations. These four variables related to bureaucratic centralization and its capacity load are the main target of this book.

Institutional Frictions in the U.S. Budget Process

Theories of bounded rationality, both incrementalist perspectives and disproportionate information-processing theory, deemed bounded rationality such as cognitive limits or emotional bias as the key reasons for either budget stability or punctuations. They also contended that prescribed political and institutional settings would invite institutional frictions. Institutional frictions will further restrict information-processing capacity of budget decision makers, which will result in more frequent budget punctuations and stability. Thus, some control factors will be investigated that might confound the impact of bureaucratic centralization as a tool to extend information-processing capacity of decision makers. Robinson et al. (2007) identified organizational size as one potential measure to tap institutional frictions. Large bureaucratic organizations are necessarily more involved in more complex decision-making settings. This is also what incrementalists regarded as the starting point of understanding governmental budgets. In large organizations, there are possibly more veto points to reach an agreeable organizational goal and strategies to achieve the goal. Consultation with a larger number of organizational members might reignite contentious controversies over the previous organizational agenda that obtained organizational consensus. It might intensify conflicts over current organizational agenda and its suggested solutions. To measure the size of the potential veto points in a large governmental bureaucratic organization, *Per Capita Employee* was constructed as per capita employees in the national executive branch. It is expected to confound information-processing capacity of budget decision makers and thus, will increase the frequency of budget punctuations. However, there is also a possibility that *Per Capita Employee* might be negatively correlated with budget punctuations as indicated in the hypothesized effects on budget punctuations in Table 4A.1. It might also measure the overall size of a bureaucratic organization that is supposed to improve the limits in human cognitive capacity as discussed in Chapter 3. Either finding will be a significant contribution to the current discourses on bounded rationality and public policy and budget outcomes.

As theories of bounded rationality clarified, political institutions also likely cause institutional frictions. At the national level, elections for President, House members, and Senators pose a fairly peculiar phenomenon. Shepsle et al. (2009) offer a very insightful clue to measure institutional frictions that might be caused by political tensions over the power of the purse in the national government. One of the central motives for elected federal legislators in distributing federal resources to states and their electoral districts is their desire for reelection (Peltzman 1976). Politicians have a good understanding of complex conditions in their states and districts, and the profile of various constituencies. The flow of federal outlays is orchestrated by many procedural and institutional structures. According to Shepsle et al., the most significant features of the structures are the bicameral arrangement in Congress, the decentralized committee systems of the House and the Senate, and the electoral calendar. Structural units in the two chamber systems are charged with first "ex ante agenda and information-gathering responsibilities and, second, with ex post bargaining and oversight authority to direct the flow of fiscal largesse" (Shepsle et al. 2009, 343). Therefore, bicameralism means that the decision-making procedures in Congress are not completely insulated from each chamber's counterpart.

Additionally, a different political tempo in the two chambers further complicates the procedures. The timing of elections places differential pressure on legislators preparing for election campaigns. There is an important electoral rhythm—the term structure of representatives and senators. On the first Tuesday after the first Monday in November of even-numbered years, elections will be held for all 435 seats in the House. In contrast, there will be elections for only a third of all Senators. They differ in terms of term length (two vs. six years) and constituency (districts vs. states). Reelection ambition, bicameral reconciliation on legislation, and chamber-specific electoral rhythms entail something that even founding fathers did not anticipate. The two chambers operate "on different time horizons and with different intertemporal perspectives" (Shepsle et al. 2009, 344). Due to the what-have-you-done-for-me- *lately* (WHYDFML) mentality of retrospectively inclined constituents, reelection-conscious politicians tend to seek to distribute federal outlays to their states or districts just in time such that constituents would appreciate the federal resources the most as legislators' reelection campaigns kick into higher gear. Shepsle et al. further formalize the framework of contested credit claiming that House representatives and Senators for a state will attempt to share the credit for appropriations to their state even when the federal resources originate in the other chamber.

Their empirical analyses show the number of projects allocated by the Senate is higher to states when incumbent senators stand for reelection than to other states by about 15–30 percent. In addition, the House counteracts about two-thirds of the bias. The findings support the model of interchamber politics and contested credit-claiming gaming between the two chambers in Congress. Therefore, election years for House representatives and Senators will intensify the interchamber politics and contested credit claiming in Congress. In this chapter, it is further assumed that Presidential elections might also augment the complexity of interchamber politics. The variable, *Election* , is the sum of three dummies for years of Presidential, Senate, and House elections. *Election* will possibly increase the frequency of budget punctuations because during election years interchamber and interbranch political tensions are likely to be heightened.

A shift in dominating political groups is likely to invite political standoff and tensions. Although such tension might be the most salient around election years, an additional variable was further tested to measure politics-induced institutional frictions. The number of Democratic legislators minus the number of Republican legislators divided by U.S. population was first created. Annual percentage changes in this variable were converted into its absolute value because either positive or negative changes might denote the level of shift in political power. Much similar to *Election* , *Political Change* is expected to increase the frequency of budget punctuations.

Finally, two indices measuring fiscal conditions surrounding budget decision-making settings were constructed. Allocation of resources to numerous claimers is heavily tangential on the availability of the resources. Governmental revenues are highly influenced by the size of the national economy (Rubin 2010). If so, governmental budgets might also grow as the economy grows. However, there is one caveat for a fiscal variable that is most frequently used as explanatory variable for governmental budget growth. If the target variable in this chapter is annual changes in each of OMB subfunctional budget authorities, then one might expect a linearly positive relationship between the fiscal variable and the annual budget changes. However, the target variable in this chapter is budget stability or punctuations that are assumed to reflect limited information-processing capacity and institutional frictions. As discussed in previous chapters, some studies indicate that more assertive agencies are more likely to get more budgets from appropriators. Upon finding a possibility of more resources, competition for claiming over public money would be enhanced, thus increasing institutional frictions. In that case, a measure of economic condition, *Per Capita Income* , will be positively correlated with budget punctuations. However, this will not be the case for annual budget changes smaller than those in budget punctuations, especially those in budget stability. As budgetary incrementalism explains, budget participants exert moderation over small, marginal deviations from budget base. Then, *Per Capita Income* might show different impacts over those observations within the zones of budget stability. The empirical findings will provide us with clues to develop further hypotheses on how resource slack will affect budget stability.

The second variable measuring fiscal conditions is *Unemployment Rate* . When unemployment rate is high, governmental outlays will also increase due to income security programs (Rubin 2010). In general, whenever there are more claimants over governmental programs, the computational burden of budget decision makers is likely to be amplified. The larger number of the claimants will also augment institutional frictions. However, one caveat is notable for this second type of fiscal variables. Politics of attention emphasizes that information oversupply is the main reason for attention-driven choice or indicator lock that will ultimately result in budget punctuations. When the information that decision makers face can be efficiently processed, higher-than-normal volumes of efficient information will not necessarily drive decision makers into indicator lock. In a private market system, a variety of information is available cost free or at the least amount of cost. The private market system might be closest to the idealized frictionless system where decision output results are highly likely to be a direct function of available information. Under this condition, observations of budget stability and punctuations are less probable and distributions of *Increment* will be closer to normal distributions.

For instance, Jones, Sulkin, and Larsen (2003) analyzed the distributions of market decision outputs such as daily percentage changes in the Dow–Jones Industrial Average, elections, and public budgets. All decisions cannot be completely immune from institutional settings. Therefore, even the Dow–Jones index, which was expected to show patterns of normal distributions, showed non-normal distributions in what is known as exponential distributions. In particular, public budgets showed Paretian distributions where budget stability and punctuations increase at the expense of more moderate budget changes. This is symptomatic that governmental budgets might be associated with bounded rationality and be exposed to stronger institutional frictions. In exponential distributions, there is a tradeoff between budget stability and punctuations. At least, moderate budget changes that are regarded as the result of more rational decisions are less heavily influenced by budget stability or punctuations. Therefore, even larger-than-normal volume, if not oversupply, of "efficient" information (e.g., Dow–Jones indices) can somehow be processed without severe cognitive limits or institutional frictions. In other words, if the increased number of income security program beneficiaries can be deemed as efficient information, then its impact on budget choices might develop somewhat exponential distributions of *Increment*. Therefore, the number of income security program beneficiaries is also likely to be negatively correlated with budget stability or punctuations.

Ryu (2009) further showed that information-processing capacity and the degree of institutional frictions might vary across different governmental funds even within the same governmental jurisdiction. More business-like operations, similar to financial OMB subfunctions, revealed distributions closer to exponential distributions that contain a lot of characteristics linked to normal distributions. Surprisingly, mandatory-type operations showed distributions closer to business-like operations, rather than general governmental-type operations that are characterized by bounded rationality and institutional frictions. Institutional frictions might increase when enacting legislations for programs such as income security programs that Democrats strongly support. Once enacted, however, expenditures over the programs are virtually automatic. In other words, there is no further contention over the legitimacy of the programs. In addition, budget decision makers only need to do the computation of budget amounts under the pre-set formula. Such computation, without doubt, does not require heavy load of information processing.

Payment of interests, another category of mandatory-type operations, is also quite similar to income security program in terms of computation and institutional frictions because decision makers have easy access to tools for financial calculations. Overall, if high unemployment rate denotes a necessity to legislate new entitlement programs, then institutional frictions will increase along with more frequent budget punctuations. Or else, if it means just increased income security payments in accordance with the number of the program beneficiaries, then institutional frictions might not peak again and computational burden on the part of budget decision makers would be manageable. Thus, its impact on budget punctuations is predicted to be in either direction. Now, what are the statistical results over the impacts of the various factors on budget punctuations? Next section reports the results.

Bureaucratic Centralization and U.S. Budget Punctuations

One aspect that starkly distinguishes OMB from line agencies is its informational capacity over budget issues. Frequently, OMB staffs have been linked to a kind of informal "information network" that spans across different partisan configurations and branches in governments in addition to its formal, programmatic analysis authority. A lot of anecdotal stories depict how central budget office staffs could be informed on budget-related issues and informal budget networks enabled them to incorporate their long-term institutional learning into budget processing. An informal network of budgeters is composed of present and past Congressional staffers, interest group lobbyists, Congressional Budget Office (CBO)/OMB staffs and retirees who shared budget information and historical memories. This informal budget network facilitated long-term learning and enabled the OMB staffs to store highly detailed histories over budget agenda. The most salient illustration is that the federal credit reform initiatives were transmitted through the informal network historically. In addition, most of the information transmitted about the history of public budget agenda was done at the *staff* level (Rubin 2003, 17–28, 97–122). This aspect of institutional memory is what makes OMB more special than several other agencies that are involved in the executive budget preparation process. For instance, the Council of Economic Advisers (CEA) retains members with high levels of economic sophistication. They bring fresh ideas on how government should work and governmental budgets should be formed. After they deposit the ideas, however, they simply leave. The situation is quite different in OMB in terms of accumulating institutional knowledge and experience. OMB budget examiners are almost always in the room where budgets are debated. Moreover, what they learned is transmitted to new members. This locates OMB certainly at the center of the executive budget process.

During the 1980s, OMB's strong top-down management practice caused some problems between agencies and OMB budget examiners. Expert knowledge over the executive agencies and programs was not coming up from the examiner level. Rather, policy options came down from the top, especially, political appointees. In particular, the program associate director at the top exerted strong influence on examiners. In many cases, careerist officials in the OMB waited for the right question and budget cues from appointed officials. As discussed above, central budget offices like the OMB have been known for mediating conflicts across agencies. However, the *centralization* in the OMB intensified hostility against the OMB from the executive agencies. Since so many decisions were top-down, OMB budget examiners lost their traditional clout with the agencies. Lacking real power over budgetary issues and pressured by the need to obtain information from the agencies, OMB examiners began to play on their budget power during the budget apportionment process. Appropriations money to be allocated to the agencies was used as a means to pressure the agencies more forthcoming with agency budget information and guarantee their compliance with OMB directives. Agency budget officers regarded such pressures as meddling infringement on their budget authorities. As a result of these frictions, the National Performance Review (NPR) drastically reduced OMB's budget power and shifted substantial budget functions to other agencies (Rubin 2003, 115–20).

The OMB tried to deal with such critiques and reform initiatives through a reorganization that would integrate management, especially financial management, into budget issues and would allow more long-term budget analyses. The reorganization, called OMB 2000, was implemented in 1994. Even after the reorganization, OMB examiners did not have such financial management skills as reading comprehensive audited financial documents. Program examiners still did not have the knack to deal with financial credit reform issues and cash management questions. However, the OMB additionally made efforts to upgrade its financial management functions by introducing a matrix structure. OMB staffs were simultaneously assigned to a division for technical managerial issues and a generalist budget analysis unit. Overall, linking management and budget issues provided the OMB staffs with more leverage for changes in budget issues in the OMB (Rubin 2003, 120–21). Thus, OMB's centralized control during the budget preparation stage is supposed to enhance information-processing capacity of budget decision makers in the executive branch.

What is the effect of the centralized staff function on U.S. budget authorities? Table 4.1 reports the results of statistical analyses. One controversial issue with respect to budget punctuations is how we can locate the cutoff points beyond which observations of *Increment* can be defined as sudden, dramatic budget changes. Earlier pioneering studies initiated by Baumgartner and Jones (1993) defined budget changes greater than 25 percent as budget punctuations (Jordan 2003). As discussed in Chapter 2, incrementalists have contended that budget changes are seldom larger than 30 percent. Therefore, the 25 percent threshold seems quite reasonable to be defined as a cutoff point to identify budget punctuations. However, we are still left unclear about how big is big enough to be "dramatic" changes. This is a controversial issue to be further sophisticated in the future research. However, Robinson et al. (2007) offer a fairly viable option for identifying such cutoff points based on disproportionate information-processing theory. Distributions of decision outputs in idealistic frictionless systems such as pure economic market systems, as noted above, will be a direct function of input information. Due to the central limit theory, the distributions of such decision outputs will be close to normal distributions (Jones, Sulkin, and Larsen 2003). Then, observations of *Increment* that falls outside the normal range would be readily defined as budget choices under bounded rationality, both budget stability and punctuations.

The cutoff points to identify observations in budget stability are already introduced above. Again, through visual and statistical analysis the threshold points for budget punctuations could be identified. In Figure 4.1, the cutoff points for budget punctuations were –.50 and .58. This means that observations of *Increment* less than negative 50 percent or larger than positive 58 percent are categorized as budget punctuations. In Figure 4.1, observations outside the points of ± 1 were deleted for visual clarity. In the final regression analyses, they were added back. Furthermore, observations with previous year's budget authority of zero dollars but current year's budget authority of nonzero dollars are automatically deleted when constructing *Increment* by typical computer programs. However, they are clear examples of positive budget punctuations via creation of new programs. There were a few such cases that were also added back into the final regression models. When *Increment* belongs to the zone of budget punctuations, a dummy variable, *Punctuation* , was coded one. If not, it was coded zero.

Since U.S. budget authorities were nested under both seventy-six OMB subfunctional categories and forty-six FYs, there is a high likelihood of clustering across the two class variables (i.e., subfunction and year). If we run a typical logistic regression analysis, the result might suffer Type-I error such that standard errors of regression coefficients might be underestimated (Raudenbush and Bryk 2002). For this reason, multilevel logit regression analysis was conducted. The first column in Table 4.1 reports the results of an unconditional means model (or intercept only model). There was a discernible random effect in the intercept variance across the class variable, OMB subfunctions.

Table 4.1 Multilevel Logit Regression Results Explaining U.S. Budget Punctuations: Executive Models (1961–2006)

Variable	Unconditional Means Model		Full Model (Cutoff: -0.50, 0.58)	
	Coefficient	Pr > |*t*|	Coefficient	Pr > |*t*|
Intercept	-2.0735	< 0.0001	-2.2324	< 0.0001
Centralization			-2.0815	0.0642
Centralization^2			2.1641	0.0490
Central Capacity Load			-0.7088	0.0026
Central Capacity Load^2			-1.3476	0.2745
Per Capita Employee			-0.1823	0.1429
Election			-0.0046	0.9221
Political Change			0.0867	0.3943
Per Capita Income			-0.2356	0.1286
Unemployment Rate			-0.1116	0.0665
Number of Observations	3,196		3,196	
Number of Punctuations	377		377	
-2 Log Likelihood	16,457.71		29,674.19	
Pearson χ^2	3,196.0		4,408.24	
Pearson χ^2/DF	1.00		0.97	

Notes: Class variables (OMB s ubfunctions). The unconditional means model is based on a random intercept model. For this model, – 2 Restricted Pseudo-Likelihood and Generalized χ^2 values are reported. The full model is based on the assumption that there is no discernible random effect in intercept variance.

A model with forty-six FYs as class variable did not converge. With –2 Res *Pseudo* -Likelihood statistics, a χ^2 test could not be conducted to compare the explanatory power of different model specification (SAS Institute Inc. 2005). Instead, generalized χ^2 values divided by degrees of freedom could be used to check whether undetected clustering across level-1 units (i.e., *Punctuation*) exists or the level-1 model is adequately specified (Raudenbush and Bryk 2002). Samples without overdispersion or underdispersion might return the values of generalized χ^2/DF closer to one (SAS Institute Inc. 2005). Virtually all models in this book were screened based on this criterion.

In the second column in Table 4.1, the key variables of bureaucratic centralization and institutional friction factors were added into the unconditional means model. For this model, there was no discernible random effect in the intercept variance.[4] Despite no discernible specification in the variance in the intercept, Pearson χ^2/DF is still quite close to one, which denotes that the explanatory power of the full model is still fairly strong. First, variables associated with bureaucratic centralization show mostly statistically significant impacts on budget punctuations in the expected directions.

Centralization, as expected, is significantly and negatively associated with budget punctuations (p = .0642). As bureaucratic centralization increases, probability of budget punctuations decreases. This implies that bureaucratic centralization might help expedite information-processing capacity of budget decision makers. However, excessive centralization hampers the information-processing capacity of decision makers. *Centralization*^{2} significantly increases probability of budget punctuation as also expected (p = .0490). Thus, the curvilinear relationship between bureaucratic centralization and budget punctuations is supported. Slightly different from the expectation, there was no curvilinear relationship between central capacity load and budget punctuations. As the amount of OMB subfunctional authorities to be reviewed by OMB staffs increases, the frequency of budget punctuations also decreases. The average amount of OMB subfunctional authority per OMB staffs was about 36 million dollars in year 2000 constant value, with the standard deviation of about 120 million dollars and the maximum value of about 1.2 billion dollars. It seems that an OMB staff can manage this level of budget amount. In other words, an OMB staff might have been assigned an adequate work load for the study period.

This capacity load needs some more careful discussions. There have been three main obstacles to keep OMB's institutional memory during recent decades. One was strengthened top-down management in the OMB, which was discussed above. The others include changing roles of budget examiners and rapid turnover among newer recruits. During the 1980s, traditional OMB budget examiners have been much replaced by policy analysts who pursued number crunching. Young policy analysts who were mostly recent graduates of graduate schools did not have any institutional memories except for their skill and zeal for number crunching. They did not know historical contexts of national programs. Some even did not notice that agencies were proposing the same budget requests that they used several years ago. Only senior members with institutional memories caught them.

Along with the declining budget analyzing capacities of new budget examiners, OMB staff number has declined throughout the 1980s. In the early part of the 1990s, it has slightly increased but tapered off during the late part of the 1990s. All these change patterns resulted in increased work load for OMB staff, especially during the 1980s when the average OMB budget examiner was assigned to review five billion dollars in 1985 (Rubin 2003, 116–17). Five billion dollars can be converted into about 7.15 billion dollars in year 2000 constant dollars (the same dollar values used for this book). Compared with the somewhat high peak of work load in 1985, about seven billion dollars, about thirty-six million dollars of work load for the study period seems to be quite manageable. In addition, like many other federal agencies the OMB has also been involved in establishing automated data and communication systems to reduce employee's workload. Such efforts include: keeping computers up-to-date, using internal/external Web sites for facilitating communications, making legislation-related information electronically accessible for OMB staff, providing electronic tools to deliver economic and fiscal data to OMB staff, and improving electronic communications between OMB staff and agencies (Rubin 2003, 119). These combined effects might explain why there is no curvilinear relationship between OMB capacity load and budget punctuations.

All other control variables except for *Unemployment Rate* do not attain statistical significance. Institutional frictions might not augment indicator lock as much as disproportionate information-processing theory suggested. Or else, future studies are strongly warranted to identify and develop indices measuring institutional frictions in the national executive budget process. The fact that *Unemployment Rate* is negatively associated with budget punctuations ($p = .0665$) implies that budget outlays needed for income security programs might be efficiently processed without posing any significant workload onto budget decision makers.

The OMB has recently been criticized for being politicized. It is thus worthwhile to briefly review the charge especially because bureaucratic centralization might exert different impact on budget punctuations depending on its surrounding partisan configurations as discussed in Chapter 3. The conventional view of the OMB is that the OMB performs more the role of budget guardian much similar to the role of Congressional House Appropriations Committees in earlier times. Based on forecast revenues and chief executive's political and policy preferences, the OMB used to exert centralized control over agency budget requests. Based on the information obtained through the informal network, however, the OMB also performs the role of mediator over conflicts between agencies. This facilitates information shared across different agencies. The OMB has been pursuing long-term accuracy in information processing but has recently been criticized for being more politicized with diminishing neutral professionalism. The OMB might serve to materialize the president's political and policy preferences as the priority task. In this sense, the OMB has recently been politicized, rather than technically professionalized based on neutral competence (Rubin 2003, 109–16).

When the national government has been suffering from record-high deficits, the OMB gained a reputation of providing politicized budget estimates, in what is known as rosy scenario. Under the budget constraints in Gramm–Rudman–Hollings (GRH), the OMB frequently prepared rosy economic forecasts by ignoring the accurate state of the economy. This led GRH's sequestration trigger to miss the budget deficit reduction targets. The politicization of the OMB, rather than neutral competence, was the most salient in the area of forming baseline budgets. When the OMB prepares President's budgets, there are likely to be many assumptions on the baseline budgets. The OMB typically uses the so-called current (or constant) service budget that delivers the same level of services next year if there are no policy changes. Constant service budgets make various assumptions on future inflation, which results in many different scenarios of executive budget proposals. Since elected officials can claim savings or suffer from spending increases depending on which assumptions are used for predicting future inflation, OMB's assumptions on baseline budgets are highly likely to reflect dominant political groups' preference on the assumptions (Rubin 2003, 109–13).

During the Clinton administration, the OMB regained some of its previous reputation for neutral competence. However, the OMB was still criticized for making fake efforts to reduce budget deficits, which also evidenced OMB's political coloring. Rubin (2003, 115) introduces an anecdotal story about the kind of political strategies possibly sustained by the OMB. Veterans Affairs Secretary Jesse Brown and NASA Administrator Dan Goldin told that they were not worried about the Clinton budget's proposed sudden cuts in their programs. Both of them received the president's personal assurance via the OMB that there would be no such budget cuts for the two agencies.

Therefore, recent stories indicate a possibility that the OMB has been substantially politicized.

There is a contrasting view, however. Even when the president nominates political appointees at the OMB, the appointees have usually accumulated several years of experience in a wide variety of policy issues as well as political conformity with president's political preferences. They are well informed about how the president's policy issues are linked to the president's national political directions (West 1995). Therefore, a certain level of politicization at the OMB might likely expedite information processing by keeping technical, programmatic issues from being overwhelmed by or mixed with political and policy issues. Overall, still compared with line agencies OMB staffs are in better positions to conduct programmatic analysis based on their superior informational advantages (LeLoup 1977, 92–107; Rubin 2003, 97–122). Despite the strong central managerial control capacity in the hierarchy of national executive branch, the OMB is also heavily swayed by partisan preferences of elected officials (Rubin 2003, 109–16). It is this political backdrop that drives one to further investigate how OMB's information-processing capacity is moderated by partisan political configurations.

Table 4.2 shows how different partisan configurations affect budget punctuations. Unified governments include partisan configurations when the president's party is the same as the majority party in both houses. Under split branch governments, the president is faced by the same majority party in both houses, which is different from the president's party. Under split legislative governments, both houses are under control of different parties. Table 4.2 indicates that the three different samples have slightly different cutoff points for budget punctuations.

One very interesting point is that bureaucratic centralization reveals hypothesized impacts on budget punctuations only under unified governments. *Centralization* exerts negative influence on budget punctuations ($p = .0182$) but *Centralization*^{2} increases budget punctuations ($p = .0179$). Results of logit model are sometimes hard to interpret. Figure 4.2 reports what happens as *Centralization* and *Centralization*^{2} increase by unit, which is one standard deviation in standardized variables, while holding all other control variables at their mean values. Under unified governments, OMB's centralized budget control reduces the probability of budget punctuations suddenly from about 94 percent to about 12 percent as *Centralization* increases from –1

Table 4-2 Multilevel Logit Regression Results Explaining U. S. Budget Punctuations across Different Partisan Configurations: Executive Models (1961 to 2006)

Variable	Unified Governments (Cutoff: -0.47, 0.40)		Split Branch Governments (Cutoff: -0.58, 0.50)		Split Legislature Governments (Cutoff:-0.42, 0.46)	
	Coefficient	Pr > |*t*|	Coefficient	Pr > |*t*|	Coefficient	Pr > |*t*|
Intercept	-2.1099	< 0.0001	-2.0078	< 0.0001	-2.8573	0.0019
Centralization	-4.7557	0.0182	-0.6631	0.7339	1.2980	0.8829
Centralization^2	4.6343	0.0179	0.6335	0.7396	-0.8777	0.9197
Central Capacity Load	-0.9004	0.0086	-0.7690	0.0414	0.3642	0.6919
Central Capacity Load^2	-1.2449	0.5224	-2.0063	0.3819	-4.8305	0.3899
Per Capita Employee	-0.0941	0.6413	-0.4213	0.1856	0.2144	0.8294
Election	0.0591	0.4062	-0.0644	0.4147	0.01136	0.9571
Political Change	0.0709	0.6505	0.1470	0.4294	-0.2041	0.6155
Per Capita Income	-0.3068	0.1274	-0.7058	0.1725	0	.
Unemployment Rate	-0.2767	0.0395	-0.1599	0.1939	0	.
Number of Observations	1,203		1,413		432	
Number of Punctuations	180		170		61	
-2 Log Likelihood	978.40		1,004.42		335.67	
Pearson χ^2	1,133.26		1,356.35		413.69	
Pearson χ^2/DF	0.95		0.97		0.98	

Notes: Class variables (OMB Sub-functions) All regressions are based on the assumption that there is no discernible random effect in intercept variance.

Figure 4.2 Bureaucratic Centralization and Probability of U. S. Budget Punctuations: Unified and Split Branch Governments

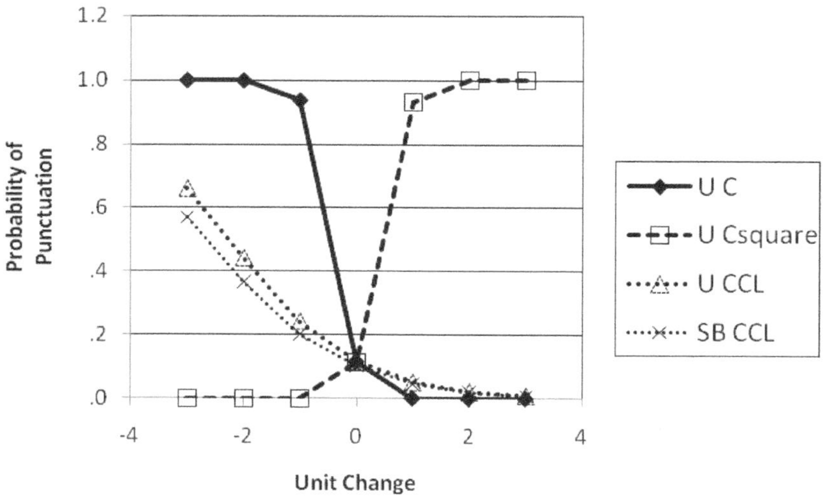

Notes: U (Unified Governments), SB (Split Branch Governments) , C (*Centralization*), CSquare (*Centralization*^{2}), CCL (*Central capacity load*).

to the mean value of zero. *Centralization*^{2} increases the probability of budget punctuations from about 12 percent to about 93 percent for the same range of changes as it increases from the mean value of zero to one. These are the most salient impact of bureaucratic centralization on budget punctuations among the three partisan configurations. This implies that maintaining the level of centralization around its mean value is the best for enhanced information-processing capacity of the central budget office under unified governments. The mean value of nonstandardized variable of OMB centralization is about .0002. This denotes keeping about two OMB employees per ten thousand executive employees would be the best condition for maximizing information-processing capacity of budget decision makers, ceteris paribus.

As the OMB was being more politicized since 1981, OMB staffs have been engaged in congressional monitoring, rather than enhancing neutral competence. OMB budget examiners spent more time on such monitoring. “One former political-level policy official estimated that examiners were probably averaging about half legislative and half budgetary activity as compared with 80 percent budgetary activity and 20 percent legislative activity before 1981” (Rubin 2003, 116).

If OMB's congressional monitoring is an important aspect of OMB activities, then OMB's information-processing capacity will also be highly tangential on how OMB can maximize its central budget coordination functions. However, this depends on different partisan configurations surrounding its budget review process. As hypothesized in Chapter 3, unified governments are more likely to make faster fiscal adjustment to external revenue shocks. This might be probably because intraparty transaction costs might be smaller than interparty transaction costs under unified control of partisan conflicts, among many reasons. When partisan preferences are uniform as in unified governments, bureaucratic centralization, which might improve performance of defender-type organizations like the huge national executive government with numerous agencies, might function the best (Andrews et al. 2009).

Empirical results in Table 4.2 also clearly show that *Central Capacity Load* reduces budget punctuations. Here again, partisan configurations do affect its impact on budget punctuations. In Figure 4.2, when central capacity load is about three standard deviations below the mean value of zero (i.e., −3 on the horizontal axis in Figure 4.2) for unified governments, the probability of budget punctuations is about 66 percent. As its unit increases up to the mean value of zero (0 on the horizontal axis in Figure 4.2), the probability steadily decreases to about 11 percent. Beyond the mean value of central capacity load, the probability decreases but to a lesser degree.

One controversial issue with respect to disproportionate information-processing theory is how we can identify the cutoff points for budget punctuations. Probably, ± 100 percent or bigger changes might be definitely huge changes. How big is big enough to be declared as budget lurch? Robinson et al. (2007) suggested a fairly reliable method of identifying cutoff points for budget punctuations, which was used for this chapter. Their study used about 30–40 percent budget changes as the cutoff points for budget punctuations. This is very close to the 25 percent threshold that disproportionate information-processing theory used (Jordan 2003). However, there are still some problems with this approach. The cutoff points will somehow change depending on whether we include in the final sample outliers or not. For instance, in Figure 4.1 budget changes bigger than ± 100 percent were excluded for a visual purpose. When outliers beyond ± 100 percent are included, the cutoff points were larger than those used in this chapter. To address this problem of varying cutoff points, the cutoff points were changed from ± 30 percent to ± 90 percent gradually by a ± 10 percent increment. The results are almost the same as those reported in this chapter. Therefore, the results reported here are very solid observations on how bureaucratic centralization affects budget punctuations.

An almost similar pattern was identified for the impact of central capacity load under split branch governments. Alt and Lowry (1994, 2000) contended that under split branch governments the governor's party in legislatures might pressure governors to take rapid action to avoid unpopular deficits or unplanned surpluses. Their empirical results show that split branch governments also make quick fiscal adjustment in response to unplanned revenue shocks although they are not as quick as unified governments do. Since partisan configurations might not be as uniform under split branch governments as under unified governments, bureaucratic centralization might not reveal its maximum effect under split branch governments. However, the results in Table 4.2 and Figure 4.2 evidence that central capacity load of OMB staffs still makes a difference in information-processing capacity under split branch governments.

As also hypothesized in Chapter 3, split legislature governments are characterized by the strongest potential for institutional frictions. Revenue adjustments to external revenue shocks are contingent on partisan preferences in legislatures and especially tangential on the last vote needed for overriding chief executive's veto in the legislature. All in all, split legislature governments might not provide the best condition for defender-type organizations to maximize their centralized control functions. Thus, as shown in Table 4.2 and Figure 4.2, features of bureaucratic centralization do not have discernible effects on budget punctuations.

Finally, only *Unemployment Rate* shows significant and negative impacts on budget punctuations under unified governments (p = .0395). Above, high unemployment rate was linked to a possibly increased number of beneficiaries of entitlement programs such as income security benefits. The programs are typically one of the most favorite programs for Democrats who tend to increase benefits for almost the same constituent groups as the entitlement program beneficiaries. Political coloring might get heightened over the assumptions of baseline budgets even for mandatory budget items that are already provided in statutory provisions. This tendency might get intensified especially under split branch or legislature governments where partisan conflicts are likely more intense. Under unified governments, such tensions over entitlement programs, either impetus for reduction or increase, might be minimized. If so, this will explain the negative impact of unemployment rate on budget punctuations.

In sum, bureaucratic centralization does reduce the frequency of budget punctuations. However, too excessive bureaucratic centralization increases budget punctuations. This section further suggests a very important finding. Whether an adequate level of bureaucratic centralization enhances information-processing capacity of decision makers substantially hinges on surrounding partisan configurations. When the surrounding conditions are similar to those when defender-type organizations perform best such as under unified governments, bureaucratic centralization does improve information-processing capacity of budget decision makers. All other control factors that were supposed to measure institutional frictions are not statistically significant. This implies that information-processing capacity of decision makers is much more important than institutional frictions in causing or reducing budget punctuations.

Bureaucratic Centralization and U.S. Budget Stability

Although disproportionate information-processing theory made a great contribution to further our understanding of policy and budget processes, incrementalism has dominated the field of policy and budget processes for recent almost six decades. Disproportionate information-processing theory posited that limited information-processing capacity of budget decision makers will drive them to pay attention to selective informational cues from budget environments. In addition, information oversupply will drive them to resort to attention-driven choice mechanisms. This was the primary reason for why sudden, dramatic budget changes take place.

Very interestingly as discussed in Chapter 2, incrementalism suggested that almost the same reasons, bounded rationality augmented by prescribed political and institutional procedures, result in extreme budget stability. Lindblom (1959, 1979) implied that due to lack (and thus, probably undersupply) of "complete" information, rather than information oversupply, budget decision makers tend to refer to an agreeable budget base as the starting point of budget deliberation. Budget actors have a tendency to not touch the budget base. If the base is debated again, all dormant political contentions might surface up again. Thus, agency budgets are not reviewed comprehensively comparing the values of the current programs with all possible alternatives. In most cases, it is based on last year's budget with a special focus on a small margin of increase or decrease. The general consensus about agency budgets is that they will continue their operation at the going level of spending. Their budget levels usually are not subject to intense scrutiny. In addition, fair share means not only this base but also the expectation that agencies will get some portion of the budget base. The fair share denotes a convergence of expectation that each agency will receive a certain amount of resources compared with other agencies. The base is either the current spending level of agencies or base-line budgets, i.e., next year's cost of delivering current year's service level (Wildavsky and Caiden 2004).

In this sense, budgeting is consensual in that there must be an agreement over the general direction of public policy. Otherwise, aids to calculation through incremental adjustment will not work. Budgeting is also historical. One way of dealing with the huge amount of information for budgetary decision making is the accumulation of experience. For example, members of Congress usually serve several years before they will work on appropriations committees. Based on their yearlong experiences, they can substantially reduce the burden of reviewing all alternatives. A line-item budgetary format is quite helpful for the historical approach. This approach is fairly consistent with how OMB's institutional memory, discussed earlier, is triggered as OMB budget examiners review agency budget requests. Overall, budget reviews and deliberations are characterized by a highly predictable process. Most of all, there will be a stabilized relationship between main budget actors. The main budget actors include, at the national level, budget and program officers in executive agencies, finance experts in the central budget office (BOB or OMB), and members and clerks of Congressional appropriations committees. The premise of classical budgeting under incrementalist perspectives is the mutual agreement on the size, scope, and distribution of scarce resources for budget claimants (Wildavsky and Caiden 2004, 43–67).

It would be very interesting to investigate whether and how bureaucratic centralization influences the steadfast budget inertia formed by the main budget actors. Table 4.3 shows the area of budget stability ranges between an 8 percent decrease to a 13 percent increase for the full sample. This is quite compatible with the range of budgetary incrementalism presented in the literature. About 1,785 observations of the total cases of 3,195 (about 55.9 percent) fall within the area of

Table 4.3 Multilevel Logit Regression Results Explaining U. S. Budget Stability across Different Partisan Configurations: Executive Models (1961 to 2006)

Variable	Full Model (Cutoff: -0.08, 0.13)		Unified Governments (Cutoff: -0.08, 0.12)		Split Branch Governments (Cutoff: -0.07, 0.13)		Split Legislature Governments (Cutoff:-0.12, 0.18)	
	Coefficient	Pr > |t|	Coefficient	Pr > |t|	Coefficient	Pr > |t|	Coefficient	Pr > |t|
Intercept	0.2248	0.0009	0.2750	0.0070	-0.0252	0.8850	2.2689	0.0056
Centralization	0.3765	0.6216	1.9976	0.1595	-0.6881	0.5921	3.9487	0.5416
Centralization^2	-0.4214	0.5738	-1.9819	0.1503	0.7036	0.5786	-4.1995	0.5125
Central Capacity Load	0.5033	< 0.0001	0.4905	0.0047	0.4238	0.0583	-1.3220	0.0743
Central Capacity Load^2	-0.0809	0.6375	-0.2105	0.2281	0.4842	0.3197	10.9577	0.0379
Per Capita Employee	-0.1082	0.1905	0.1499	0.3167	-0.0195	0.9245	-1.0234	0.1459
Election	0.0152	0.6298	-0.0095	0.8539	0.0953	0.0719	-0.0221	0.8872
Political Change	-0.1095	0.1239	-0.1050	0.3459	-0.1571	0.2259	0.1309	0.6638
Per Capita Income	0.0292	0.7793	0.3162	0.0341	0.3516	0.2877	0	.
Unemployment Rate	-0.0104	0.7982	0.1174	0.2048	0.0875	0.2852	0	.
Number of Observations	3,195		1,203		1,413		432	
Number of Budget Stability	1,785		688		768		280	
-2 Log Likelihood	4,282.18		1,612.42		1,862.82		533.47	
Pearson χ^2	3,208.18		1,205.09		1,414.72		411.24	
Pearson χ^2/DF	1.01		1.01		1.01		0.97	

Note: Class variables (OMB Sub-functions) All regressions are based on the assumption that there is no discernible random effect in intercept variance.

budget stability. This implies that the budget inertia induced by the main budget actors is still widely observed in the national budget process. The column for the full sample in Table 4.3 reveals that the only statistically significant variable is *Central Capacity Load* ($p < .0001$). Given the fact that work load for OMB staff has been within a manageable range for the study period, it is surprising at first glance to find that OMB staff's *manageable* workload increases the probability of budget stability.

When OMB staffs' workload increases, in other words OMB staffs can process more budget information, the probability of budget punctuations significantly dropped under unified and split branch governments as discussed in Figure 4.2. This could be true because OMB staff can process budget information in a timelier manner, which prevents attention-driven choice and ultimate budget punctuations. As clarified in equation (2.5), however, bureaucratic centralization and adequate capacity load of budget decision makers might have different patterns of affecting budget stability. Under the strongest incrementalist perspective, the main budget actor parameter in the second part of the right-hand side in equation (2.5) will be zero: i.e., $M.B.A. * (\beta_1 \cdot Z_{1t} + \beta_2 \cdot Z_{2t} + \ldots + \beta_m \cdot Z_{mt}) = 0$, as discussed in Chapter 2. If so, the first part of the right-hand side in equation (2.5) denotes that the main budget actors do not pay adequate attention to budget information cues that they receive from budget environments. Instead, they pay attention to marginal deviations from a certain reference point (i.e., $(\beta_0 - 1)$ in equation (2.5)) upon which they agree. The reference point will be close to the budget base, which is likely to be previous year's budgets for agencies. The results in Table 4.3 support this expectation. OMB staffs' capacity load cannot influence the steadfast and sticky budget base among the main budget actors. As OMB staffs work harder to process more budget information, it only helps increase main budget actors' bias toward budget inertia by rendering budget decision makers to focus only on small changes from the budget base. Budget decision-making systems under this condition look very close to what characterizes reactor-type organizations or programmed decision environments discussed in Chapter 2. Reactor-type organizations do not have a consistent and stable strategy for responding to the changes and uncertainty in their surrounding environments. Reactors seldom make any environmental adjustments until they are forced to do so. Bureaucratic centralization is observed to expedite information processing and reduce institutional frictions vis-à-vis budget punctuations. In stark contrast, it does not replicate its effect on budget choices that pertain to budget inertia or stability. In the above, it was clarified that OMB staffs' workload might be within their capacity limit. Therefore, as OMB staffs are working harder, the probability of budget stability increases.

Here again, the impact of central capacity load is clearly swayed by partisan configurations. Under unified and split branch governments, *Central Capacity Load* increases the probability of budget stability (p = .0047 and p = .0583, respectively). Alt and Lowry (1994, 2000) reported that political conditions under split branch governments are very similar to those under unified governments such that majority party's preference for fiscal scale will press budget actors to make quicker adjustment to external revenue shocks. This might be relevant for explaining how the second part of the right-hand side in equation (2.5) functions in a different manner under unified and split branch governments: i.e., expedited information processing under majority preferences for fiscal conditions. When the second part is null, the first part in the right-hand side of equation (2.5) will also have a different connotation. The tendency of the main budget actors to stick to the budget base and consequently focus only on marginal changes might be stronger whenever there is a majority preference toward fiscal scale. Again considering that OMB staffs' workload might have been adequate, the probability of budget inertia increases as OMB staffs work more. This aspect is starkly contrasted with the findings for split legislature governments.

Under split legislature governments, *Central Capacity Load* reduces budget stability (p = .0743) and *Central Capacity Load*^{2} increases budget stability (p = .0379). As discussed in detail in Chapter 3 and above, there are more veto points for decision making under split legislature governments. This makes each of the main budget actors have an increased influence to voice and make the case for its own budget preferences. Under this condition, main budget actors' tendency toward budget inertia or stability might weaken whenever OMB staffs work more by now questioning what was previously deemed and agreed upon as unquestionable. Excessive workload of OMB staffs under split legislature governments might end up weakening OMB staffs rather than the main budget actors. This will result in enhancing budget inertia under split legislature governments. In any case, the results reveal that there are different explanatory factors that affect budget stability and punctuations as Robinson et al. (2007) implied.

The literature suggests that whenever resources are scarce, budget processes become more contentious (Rubin 2010). When there are more resources, fighting over budget resources might dampen. This might be especially the case under unified governments where the main budget actors might have already established how they can share budget pies. This could explain why *Per Capita Income* significantly increases the probability of budget stability under unified governments ($p = .0341$). Finally, *Election* significantly increases the frequency of budget stability only under split branch governments ($p = .0719$). *Election* was hypothesized above to augment institutional frictions based on contested credit claiming especially between the House and the Senate. It is very difficult to explain how such institutional frictions increase budget stability. However, there is one potential explanation. Under split branch governments, contested credit claiming between the two chambers might still materialize. In addition, the institutional power tension and game between the president and Congress might still be in operation. As the budget literature suggests, whenever one budget aspiration is pitted against other fiscal aspirations, the result is almost always budget stability: i.e., the status quo cannot be easily challenged (Rubin 2010; Wildavsky and Caiden 2004). This might explain why *Election* increases the probability of budget stability only under split branch governments. This must be a significant future research topic.[5]

Conclusion

In this chapter, we have investigated how bureaucratic centralization in a large bureaucratic organization such as the national executive branch can extend information-processing capacity of budget decision makers. Although bureaucracy has been criticized from multiple viewpoints, bureaucratic organizations were oftentimes developed as a way to improve the limitations in human cognitive capacities. In particular, an empirical study shows that in a defender-type organization such as the national bureaucracy a certain aspect of bureaucratic centralization improves organizational performance. Empirical findings in this chapter strongly support the previous report.

Bureaucratic centralization tends to significantly reduce budget punctuations but excessive bureaucratic centralization increases budget punctuations. Disproportionate information-processing theory recently illuminated how we can interpret why budget punctuations occur and what factors might explain the presence of such sudden, dramatic budget changes. Based on the theory, bureaucratic centralization seems to enhance information-processing capacity of budget decision makers. With the augmented information-processing capacity, decision makers can process budget informational cues flowing from budget environments in a more timely fashion. However, excessive bureaucratic centralization seems to detract from the information-processing capacity of budget decision makers. In addition, as budget examiners and staff in the central budget office, OMB, review more budget information, budget punctuations are less likely as far as the work load is within their capacity.

Overall, bureaucratic centralization is found to be a tool to improve bounded rationality of decision makers but with a certain constraint. In addition, whether and how bureaucratic centralization affects budget punctuations is highly dependent on political backdrops surrounding bureaucratic organizations. Bureaucratic centralization tends to augment information-processing capacity of budget decision makers mostly under unified governments where interparty transaction costs are likely to be minimized. Bureaucratic centralization is by construction compatible with hierarchical structures in bureaucratic organizations. The unified political control under unified governments also contains some features similar to the hierarchical structures. Thus, when there is a match between bureaucratic centralization and its surrounding political backdrops, it is likely to expedite information processing and reduce institutional frictions. Finally, bureaucratic centralization cannot help shake loose budget inertia or stability that is observed to be induced by the budget base agreed upon among the main budget actors in terms of budgetary incrementalism. Bureaucratic centralization even increases the frequency of budget stability here again mostly under unified governments. Therefore, a certain aspect of bureaucracy can improve bounded rationality. However, one clear message is that "*bounded* bureaucracy" can improve bounded rationality in the national executive budget process.

Notes

1. Note that these offsetting receipts are collected from customers, not from other governmental agencies.
2. As detailed later in this chapter, observations of previous year's budget authorities with zero values but current year's budget authorities with *non*zero values are clear examples of positive budget punctuations. These observations are added back into the final regression models. The percentage here is computed with the full sample including such budget punctuations.

3. Partisan configuration variables were not lagged. The OMB is reviewing agency budget requests throughout the fall of a typical calendar year and the spring of the next calendar year when agencies request their budgets for the third calendar year. Therefore, either lagged or current partisan configurations can be used for the research question in this book. When partisan configuration variables were lagged, the results reported in this chapter were not obtained. This implies that partisan configurations in the second calendar year exert more influence on OMB's central budget coordination activities.
4. SAS PROC GLIMMIX was used for estimation with the RANDOM _RESIDUAL_ option in place of random intercept variation. When three dummy variables for financial subfunctions, mandatory subfunctions, and national security subfunctions were added in regression models, model-fit statistics deteriorated in terms of the values of generalized χ^2/DF.
5. Detailed discussions of all control factors in this chapter and the following two chapters are beyond the scope of this book. A detailed summary table is available upon request to the author. The summary finding clearly shows that most of expectations regarding centralization and central capacity load are strongly supported. Most of control factors also exert expected influence on budget choices and there is an overall common pattern between unified governments and split branch governments over budget stability.

Appendix

Table 4A.1 Descriptions of the Explanatory Variables in National Models

Variable	Definition	Hypothesized effects on budget punctuations	Data source
Centralization	OMB or CBO staff/Executive or Congressional employees	–	OPM/Dwyer and Peterson (2001)
Centralization^2	*Centralization* squared	+	OPM/Dwyer and Peterson (2001)
Central capacity load	OMB Subfunctional Budget Authority/OMB or CBO staff	–	OPM/Dwyer and Peterson (2001)
Central capacity load^2	*Central capacity load* squared	+	OPM/Dwyer and Peterson (2001)
Per capita employee	Per capita executive or congressional employees	+/–	OPM/*Statistical Abstract of United States*/Dwyer and Peterson (2001)
Election	Sum of Three Dummies: Year of Presidential Election, Year of Senate Election, and Year of House Election	+	*Statistical Abstract of United States*
Political change	Absolute value of annual changes in the variable: (Democratic House members + Democratic senators—Republican House members—Republican senators)/U.S. population	+	*Statistical Abstract of United States*
Per capita income	U.S. personal income/U.S. population	+	*Statistical Abstract of United States*
Unemployment rate	Unemployment rate	+/–	DOL

Source: Dwyer, P., and R. E. Peterson. *Legislative Branch Employment: Trends in Staffing, 1960–2000.* CRS Report for Congress. Washington, DC: The Library of Congress, Congressional Research Service, 2001. Order Code RL30996.

OPM: Office of Personnel Management. *Federal Civilian Workforce Statistics: Employment and Trends* (various versions).

DOL: U.S. Department of Labor, Bureau of Labor Statistics.

5

Bureaucratic Centralization and the Congressional Budget Process

Bureaucracy has been criticized for various malfunctions. But as shown in Chapter 4, a certain aspect of bureaucracy, bureaucratic centralization with an adequate level of work load, produces some benefits. Bureaucratic centralization likely improves information-processing capacity of budget decision makers during the executive budget process in the national government. It also likely reduces institutional frictions over national budget decision making. Bureaucratic centralization significantly reduces the frequency of budget punctuations that are possibly the ramifications of constrained capacity of decision makers and heightened institutional frictions. Despite the advantages, bureaucratic centralization is not without its limits as well. Its effectiveness in enhancing information capacity and reducing institutional frictions is substantially constrained by three contingencies: i.e., the effect of bureaucratic centralization to a certain threshold point, the effect being contingent on partisan environments, and limited impacts on budget stability.

Bureaucratic centralization in the national executive branch reduces the probability of budget punctuations, but excessive centralization of budget review power or excessive central budget coordination in the Office of Management and Budget (OMB) increases the frequency of budget punctuations. It is likely that the benefits from augmented information-processing capacity of budget actors and reduced institutional frictions are offset by the extra costs incurred from excessive centralization. Excessive centralization in a notably hierarchical bureaucratic organization might invite institutional frictions during the executive budget process. Those frictions are strong enough to nullify the informational advantages rendered by bureaucratic centralization.

Second, the benefits from bureaucratic centralization are obviously contingent on partisan configurations surrounding the whole budget preparation and review cycle. Bureaucratic centralization shows its expected impacts on budget punctuations, but only when its surrounding environments are compatible with presumably ideal conditions for bureaucratic organizations. The national executive branch clearly exemplifies bureaucratic centralization that is highly characteristic of bureaucratic hierarchies. Under unified governments, the president and both chambers in Congress come from a same party. The streamlined and unified partisan control will not cause any conflicts with the hierarchical backdrop featuring bureaucratic organizations in the executive branch. Therefore, it does not sound strange that bureaucratic centralization likely enhances information-processing capacity of budget actors and reduces institutional frictions under the unified governments where hierarchical systems during the executive budget process are least likely to be disturbed.

Third, bureaucratic centralization has no impacts on budget inertia. According to budgetary incrementalism, it has been empirically evidenced that budget decision makers do not review the budget base. They focus on the alternatives that are marginally deviating from the status quo. Budgetary incrementalism also normatively contends that starting from the budget base will minimize political conflicts that have already passed a political viability test and are reflected into the status quo. Empirical findings reveal that bureaucratic centralization does not control budget inertia. Instead, under unified governments central budget staffs' work load tends to accelerate such budget stability. Perhaps, many allegations poured over OMB's politicization might gain some support here. OMB staffs might serve the dominant political will under unified governments, which would protect their current political interests.

How can then bureaucratic centralization in the Congressional budget process affect information-processing capacity of budget decision makers and institutional frictions? How can it influence budget punctuations and stability? We can expect a result probably almost similar to the findings from the national executive budget process, because governmental organizations, including Congressional organizations, are basically defender-type organizations as discussed in Chapter 3. However, there is one clearly different dimension in organizational structures in U.S. Congress. If the national executive agencies can be characterized by hierarchies and functional specialization, then

Congress might be featured by its fundamental raison d'être, that is representation.

Congress is inherently a decentralized institution. Due to its diverse geographical basis for member election, Congress allows numerous committees and their members a voice during the Congressional budget process. In this sense, fragmentation is not necessarily a legislative disorder. Senators come from the fifty states and representatives from 435 different electoral districts. Therefore, "the political job of Congress is to give voice, representation, and access to the diversity of interests in American life" (Schick 2007, 119). Congress' practice has been such that many budget-related measures are debated and approved one at a time. This practice reinforces the tendency of decentralization. It is least likely that a single set of Congressional committees controls all budget legislation. In that case, the rank-and-file majority will eventually regain the power away from the few who had budget control power. Budgetary fragmentation has worked reasonably well in forming Congressional budgets. During every step of budget review stages Congress has used the president's budget as the starting and guiding point, especially in making appropriations and writing tax legislation. Numerous pieces of congressional budget decisions made up budget totals that are not a far departure from the president's budget. Overall, fragmented Congress seemingly produced fairly coordinated budgets (Schick 2007, 119–20). However, there was a radical change in the Congressional budget process with the enactment of the 1974 Congressional Budget and Impoundment Control Act (CBA). The next section describes how the Congressional initiative to centralize the budget process influenced the decentralized and fragmented nature of the Congressional budget process and budget actors.

Congressional Macrobudgeting: Institutions and Partisan Politics

Before the enactment of the CBA, there were three main committees in Congress, Authorization Committees, Appropriations Committees, and two tax committees (House Ways and Means and Senate Finance Committees). A conventional view of Appropriations Committees, especially the House Appropriations Committee, is somewhat bifurcated. Both Republicans and Democrats shared a general ideological consonance over their budget-cutting tendency. In particular, the House Appropriations Committee was the least partisan committee and the norms of specialization and reciprocity dominated appropriations processes. Members developed specialized expertise on the areas of the executive budget. The House Appropriations Committee was viewed as guardians of the Treasury, who exerted tight reviews over agency budget padding. In addition, Appropriations Committees in both chambers also played a similar, watchdog role over legislative proposals that Authorization Committees prepared. However, the Senate Appropriations Committee slightly differed from the House Appropriations Committee. Senators were somewhat more interested in constituency service. Decision making is more individualistic and the committee is less dominant over its members. The Senate Appropriations Committee acted like an appeal court where budget claimants who got hurt by House actions can appeal for recovering their budgets. Senate Appropriations Committee members tended to view themselves as the responsible legislators who tried to keep the House Appropriations Committee from doing too much damage to constituency or national interests (Fenno 1966; LeLoup 1977, 1980, 113–21; Wildavsky and Caiden 2004, 57). In the late 1960s even before the enactment of CBA, however, committee advocacy for specific programs increased and the guardianship role of the House Appropriations Committee much declined (LeLoup 1980, 121).

The introduction of Congressional macrobudget reforms in the CBA was partly ignited by Nixon's abuse of presidential impoundment power. In addition, enactment of too many entitlement programs gradually shifted a substantial portion of budget review and control power conferred Appropriations Committees. The Congressional reaction to the declining budget authority was the creation of central budget control mechanism, or Congressional macrobudgeting systems. The enactment of the CBA brought about numerous changes in the relationship between central budget control towers (i.e., House and Senate Budget Committees) and all other committees, especially Appropriations Committees primarily and Authorization Committees secondarily. It also changed the conventional roles of Appropriations Committees in particular. Bureaucratic centralization in the Congressional side was embedded in the setting totally different from the hierarchical context in the executive branch. Congress is ultimately nothing more than a coalition of "co-equals." Furthermore, the CBA entailed another layer of complexity in terms of both partisan and institutional conditions as discussed in this chapter. Therefore, it seems imperative to explore first the changing partisan and institutional settings in Congress since the inception of the CBA, under which bureaucratic centralization in Congress has been expected to influence information-processing capacity of budget decision makers and reduce institutional frictions.

LeLoup (1980) made a succinct yet clear discussion of what happened in the aspiration and behaviors of budget actors in Congress immediately after the enactment of the CBA up to the late 1970s. In particular, LeLoup made a thorough comparison between the House Budget Committee (HBC) and the Senate Budget Committee (SBC) over five dimensions: i.e., membership, goals, strategies, environments, and decision making. The comparison over the five dimensions offers an information-rich depiction of the partisan and institutional backdrops where bureaucratic centralization in Congress played out. The comparison is also important because the two Budget Committees were at the center of the Congressional macrobudgeting system through budget resolution and reconciliation procedures.

The HBC overall reflected patterns somewhat comparable to the conventional view of the Senate Appropriations Committee, which was constituency-oriented. But there were more features that distinguished the HBC from other committees over the five dimensions. In terms of membership, there was a term limit to four years in the HBC although later it was lessened. Due to the term limit, HBC members regarded their membership assignment as part time. According to the CBA, five members of the HBC must also serve on the Appropriations Committee and five on the Ways and Means Committee. The remaining seats must be allocated to the majority and minority leadership. The CBA provisions were designed to prohibit HBC members from using the budget committee as a power base (LeLoup 1977, 144; 1980, 59–62; Schick 2007, 132). In contrast, there was neither term limit nor direct representation of other committees or party leadership in the Senate. The SBC was represented more by the Appropriations Committee. Membership does not rotate and the committee seems to be more stable than the HBC (LeLoup 1977, 144; 1980, 86; Schick 2007, 132).

In terms of goals and strategies of Congressional members, there was a subtle but fairly significant departure of the HBC from the SBC. Fenno (1966) identified three goals of Congressional members: i.e., constituency (fostering chances for reelection), power (gaining influence within Congress), and policy (shaping major national policies). LeLoup adds the fourth goal, process (changing practices and procedures within Congress through budget resolution and reconciliation procedures). One subtle and interesting point is that HBC Republicans were policy oriented while HBC Democrats were concerned with process (LeLoup 1980, 62–67). The goal difference resulted in differing strategies. HBC members, especially Democrats, were more concerned about the process provided in budget resolutions. Their first strategy was to write a budget resolution that could pass the House. Too high budget totals might alienate conservative Democrats, while too low budget targets might alienate liberals. The second strategy was to accommodate most spending objectives of standing committees. This clearly posed some tensions between its watchdog stance and the need to safeguarding the budget process in the earlier years (LeLoup 1980, 72–75).

In contrast, the SBC was more policy oriented. Even SBC Democrats were less concerned with process unlike HBC Democrats who were concerned about keeping budget resolution and reconciliation procedures. SBC Democrats and Republicans were focused on both fiscal policy and budget control. Budget resolutions were supported by large majorities and backed by bipartisan support. Due to their six-year terms, senators were more stable in their membership and felt less constituent pressure than their House counterparts. Overall, SBC's strategies were much akin to the tension that the Appropriations Committee experienced during the 1960s. That is, the SBC remained as a budget-cutter but tried to leave some room in budget resolutions to satisfy legitimate spending needs. In addition, the SBC tried to establish a solid, bipartisan front on the Senate floor. This strategy preserved the strength of the SBC and increased its chance for legislative success on the floor (LeLoup 1977, 88, 97).

In terms of the budget environments surrounding the committee decision structures, differences between the HBC and the SBC were more emphatic. HBC Republicans overwhelmingly voted against budget resolutions. Partisan divide in the HBC exerted significant influence on budget resolutions. Institutional features further accelerated the partisan divide. When the HBC made some budget cuts, other House committees padded their requests to protect their programmatic options. In addition, the Appropriations Committee was more affected by budget resolutions because expenditures were categorized into functional subtotals that come close to the committee jurisdiction. Thus, there was a heightened tension between the HBC and the House Appropriations Committee. There was greater support for budget resolutions and reconciliation procedures in the

SBC, though. No budget resolutions failed to gain minority support in the SBC. One potential reason might be that SBC Republicans were less cohesive than HBC counterparts. This means that they were less swayed by partisan lines than their individual policy preferences. The SBC was also more aggressive toward the Authorization Committee rather than the Appropriations Committee. The SBC was generally in good relationships with the Appropriations Committee primarily because appropriations bills were rarely the target of SBC opposition (LeLoup 1980, 67–70, 89–94).

There were some other disparities along the line of decision environments. The HBC is not as independent as other standing committees. In this sense, party leadership in the HBC was crucial for the success of the HBC. In the HBC, a variety of interest groups, such as organized labor and state/local governments, attempted to influence the targets and ceilings recommended by budget resolutions. Although interest groups exerted influence on the HBC, they were not as active as for other typically client-oriented committees. This was because the HBC at least was focused on budget target totals and responsible in minimizing the parochial spending appeals that were rampant in the rest of the Congress. Despite the Congressional desire for independence from the president's budget, the HBC usually adopted it as the reference point for national fiscal policy. In contrast, SBC members were not as dependent on party leadership as in the HBC. The SBC attempted to use the Congressional current policy estimates as markup although it also relied on the president's budget as the most important budget referent. Party leaderships, the executive branch, and interest groups were less salient in the SBC (LeLoup 1977, 143–44; 1980, 70–72, 95–96).

Finally, in the process of decision making, there was a difference between the HBC and the SBC when dealing with the Congressional Budget Office (CBO). The HBC assembled staffs with more technical expertise while the SBC blended budgetary expertise with legislative experience. In addition, the HBC staffs tended to compete with the CBO staffs, so the CBO had been more devoted to paying more attention to the SBC. SBC staffs were more open to CBO reports than HBC staffs. Furthermore, in the individualistic Senate, members could have their own staff in conjunction with the core committee staff and the CBO staff assistance (LeLoup 1977, 144–45; 1980, 102, 144–45).

So, Congressional macrobudgeting initiatives put another layer of complex institutional structures, with a need to account for the aspirations and behaviors of new budget actors, the HBC and the SBC, during the Congressional budget process. This complexity has somewhat different connotation compared with that describing hierarchical structures and processes during the executive budget process. Although the latter is complex enough in terms of budget size and program scope, the provisions of Congressional macrobudgeting also raised a practical issue of new institutional layers, new potential veto points, and institutional conflicts.

Under bureaucratic hierarchies, commands are delivered from top, central divisions. In many senses, those commands are imperative to organizational members: i.e., the members are subjected to central control based on a hierarchical, command and control system. Therefore, the complexity of organizational layers and functional divisions is more likely to be a matter of numeric sum of the layers and divisions under hierarchical organizations. However, on the Congressional side, as discussed above, hierarchies are replaced by fragmentation, decentralization, and most of all autonomy, considering that Congress is fundamentally representing constituency interests. The tendency is especially the case on the Senate side. Congressional macrobudget tools such as budget resolution and reconciliation along with the two budget committees do not guarantee that a simple arithmetic sum of complex provisions, procedures, and organizations can measure potential institutional frictions.

More importantly, the centralized Congressional macrobudgeting also changed the aspirations and behaviors of the remaining Congressional committees. Of course, there were some positive effects of the Congressional macrobudgeting. Implementation of the Congressional macrobudgeting clarified the role of the Authorization Committees such that they had a better sense of how their budget requests were linked to budget totals and appropriations (LeLoup 1980, 116–17). However, its impacts on Appropriations Committees were slightly different. Appropriations Committees were traditionally focused more on policing over budget padding, and as such they were depicted as guardians of the public purse. However, Appropriations Committees realized that there were other central committees that were supposed to provide budget totals and check whether all standing committees remained within the budget targets. Appropriations Committees now became less vigilant to policing budget padding by Authorization Committees and executive agencies. What was once a guardian now turned out to be a claimant of parochial interests, and the potential for increased institutional frictions was elevated (Schick 1980).

What happened immediately after the enactment of the CBA has remained almost unchanged in the recent decades. Institutional differences between the SBC and the HBC, partisan divide during floor action as well as within the SBC and the HBC, and assertiveness of Appropriations Committees have been persisting for over thirty years after the establishment of the CBA. Congressional macrobudget mechanisms have often been used as tools to control budget deficits. In terms of control orientation, the SBC has been stricter. As discussed above, during the late 1970s the SBC pursued policy goals in budget resolutions, such as fiscal policy and budget control. This has been evidenced again during recent decades. The SBC, with its permanent committee assignments, has been stronger than the HBC. It has been fighting for its own institutional budget control power while the HBC has tried to accommodate other committees' budget goals. The SBC has retained stricter rules over budget enforcement. Many points of order to enforce budget resolution targets provided in the Byrd rule for protecting against extraneous provisions in reconciliation bills need a three-fifth majority to be waived. For instance, budget measures that violate the budget targets in budget resolutions are subject to points of order by a single member during floor action. In the Senate but not the House, a point of order can only be waived by a three-fifth majority. The House has retained the power to decide upon its own rules. This relatively lax House budget rules reflected the stronger party leaders in the House and the weakness of the HBC in imposing budget totals onto other standing committees. The difference is partly attributable to the difference in institutional culture between the House and the Senate in general. The House rules are basically designed to facilitate the passage of programs that House members prefer. The Senate rules have more room for floor amendments and thus, result in less partisan divide. In the Senate, minority members can filibuster legislative measures despite stricter budget control rules. Senate members tend to be more individualistic and less partisan-driven (Schick 2007, 155–59).

As was observed during the late 1970s, party leadership was very strong in the HBC. The tendency has not changed during recent decades. Budget committee chairs have almost always developed the majority party's position on budget issues. After obtaining a sufficient understanding of the majority party's preference, committee chairs have convened budget committees to mark up budget resolutions. Especially in the House, the pre-resolution consultations have been fairly partisan. In the Senate during the late 1970s, SBC chairs reached out to minority members to broaden SBC's support for budget resolutions. However, there has been a change in the SBC since the early 1990s. A partisan wedge between Republicans and Democrats has been widened in the SBC as well (Schick 2007, 136). An almost similar pattern of partisan divide was observed during floor actions.

From 1976 to 2008 in the House, almost all the votes of the majority party were cast to gain support for budget resolutions while the minority party cast almost all of their votes against budget resolutions. This pattern persisted during the 1970s and 1980s when Democrats were the majority in the House. Since the mid-1990s when Republicans were the majority, the pattern also persisted. During recent years, there was a fissure even between Republicans. Some of them preferred downsizing government and others opted for maintaining current programs. During the early years after the implementation of the CBA, bipartisan cooperation facilitated the adoption of budget resolutions in the process of Senate floor action. As mentioned above, such bipartisan cooperation during floor action in the Senate was substantially supported by the SBC leadership and members. Since 1981 when the Republicans gained control in the Senate, partisanship has emerged in the Senate as well. During some recent years, every minority Senator voted against budget resolutions (Schick 2007, 136–40).

Overall, the SBC and the HBC have evolved into instruments of party leaderships in Congress. Schick (2007, 132) lists three potential reasons for the influence of party leaderships. First, unlike each piece of legislations, budget resolutions are a picture of total budgets. As such, they cover the gamut of defense, income security programs, transportation programs, international programs, etc. Therefore, budget resolutions are, by construction, vulnerable to partisan interests and conflicts. This is especially the case because Congress has been characterized by partisan fragmentation. Not surprisingly, party leaders have often ironed out political disputes over budget aggregates and functional allocations in their favor. Second, budget resolutions have always been the Republican budget or the Democratic budget, not fiscal preference of one or another committee. Since the enactment of the CBA, divided governments (i.e., split branch governments and split legislature governments) have been the case for more than two-thirds of the years. Under the political gridlock, "only party leaders can represent the range of views needed to formulate and defend the party's position on the budget" (Schick 2007, 132). Finally, it was also party leaderships that could silence party line voting and political fissures between Democratic and Republican ranks. Therefore, partisan configurations within Congress as well as new institutional features were symptomatic of the Congressional budget process since 1974.

In addition, Appropriations Committees have repeated aspirations and behaviors much similar to those observed during the late 1970s. They have been less vigilant to policing over budget padding and the committees themselves have consistently joined the list of budget claimants (Cogan, Muris, and Schick 1994). Furthermore, the majority preference over fiscal targets in such power committees as Appropriations Committees prevailed over the will of the budget committees. As Schick clarifies (2007, 161):

> The congressional budget process is a malleable tool. It served Congress during the decades of high deficits and assisted Congress in balancing the government's books in the late 1990s. If it survives, it will be because the process enables Congress to set the policies and priorities it wants, not because it prevents a legislative majority from working its will.

Clearly, Congressional budget procedures have become more complicated from both institutional and political perspectives. Bureaucratic centralization in Congress cannot be accurately depicted and investigated without keeping in mind such recent radical shifts in Congress and the fundamental differences of Congress from the bureaucratic hierarchies in the executive branch. What are the roles, aspirations, behaviors, and strategies of the CBO under such backdrops in Congress? One can never answer this question without scrutinizing political coloring over the new institutional features in the CBA.

The Congressional Budget Office (CBO): A Bipartisan Information Processor

The Congressional macrobudget initiatives were the results of Congressional efforts to regain institutional budget power from the president by having Congressional budgets that are not necessarily the same as the president's budgets. The budget committees, at the beginning stage of Congressional budget reviews, developed their own budget targets. One of multiple reasons why Congress had relied on the president's budgets as reference points was partly attributable to the lack of its own informational power. The CBO was created mainly for the purpose of providing Congress with sophisticated budget information and policy analysis. The main institutional tools of the Congressional macrobudget systems, budget committees, have not been successfully imposing budget totals on parochial assertiveness of legislative standing committees as discussed above.

In contrast, since its inception the CBO was formed into a fairly effective information-processing center in Congress despite the continued bipartisan political pressures upon its operation. As LeLoup (1977, 147) depicts, "the new congressional bureaucracy has been one of the most controversial creations of the budget act and the subject of continuing criticism." The main functions of this new *bureaucratic* organization in Congress were largely targeted on serving as the principal source of budget information on revenues and expenditures. The CBO assisted primarily the Budget Committees with information on budget authority, outlays, tax expenditures, revenues, etc. But it also assisted the Appropriations, Ways and Means, and Finance Committees with the same information sources. CBO's main functions were scorekeeping, bill costing, five-year projections, report on budget alternatives, and policy analysis reports. Although CBO's role was to provide neutral information, it soon became known for its liberal advocacy, such as Keynesian slant, and bias against military budgets. Hence, the antagonistic House Appropriations Committee substantially limited its staff size. During its early years, SBC staffs were more open to CBO reports than HBC staffs. The Appropriations Committees and other standing committees did not use such reports often. Since 1976, cost estimating has been enhanced, thus it has helped Congressional members understand long-term fiscal impacts of legislation. However, the CBO was not highly successful in fulfilling its main missions during its early years of operation. CBO staffs were predominantly lacking Congressional experience. In addition, CBO staffs had great difficulty serving diverse political preferences along the partisan lines (LeLoup 1977, 147–48; 1980, 143–47).

Throughout the more recent decades since 1974, CBO's main functions were tightly focused on three dimensions. First, the CBO has been responsible for fiscal noting, which includes estimating the budgetary cost of proposed legislation. Second as discussed below, the CBO has picked up in its responsibility in checking if new legislations were being within acceptable budget rules, most likely specified in budget resolutions. This responsibility includes scoring for single pieces of legislation and scorekeeping for accumulated, past, and current legislations. Legislators frequently contacted the CBO to see if their legislative proposals were in compliance with budget targets in budget resolutions and requirements for Pay-as-you-go (PAYGO) offsetting.[1] These issues have been very contentious partly because the interpretation of such rules and requirements was highly dependent on CBO's estimation. CBO's role as scorekeeper put this rather small agency to a highly visible place, of course, with heightened political pressures to drive the CBO in their favor. Third, the CBO also estimated whether the president's budget proposals remained within an acceptable degree of fiscal balance. This responsibility also placed the CBO at a political crossfire (Rubin 2003, 99; Schick 2007, 154–55).

As in its early years, the CBO has been almost always in the line of political fire during the recent decades as well. Numerous anecdotal stories show, however, that despite the political pressures the CBO has also been fairly successful in maintaining its neutral competence. It is very ironic that the very political crossfire in turn created a safeguard for the CBO against lopsided political pressures. Or, at least it has been quite successful in appearing neutral.

One of CBO's initial functions was to make policy analysis. Unlike the OMB, however, the CBO cannot make policy recommendations because a budget office for the entire Congress must remain bipartisan. The CBO has been maintaining its role as politically neutral information processor and analyst. For instance, while the OMB has been criticized for its too rosy economic forecasting, the CBO has gained reputation for more accurate, objective economic forecast. However, CBO's scoring and scorekeeping were inevitably swirled into political debates. For instance, the Clinton administration proposed health care reform initiatives. The CBO estimated that the measures would cost governmental resources although much of the burden expected from the legislative proposals was supposed to be borne by the private sector. This was partly driven by the political power opposed to the Clinton initiative. Thus, the CBO was in the middle of political and policy debates.

There were many reasons why the CBO could not be politically neutral. In a sense, the CBO, much like the OMB, is a mediator between those with potentially conflicting budgetary interests. It had been guiding Congressional budget actors on what they could or could not do given budget rules. Second, CBO's scoring and scorekeeping, by nature, are prospectively predicting future economic conditions and revenue potentials of the national government. Whatever touches on prospective forecast is doomed to political tensions because of the arbitrariness inherent in prediction. Therefore, for the CBO maintaining neutral political stance, or at least appearing to do so, is crucial for its survival (Rubin 2003, 100–1).

Probably, no political pressures placed over CBO scoring might have been more intense than the demands for the so-called *dynamic* scoring. Supporters of the supply-side economics consistently contended that federal tax cut will induce taxpayers to save more resources that could further be used to stimulate private business investments. Republicans argued that tax cuts might increase federal deficit in the short run but tax cuts will ultimately boost the national economy. The growing national economy will surely increase federal tax revenues, if all other things are equal. The tax cut made by the Reagan administration was substantially propelled by the logic (Gosling 2009, 69–85). The logic of incorporating tax cuts into the multiyear fiscal scoring is what is more widely known as dynamic scoring.

Republicans have been consistently pressing the CBO to produce multiyear budget forecasts based on dynamic scoring. It is well known that there are little underlying data or accurate assumptions on dynamic scoring. However, whenever politicians were pressed by budget rules or driven by their political motivations and needs, neutral scoring was significantly jeopardized. For instance, the 1990 Budget Enforcement Act (BEA) prescribed that the cost of all new direct spending and revenue bills in a fiscal session must be fiscally neutral through the PAYGO procedure. In other words, new direct spending increases must be offset by an equivalent decrease in previous direct spending or a revenue increase. Or, new revenue decreases must be fully offset by revenue increases in other legislative proposals or decreases in previous or current direct spending. Republicans frequently pressured the CBO to apply dynamic scoring to tax breaks so that tax breaks would bring about future revenue increases. In that case, there is no need to comply with the deficit-neutral PAYGO procedure that requires an offsetting measure to be taken. The pressure for dynamic scoring picked up significantly after the 1998 balanced budget agreement. It is very surprising to find that even the SBC, which has been less likely to be partisan-driven, also called for the CBO to estimate cost savings and revenue increases if the national budget were balanced in 2002 (Rubin 2003, 102–4). Some Congressional members criticized the pressures for CBO's dynamic scoring in that they might detract from CBO's political neutrality. However, political tensions and conflicts over dynamic scoring persisted. As Rubin (2003, 105) notes, "Republicans pointed out that with static budgeting, revenue tended to be overestimated when tax rates increased; the Democrats countered that Republicans overestimated revenue when tax rates were cut, when they used dynamic scoring."

The CBO has fairly tactfully, sometimes with the help of institutional provisions, navigated through such political labyrinths. As mentioned above, the Congressional macrobudget process has more or less languished. In contrast, the CBO has flourished as an objective and skilled producer of budgetary information and policy analysis. CBO's survival since the enactment of the CBA in 1974 could be ironically attributable to the prominence accorded scoring and scorekeeping that also placed the CBO in the middle of political crossfire. CBO's scoring can doom legislative proposals or pave the way to their passage. Even after political negotiations and compromises between committees and their members were made, the CBO could compel them to modify pending legislations. The CBO has been trying to survive under such Congressional environments by being both independent of Congress and subservient to it. If the CBO is not subservient, Congress might not provide the CBO with the resources it needs, withdraw or dilute CBO's authority, or CBO staffs might be kept at a distance from the Congressional budget process. If the CBO is not independent, it will lack the pronounced legitimacy and stature over scoring and scorekeeping.

In some sense, other Congressional macrobudget systems helped the CBO augment its independence as an information processor. The statutory PAYGO procedures under the 1990 BEA were repealed in 2002 but rule-based PAYGO has been in operation in the Senate since 1993. The latter has obviously maintained Congressional interests in scoring. Budget reconciliation in the Congressional Budget Act (CBA) also elevated the weight of scoring because legislative proposals, which were within the reconciliation instructions, were free from the Senate filibuster. During more recent times, Congress has been moving into stronger partisanship and CBO's need for independence became more urgent, but at the same time much more difficult. However, the CBO has been walking the tight institutional and political rope fairly well during the recent decades (Schick 2007, 132–34).

Schick (2007, 134–35) takes two recent, illustrative incidences that clearly evidence how the CBO fail, or give life to, presidential legislative initiatives. In his early years, President Clinton strongly supported his universal health care reform initiative as his priority project. Clinton's FY 1995 budget estimated that his reform proposal would save as much as about fifty billion dollars over the next six years. In stark contrast, the CBO director, Robert Reischauer, estimated that the proposal would cost the national government additional seventy billion dollar spending. One cannot say that the CBO score blocked Clinton's initiative. However, it seems quite probable that the CBO scoring caused substantial levels of influence over the president's fiscal task.

In 2003, the CBO played another decisive role in determining the fate of pending legislation, adding prescription drug benefit to Medicare. Under the legislation, there is a part of benefit provisions, which caused computational nuisance. For instance, under the 2007 price schedule, participants must pay the first 265 dollars. Medicare reimburses 75 percent of costs ranging from 265 dollars and 2,400 dollars—this range was called a donut hole. Individuals are to pay all expenses between 2,400 dollars and 5,451 dollars. Beyond the upper limit, Medicare pays most costs. The CBO previously scored costs from the new legislation to be about 395 billion dollars for a 10-year period. It ultimately turned out that CBO's estimation of costs eventually dictated the range of the donut hole as well as the fate of the initiative.

CBO's strategies, whether developed by CBO's own decisions or rendered by mere chances of given political conditions, cast more subtle political nuance that needs further discussion. In 1995, Republicans triumphantly regained the majority control in Congress. The political expectation at the moment was that many of CBO staffs might be fired and replaced by those who might show more loyalty to Republican political agenda. However, it was only the CBO director, Robert Reischauer, who was not reappointed but most other staffs retained their jobs. Republicans' maneuver not to pressure the CBO to be more political was substantially due to the emerging understanding in Congress. Republicans somehow believed that CBO's neutrality might be very useful in demanding the president's proposal for a balanced budget by 2002 pass CBO's scoring hurdle. Republicans opted for CBO's more neutral and technically accurate scoring reports rather than the president's politically biased OMB estimation (Rubin 2003, 101). The institutional power struggle between the president and Congress, therefore, allowed a substantial leeway on the part of the CBO in maintaining neutral competence. It also enabled the CBO to remain an effective information processor in Congress, *especially* under split branch governments. Overall, political tensions that might have thrown the CBO into political mire ironically allowed a safeguard against the political crossfire (Rubin 2003, 107–9).

In addition to such political conditions that rendered the CBO able to maintain its neutral competence, the CBO itself has also kept efforts to maintain its reputation as a politically neutral information processor. As Rubin (2003, 109) notes, while the CBO was subjected to substantial pressure for dynamic scoring that was not technically acceptable, the pressure was somewhat under control. Overall, where the OMB has been dedicated to serving political and policy preferences of the president, the CBO has fundamentally been trying to serve two parties in Congress. Partisan configurations between the president and Congress, as well as partisan conditions within Congress, are thus highly likely to define the peculiar features of the Congressional budget process. Whether and how bureaucratic centralization in Congress, CBO's creation, affects the information-processing capacity of budget decision makers will substantially hinge on such partisan configurations. There is one final caveat over the impact of the CBO on Congressional budget choices. As discussed in Chapter 4, the OMB was expected to function as an information processor and a friction reducer. In contrast, the CBO might function more as an information processor. The CBO does not retain the central command power of the OMB. The CBO only takes advantages of political crossfire to survive as a neutral information processor. Therefore, if we find the CBO affects budget punctuations and stability, it will be more likely the result of its information-processing capacity.

Bureaucratic Centralization and U.S. Budget Punctuations

Bureaucratic centralization is expected to facilitate communications within large bureaucratic organizations, especially for defender-type organizations such as the national executive branch agencies or Congressional organizations. Under the executive budgeting system, the OMB retains institutional authority to coordinate interdepartmental conflicts, and expedite communications and information sharing among executive agencies. OMB's information-processing capacity is significantly linked to its institutional authority. The kind of institutional authority that the OMB exerts might function the most effectively under institutional settings closer to hierarchical bureaucratic structures, as was found in Chapter 4. Bureaucratic centralization in the national executive branch increases the information-processing capacity of budget decision makers and consequently reduces the frequency of budget punctuations primarily under unified governments. However, whether bureaucratic centralization in Congress will reveal exactly the same results is utterly an open question. This is especially the case because the fundamental nature of the Congressional budget process is characterized by decentralization and fragmentation, in part defined by Congress' main mission of representation. The basic nature has been more complicated by new institutional layers and partisan politics that the Congressional macrobudget system brought about. This section shows empirical findings on how bureaucratic centralization in Congress affects U.S. budget choices.

The CBO was not organized until February 1975 (LeLoup 1977, 147). For this reason, data to construct bureaucratic centralization was available only after 1975. Therefore, the total sample for the Congressional model in this chapter covers thirty-one years for the period from 1976 to 2006, constrained by the data availability of CBO staffs. U.S. budget authorities on seventy-six OMB subfunctions are also tested to see how bureaucratic centralization in Congress affects budget punctuations. U.S. budget authorities for the subfunctions include new annual budget authority, permanent budget authority, and other legal authorities to borrow and contract. The data set, as described in Chapter 4, covers four macrofunctions: e.g., domestic discretionary subfunctions, financial subfunctions, mandatory subfunctions, and national security subfunctions. Some OMB subfunctions such as Postal Service covered in financial subfunctions include offsetting receipts. Thus, some annual changes in U.B. budget authorities are less than −1.[2]

Figure 5.1 shows the distribution of *Increment* in U.S. budget authorities for the Congressional model. Here again, the range of *Increment* is limited within ± 1 for a better visual purpose. There were 2,080 observations of *Increment* in this limited sample for the Congressional model. The mean value of *Increment* was about .4 percent. The Kurtosis value was about 5.08 that are slightly larger than that reported for the executive model in Figure 4.1. The distribution of *Increment* again shows a distribution of budget changes typical for governmental budgets. It is characterized by its high peak denoting

Figure 5.1 Distributions of *Increment* in U. S. Budget Authority: 1977 to 2006

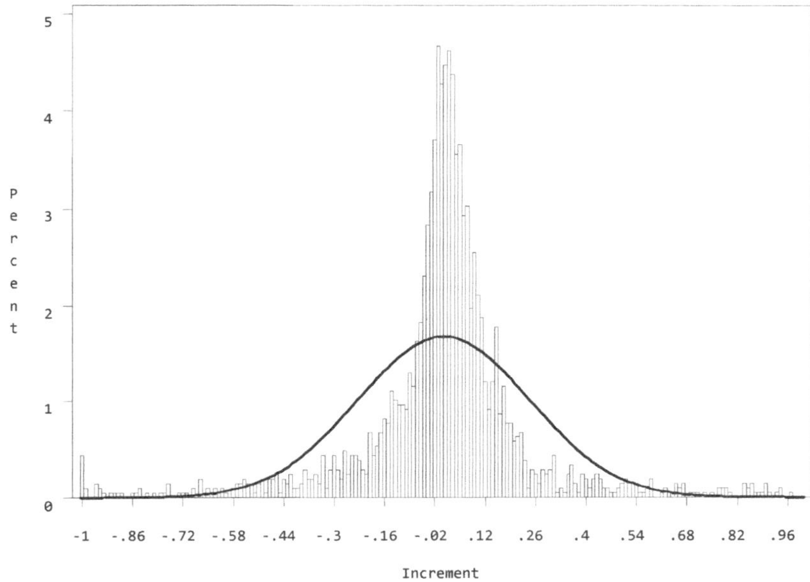

Notes: N: 2,080; Mean (.4 percent); Std. Dev. (23.7 percent); Kurtosis (5.08). Since key variables are one-year lagged, the first year of analysis is 1977.

that a disproportionately larger portion of the changes in U.S. budget authorities falls within the zone of budget inertia or stability. Relatively less frequent observations are found in the area of moderate budget changes. The stretched and thick tails in the positive and negative directions imply that unlike the budgetary incrementalism, there are many observations of *Increment* falling within the range of sudden, dramatic budget changes or budget punctuations.

As discussed in Chapter 4, some observations of *Increment* were added back into final regression analysis. When past year's budget authority is zero while current year's budget authority is nonzero, this case will be missing in typical computer programs. However, these cases are clear examples of positive budget punctuations. When those values are added back into the sample used in Figure 5.1, the sample number increased to 2,190. Again based on Robinson et al. (2007), the area of budget punctuation is identified as the range where actual observations cross over the normal approximation curve in both positive and negative tails in Figure 5.1. The cutoff points for budget punctuations were identified visually and statistically as –.50 and .51. About 11.5 percent of annual changes in U.S. budget authorities fall within this range of sudden, dramatic budget changes. As shown in Figure 5.1, a substantial portion of *Increment* falls within the range of budgetary incrementalism. The cutoff points for this range were –.18 and .13. The high peak of actual frequency for the observations between the cutoff points, which crosses over the normal approximation curve, denotes that still most of changes in U.S. budget authorities fall within this area of budget inertia or stability. About 58.5 percent of *Increment* falls within this range. The remaining cases, about 30 percent of *Increment,* were within the area of moderate budget changes.

Then, what might be the impacts of bureaucratic centralization in Congress on budget decision makers' information-processing capacity and budget punctuations? As LeLoup (1977, 147) indicates, the creation of a new *bureaucracy,* the CBO, was one of the most controversial issues since the inception of the CBA in 1974. While budget resolutions and budget reconciliations directed by the budget committees were not highly functional as originally intended, the CBO has been substantially successful in securing its status as a bipartisan information processor in Congress through the functions of scoring and scorekeeping. Bureaucratic centralization in Congress is measured in the virtually same way OMB centralization was constructed. Appendix 4.1 provides more details about variable construction and data sources for explanatory variables used in the regression models in this chapter.

Centralization is measured as the CBO staff number divided by the number of Congressional employees. In 1976, there were 197 staff members at the CBO. During the early 1980s, the number of CBO staff ranged around about 210 and has been hovering between 210 and slightly less than 240 since the mid-1980s. Thus, the number of CBO staff has been fairly stabilized and there was no significant fluctuation. However, the number of Congressional employee has been substantially fluctuating since 1976. In 1976, there were about 20,808 employees working in the House and the Senate. The number has been gradually declining up to about 18,365 in 1986 and then increased up to about 20,100 in 1993. Since 1993, the number has been ranging between 16,541 (in 1998) and 18,723 (in 1994). The mean value of *Centralization* was about .012 denoting that there were about twelve

CBO staff members per one thousand Congressional employees. *Centralization*^{2} is the squared value of *Centralization.*

In defender-type organizations, bureaucratic centralization is expected to exert curvilinear impacts on budget punctuations. Up to a certain point that needs to be empirically investigated, centralization might speed up decision-making processes, clarify goals, and establish hierarchical (or political in the case of the CBO) authority lines such that it can expedite interdepartmental communications and coordination. Beyond the tipping point, however, bureaucratic centralization might detract from such positive functions that can be secured within an adequate level of bureaucratic centralization. *Centralization* will decrease but *Centralization*^{2} will increase the probability of budget punctuations in the Congressional budget process.

As implied in Gulick's span of control, bureaucratic members are exhorted to be given an adequate work assignment for maximizing their professional capacities supervising subordinates. This will not be an exception for even those working in central bureaucratic organizations. *Central Capacity Load* is constructed as each budget authority amount of OMB subfunctions divided by the number of CBO staff. This way, it measures the dollar amount of U.S. budget authorities for each of OMB subfunctions, which CBO staffs are supposed to review and process budget information on. Each CBO staff member, on average, has been dealing with about 104 million dollars for each of the subfunctions. *Central Capacity Load* will decrease the probability of budget punctuations, as far as the work load is within CBO staffs' work capacity. As Meier and Bohte (2000) also showed, within the range of adequate work load bureaucratic members will fulfill their work responsibilities efficiently and effectively. Beyond the adequate work load, however, performance of bureaucratic members will be hampered. Therefore, the squared value of *Central Capacity Load, Central Capacity Load*^{2}, will detract from budget decision makers' information-processing capacity, and increase the frequency of budget punctuations.

The Congressional macrobudget procedures have affected Congressional partisan configurations since the enactment of the CBA in 1974. The SBC and the HBC brought about a new layer of partisan differences. As discussed above, the partisan lines in the SBC and the HBC have been largely a reflection of the differences in institutional culture and partisan preferences between the House and the

Senate in general. However, peculiar observations regarding CBA's macrobudget tools were related mostly to institutional procedures, especially budget resolution and reconciliation. The new institutional procedures engendered new aspirations and behaviors of standing committees as well as the SBC and the HBC. They might have caused additional rounds of institutional conflicts. This possibility might also have been reinforced by similar Congressional macrobudget tools, such as Gramm–Rudman–Hollings (GRH) of 1985, the BEA of 1990, and other attempts to control federal deficits including the Line Item Veto Act of 1996, the Balanced Budget Act of 1997, and Congressional rule-based PAYGO procedures throughout the 1990s (Schick 2007; Wildavsky and Caiden 2004).

To control for these potential influences of the Congressional macrobudget tools on institutional frictions, additional variables that might tap the macrobudget procedures were further tested in the Congressional regression models. According to the CBA of 1974, budget bills that violate the budget reconciliation instructions included in budget resolutions will be packaged into omnibus reconciliation bills by the Budget Committees. As discussed above, the lengthy process to pass budget resolutions and reconciliations has caused substantial levels of institutional frictions. In addition, according to the Senate Byrd rule any provisions of, or amendment to, reconciliation bills which are deemed "extraneous" to amending entitlement or tax laws are vulnerable to a point of order. Therefore, the number of actions to either strike or retain such extraneous provisions will be reflecting institutional conflicts and frictions. These aspects are starkly contrasted with budget preparation procedures in the national executive branch. Three variables (number of annual omnibus reconciliation act, number of actions to strike extraneous provisions, and number of actions to retain extraneous provisions) were controlled for in the Congressional models. In addition, two dummy variables measuring the GRH and the BEA were also controlled for as potential sources of institutional frictions. Virtually none of these variables exerted significant impacts on budget punctuations in the Congressional models, with the main findings unchanged. For this reason, these variables are not included in the final regression analyses. All other variables are the same variables used for the executive models. This also makes possible a direct comparison between the Congressional model and the executive model. As in the case for the findings in Chapter 4, all control factors are one-year lagged variables.

Table 5.1 empirically shows how bureaucratic centralization in Congress affects budget punctuations in U.S. budget authorities. Compared to the unconditional means model under the first column, the full model has a stronger explanatory power in terms of Pearson χ^2/DF. None of explanatory variables except for bureaucratic centralization in Congress shows statistically significant impacts on budget punctuations. Congress has been depicted as an institutional setting that is least amenable to hierarchical arrangements. As discussed above, however, the CBO has been deemed as a new addition of *bureaucratic* layer in Congress. CBO's functions as a *centralized* bipartisan information processor, especially for scoring and scorekeeping, were

Table 5.1 Multilevel Logit Regression Results Explaining U. S. Budget Punctuations: Congressional Models (1977 to 2006)

Variable	Unconditional means model		Full model (Cutoff: −.50, .51)	
	Coefficient	Pr > $\|t\|$	Coefficient	Pr > $\|t\|$
Intercept	−2.9004	< .0001	2.4018	<.2789
Centralization			−13.5875	.0297
Centralization^2			6.9025	.0320
Central capacity load			−.4541	.1241
Central capacity load^2			−2.1297	.1610
Per capita employee			−.5902	.2909
Election			−.0008	.9892
Political change			−.0019	.9881
Per capita income			−.2661	.3820
Unemployment rate			.0147	.8918
Number of observations	2,197		2,197	
Number of punctuations	252		252	
−2 Log likelihood	12,613.33		1,518.56	
Pearson χ^2	1,324.05		2,060.44	
Pearson χ^2/DF	.60		.94	

Notes: Class variables (OMB Sub-functions). The unconditional means model is based on a random intercept model. For this model, −2 Restricted Pseudo-Likelihood and Generalized χ^2 values are reported. The full model is based on the assumption that there is no discernible random effect in intercept variance.

expected to augment the information-processing capacity of budget decision makers in Congress.[3]

Centralization, as expected, significantly and negatively reduces the probability of budget punctuations in Table 5.1 ($p = .0297$). *Centralization*^{2}, in contrast, increases the frequency of budget punctuations ($p = .0320$). Therefore, bureaucratic centralization in the Congressional budget process seems to expedite information processing but excessive centralization, as in the case for the executive budget process, tends to hamper efficient information processing. What is somewhat surprising in Table 5.1 is that the two measures tapping the work load of CBO staff are not significantly correlated with budget punctuations. As explained above, the CBO has been depicted primarily as a bipartisan information processor in Congress. As such, one might expect that the level of CBO staff's work load might significantly sway the information-processing capacity of budget decision makers during the Congressional budget review process. This might be because CBO's scoring likely contains interpretations regarding centrally formed budget targets. OMB's central budget coordination covers the gamut of revenue forecasting, agency budget review, and streamlining such budget conditions into the president's policy preferences. However, CBO's scoring and scorekeeping are relatively confined to whether the costs of proposed bills are within the limit of budget targets. As such, CBO's work load might not be as tight as that for OMB staffs. This might explain why there are no systematic impacts of the CBO capacity load on budget punctuations. Quite similar to the case for the executive models, all other control variables did not attain statistical significance.

Another interesting point with respect of the impact of bureaucratic centralization on budget punctuations in Congress is the fact the findings are strictly contingent on partisan configurations. Table 5.2 shows how the effect of bureaucratic centralization on budget punctuations is moderated by partisan configurations. A difference between Table 5.2 and the equivalent tables in Chapter 4 is that split branch governments and split legislature governments are combined into one category of divided governments. Only when the two categories were combined, bureaucratic centralization exerted significant impacts on budget punctuations. In any case, Table 5.2 clearly indicates that CBO's centralized information-processing functions are highly tangential on partisan configurations that surround CBO's role as a bipartisan information processor as

Table 5.2 Multilevel Logit Regression Results Explaining U.S. Budget Punctuations across Different Partisan Configurations: Congressional Models (1977–2006)

Variable	Unified governments (Cutoff: −.50, .50)		Divided governments (Cutoff: −.18, .50)	
	Coefficient	Pr > $\lvert t \rvert$	Coefficient	Pr > $\lvert t \rvert$
Intercept	27.0423	.2636	3.3280	.2871
Centralization	−56.6483	.2050	−18.0486	.0570
Centralization^2	18.1883	.2195	9.8504	.0494
Central capacity load	−.4626	.3838	−.4332	.2697
Central capacity load^2	−2.3014	.4077	−2.4179	.2586
Per capita employee	−10.2744	.2624	−.1365	.8545
Election	.9179	.1810	−.0297	.7035
Political change	−2.2529	.2205	.2302	.4569
Per capita income	−4.2459	.3090	−.0938	.8140
Unemployment rate	−.9579	.1310	.0394	.8137
Number of observations	659		1,390	
Number of punctuations	79		159	
−2 Log likelihood	466.04		957.57	
Pearson χ^2	616.98		1,307.95	
Pearson χ^2/DF	.95		.95	

Note: Class variables (OMB Sub-functions). All regressions are based on the assumption that there is no discernible random effect in intercept variance.

discussed in length earlier. Although the findings are slightly at variance with the hypothesized influence of partisan configurations on budget choices, they do not defy our interpretation if we consider that the CBO is a "bipartisan" information processor. Under unified governments, the CBO has experienced heightened pressure for dynamic scoring. Under split branch governments, however, the CBO has been much freer from the pressure. The CBO might also be less pressured for dynamic scoring under split legislature governments.

Bureaucratic centralization significantly reduces budget punctuations ($p = .0570$) but here again excessive bureaucratic centralization increases budget punctuations (p = .0494) only under divided governments. Clearly, when one partisan interest is pitted against another, this situation might create a political condition where the CBO can retain its bipartisan role of information processing.[4] Since logit model coefficients are hard to interpret, Figure 5.2 shows how unit changes in bureaucratic centralization in Congress affects the probability of budget punctuations. When *Centralization* increases from the unit value of 0 (mean value of the standardized variable) to 1, the probability of budget punctuations drops from about 96 percent to almost zero. When *Centralization*^{2} increases from the unit value of −1 to 0, the probability increases from almost zero to about 96 percent. In sum, bureaucratic centralization likely enhances the information-processing capacity of budget decision makers but excessive centralization might detract from the gains obtained from bureaucratic centralization. Second, the impact of bureaucratic centralization on the information capacity of decision makers is strictly dependent on partisan configurations surrounding budget decision makers.

Figure 5.2 Congressional Centralization and Probability of U. S. Budget Punctuations: Divided Governments

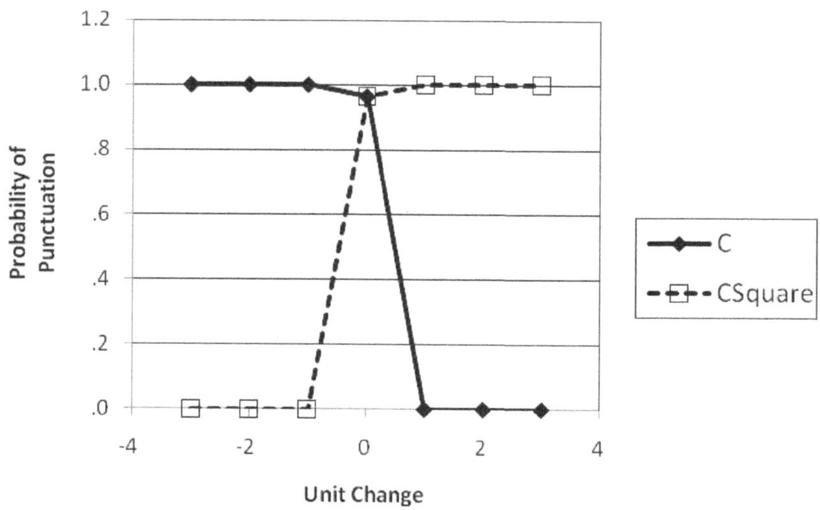

Notes: C (Centralization); CSquare (Centralization^2).

Bureaucratic Centralization and U.S. Budget Stability

As budgetary incrementalism suggested, there has been a strong tendency that main budget actors are likely to leave the budget base out of annual scrutiny. If not, old political conflicts will surface up again. In addition, the tendency was partly attributable to the bounded rationality of decision makers. According to disproportionate information-processing theory budget decision makers pay selective attention to budget information cues, as shown in the second part of the right-hand side in equation (2.5). According to incrementalism, however, budget decision makers do not pay attention to budget information cues flowing from budget environments. This was one of the strongest assumptions of budgetary incrementalism. In addition, prescribed political and legal institutions might drive budget decision makers to resort to an agreed-upon level of budget choices. Therefore, the key point in budgetary incrementalism is the role of the budget base. For instance, the first part of the right-hand side in equation (2.5) will exert strong and steadfast influence on budget decision makers as reference points. Here, the question is whether budget decision makers are likely to pay additional attention to budget information cues when they are supported by tools that might enhance their information-processing capacity. Can bureaucratic centralization in Congress significantly increase the information-processing capacity of budget decision makers and reduce institutional frictions, and consequently reduce the frequency of the extreme budget inertia?

Table 5.3 gives us some answers to the question. Under the full model column, *Centralization* and *Centralization*^{2} do not exert any statistically significant influence on budget stability. As in the case of the executive models, however, partisan configurations do present discernible effects on how bureaucratic centralization modifies the patterns of budget inertia. Under unified governments, the cutoff points for budget stability were –.09 and .12. Observations of *Increment* between the range of 9 percent decrease and 12 percent increase fell within the zone of budget inertia. *Centralization* significantly increases the probability of budget stability under unified governments (p = .0615). *Centralization*^{2} significantly reduces the frequency of budget stability (p = .0878). The two variables under divided governments do not attain statistical significance. Under the strongest assumption of budget incrementalism, the main budget actors are expected

Table 5.3 Multilevel Logit Regression Results Explaining U.S. Budget Stability across Different Partisan Configurations: Congressional Models (1977–2006)

Variable	Full model (Cutoff: –.18, .13)		Unified government (Cutoff: –.09, .12)		Divided government (Cutoff: .07, .12)	
	Coefficient	Pr > |*t*|	Coefficient	Pr > |*t*|	Coefficient	Pr > |*t*|
Intercept	–1.096	.4689	–31.1215	.0549	–2.5689	.2200
Centralization	3.1585	.4624	56.1436	.0615	7.3478	.2522
Centralization^2	–1.1569	.6042	–17.1917	.0878	–3.3552	.3252
Central capacity load	.2750	.0975	.0981	.7322	.1695	.4377
Central capacity load^2	.3398	.1720	.331	.4101	.6819	.0690
Per capita employee	.4583	.2118	12.4501	.0414	.3608	.4682
Election	–.0331	.3990	–.6867	.1077	.0147	.7760
Political change	–.0326	.7096	2.0469	.0837	–.2269	.2893
Per capita income	.1470	.4499	5.7802	.0406	.0150	.9528
Unemployment rate	–.1214	.0909	.2085	.5968	–.1032	.3361
Number of observations	2,197		659		1,390	
Number of budget stability	1,285		403		765	
–2 Log likelihood	2,903.33		863.35		1,845.85	
Pearson χ^2	2,202.59		656.21		1,378.13	
Pearson χ^2/DF	1.01		1.01		1.00	

Notes: Class variables (OMB Sub-functions). All regressions are based on the assumption that there is no discernible random effect in intercept variance.

to pay no attention to budget information cues flowing from budget environments. In that case, the second part of the right-hand side in equation (2.5) will be virtually zero. The first part of the right-hand side in equation (2.5) typically denotes the budget base. The budget base has been deemed as a symbol for bounded rationality and budget stalemate caused by prescribed institutional procedures and political gridlocks. The findings in Table 5.3 indicate that bureaucratic centralization is completely overwhelmed by the political will of the majority partisan control under unified governments.

Under unified governments the mechanism which allowed the CBO to secure a safeguard between two opposing political powers (i.e., one partisan interest is pitted against another), simply collapses. Now, the CBO is vulnerable to a lopsided political influence. When there is a strong coalition in the body politics, a typical pattern of policy or budget choices would be in favor of the main budget actors. This feature is contrasted with what was found under split legislature governments in Table 4.3. When there were more veto points that function as oversight points to each of main budget actors, OMB's increased professional work tends to increase the information-processing capacity of decision makers or reduce institutional frictions. When this scenario of multiple veto points is less probable under unified governments, the CBO seems to be more sensitive to the aspirations and behaviors of the main budget actors. The generic sensitivity of the CBO to dominating political power is lessened only when bureaucratic centralization in Congress reaches an excessive threshold, however. As *Centralization*^{2} exerts a negative influence on budget stability, the CBO seems to be less swayed by the dominating political power and trigger the mechanism as a politically neutral information processor and friction reliever under unified governments.

Only in the full model, *Central Capacity Load* significantly increases budget stability, without the impact of partisan configurations (p = .0975). Only under divided governments, *Central Capacity Load*^{2} increases the frequency of budget stability (p = .0690). With these empirical results, it is extremely difficult to assign a meaningful interpretation on how the work load of CBO staffs affects budget stability. One thing clear is, however, budgetary incrementalism might still explain something with the findings. In other words, main budget decision makers might not pay any meaningful attention to budget information cues flowing from budget environments: i.e., the second part of the right-hand side in equation (2.5) is highly likely to be zero. Under the two scenarios, most of the environmental factors do not significantly impact budget choices. In addition, central capacity load and its squared value do not return meaningful interpretation.

The negative sign of *Unemployment Rate* in the full model also denotes that unemployment rate might be associated with increased spending on income security programs as discussed in Chapter 4. The computation of the annual number of program beneficiaries might not surpass the computational capacity of budget decision makers. The annual patterns of the number might likely reflect budget information cues from budget environments, which can be efficiently processed. This will explain the negative effect of unemployment rate on budget stability.

The positive sign of *Per Capita Employee* under unified governments signals that a larger number of Congressional employees might induce institutional frictions due possibly to the potentially larger number of organizational veto points (p = .0414). This institutional friction will cause budget stability if, as budgetary incrementalism predicted, multiple budget actors accept the status quo when they collide with each other with different budget aspirations and behaviors. The momentum for stability will, of course, be stronger under unified partisan control. *Political Change* significantly increases the probability of budget stability under unified governments (p = .0837). At first glance, it is also somewhat difficult to interpret. One can expect that political turbulence from political change and the momentum to drive budget choices in the direction of conflicting political preferences might be much stronger under divided governments. That will probably reduce budget stability. Although the coefficient is not statistically significant, the sign of *Political Change* under divided governments is negative. Under unified governments, however, political preferences shift from majority preferences to still the same majority preferences. This might result in budget stability and explain the positive sign of *Political Change* over budget stability. With more resources, fighting over budget resources might be lessened. Under unified governments, the main budget actors might have already reached an agreement on how they can share budget pies. This will lead to budget inertia, which can explain why *Per Capita Income* significantly increases the probability of budget stability under unified governments (p = .0406). For more detailed discussions of control variables, readers are referred to note 5 in Chapter 4.

Conclusion

In this chapter, we have investigated how bureaucratic centralization in a large bureaucratic organization in Congress can augment the information-processing capacity of budget decision makers or relieve institutional frictions. Despite many limitations, bureaucratic organizations have been suggested as a way to improve the limitations in human cognitive capacities and reduce conflicts among their subdivisions. According to disproportionate information-processing theory, sudden, dramatic budget changes take place due mainly to bounded rationality of budget decision makers and institutional frictions. According to budgetary incrementalism, the almost same reasons lead to budget inertia. The empirical findings in this chapter show that a certain aspect of bureaucratic organizations, bureaucratic centralization, does enhance the information-processing capacity of budget decision makers or reduce institutional frictions. Again as in the case for the executive models, however, the merits of bureaucratic centralization depend on three contingencies.

First, the centralized information processing and conflict relieving by the CBO tends to significantly reduce budget punctuations, but excessive bureaucratic centralization increases budget punctuations. As the CBO can serve as a centralized information processor or friction reliever, the information-processing capacity of budget decision makers tends to be enhanced or the institutional frictions seem to be weakened. This might be due possibly to CBO's functions to facilitate communications between political claimants for budget pies. However, excessive bureaucratic centralization detracts from the merits. Second, the impact of bureaucratic centralization on budget punctuations is strictly tangential on partisan configurations. Only under divided governments where the CBO can secure a safeguard against political crossfire, bureaucratic centralization shows the same impacts on the information-processing capacity of budget decision makers and institutional frictions. Therefore, partisan contextual configurations are a significant pre-condition that decides whether and how bureaucratic centralization influences budget punctuations in the Congressional budget process.

Finally, as in the findings in Chapter 4, bureaucratic centralization cannot help shake loose budget stability that is the budget base agreed upon among the main budget actors according to budgetary incrementalism. Bureaucratic centralization even increases the frequency of budget stability; here again, mostly under unified governments. Overall, the message from the combined empirical observations is clear. Bureaucratic centralization can improve bounded rationality or reduce institutional frictions. "*Bounded* bureaucracy" can help improve bounded rationality in the Congressional budget process and reduce institutional frictions, which have been contended to be the ramifications of bureaucratic organizations.

Notes

1. The PAYGO offsetting was provided in the Budget Enforcement Act of 1990.
2. The dependent variable in equation (2.2) can simply show this aspect. When there is offsetting revenue in year *t*, the value will be recorded as negative value in the numerator. In that case, *Increment* will be smaller than −1.
3. For details of model specification, refer to Chapter 4.
4. As discussed in Chapter 4, there is still a possibility that the results reported in this chapter might depend on the cutoff points for budget punctuations. Again, the cutoff points were changed from ± .3 to ± .9 by an increment of ± .1. The results were virtually the same as those reported in Table 5.2.

6

Bureaucratic Centralization and the State Budget Process

Despite various critiques of bureaucracy, it still has some merits. Bureaucratic centralization can expedite information-processing capacity of budget decision makers and reduce institutional frictions. Budget processes have been highly centralized at various levels of the federal tier, especially in the national government and state governments. Centralized control of budget review over agency budget requests through central budget coordination somewhat expedites communications among departments and agencies based on central administrative authority. It also coordinates potential interdepartmental conflicts arising from the competition for scarce resources. Most of all, one of the main functions of central budget offices is assisting line agencies with enhanced information-processing capacity. Central budget offices assist agencies in distinguishing relevant from nongermane budget information and substantially relieve them of the heavy computational burden.

The merits of bureaucratic centralization are also highly dependent on various contingencies, as shown in Chapters 4 and 5. Although bureaucratic centralization can expedite the information-processing capacity of budget decision makers, excessive bureaucratic centralization might hamper the capacity of decision makers and increase institutional frictions. Excessive centralization might deprive departments and agencies of the chance to develop their own discretionary judgments over program-specific budget details. As disproportionate information-processing theory suggests, when budget decision makers have sufficient information-processing capacity and institutional frictions do not further delay processing of budget information cues flowing from budget environments, sudden budget punctuations are least likely to take place. With excessive bureaucratic centralization the frequency of budget punctuations will increase. These were what were empirically observed from the national budget process in both the executive budget process and Congressional budget process.

In addition, whether bureaucratic centralization reduces budget punctuations or not is highly tangential on partisan configurations surrounding budget decision-making processes. Under unified governments, political environments are much compatible with the fundamental nature of bureaucratic organizations: i.e., hierarchical command-control systems. Bureaucratic centralization expedites information processing and reduces institutional frictions under unified governments in the national executive budget process. More interestingly, bureaucratic centralization in Congress, through the Congressional Budget Office (CBO), reduces budget punctuations only under divided governments. This is largely because of the political situations that enable the CBO to function as a bipartisan information processor under divided governments. Finally, bureaucratic centralization cannot shake loose the steadfast agreement on the budget base as frequently contended in budgetary incrementalism. Thus, even an adequate level of bureaucratic centralization cannot induce main budget actors to review status quo programs. Under unified governments, bureaucratic centralization even reinforces such momentum for budget stability.

For virtually the same reason, bureaucratic centralization might exert similar impacts on budget punctuations in state governments. Much spurred by the Taft conservative reform initiative for executive budget systems in the early twentieth century, Maryland adopted the first state executive budget system in 1916. The basic structure and procedure of the state executive budget systems, which now are adopted by almost all state governments, share fundamentally similar features in common (Abney and Lauth 1998). Since state governments offer opportunities for natural experimentation for public policies, there is one caveat with state executive budget systems: i.e., each of the state executive budget systems is one of a kind. Therefore, one needs first to investigate such diversity in the practice of state executive budget systems. It is notable that while such multiple systems might result in different findings regarding the impact of bureaucratic centralization on budget punctuations, fairly common characteristics emerge from bureaucratic centralization in state executive budget processes. Later in this chapter, such disparities and commonalities will be carefully reviewed for some selective states.

In addition, there is another significant feature in state budget processes. Unlike the national budget process, state governors have line-item veto power. Originally, gubernatorial item veto power is conferred on governors to police budget padding by legislators for their pork-barrel projects. In some states, the item veto power provides governors with de facto authority of legislating public programs or writing public law. As discussed later in this chapter, the enhanced gubernatorial budget power causes institutional conflicts and tensions between the executive branches and state legislatures. In some states, it has been used as tools for budgetary negotiation between governors and legislators. All these state-specific contingencies need to be further examined so as to more accurately investigate how bureaucratic centralization affects the information-processing capacity of budget decision makers and institutional frictions. Before starting such investigation, the next section reviews state budget outcomes with state subfunctional budget data that are close to agency-level expenditures.

State Budget Outcomes: 1993, 1996, 1998, and 2000

Fiscal data to test whether bureaucratic centralization affects budget punctuations and stability were obtained from the Census Bureau. The original electronic data file covered state subfunctional expenditures from the late 1940s to 2004. The expenditures include various sorts of *direct* state government outlays including current, capital, and interest expenditures. Sums of these *direct* expenditures are the primary categories of expenditures used in this chapter. According to the data codebook, subfunctional categories were inconsistent before 1980 and thus, observations before 1980 were deleted. In addition, data to construct measures of bureaucratic centralization in the state executive branches were available only for 1992, 1995, 1997, and 1999. In Chapters 4 and 5, U.S. budget authorities were used for empirical tests. Budget authorities are direct reflection of an agreement on agencies' discretion over spending, reached between main budget actors. As such, they might be more adequate for testing the main research question in this book. However, obtaining such budget authority data for a prolonged time period, probably in terms of legislative appropriations for the fifty states, is virtually impossible. As also noted in Chapter 4, budget authorities are likely to be very close to actual outlays. For this reason, state subfunctional expenditures will still be good measures to investigate budget punctuations and stability.

Under typical state executive budget systems, state agencies and central budget offices initiate their budget preparation more than one year before the final appropriations decisions. For this reason, annual percentage changes in state subfunctional expenditures, *Increment*, were developed for 1993, 1996, 1998, and 2000 to test how one-year lagged centralization measures impact budget outlays. As shown in Table 6A.1, there were thirty-one categories of state subfunctional expenditures. They cover such state programs as elementary and secondary education, higher education, health, highways, state-operated utilities, interest payments, employee retirement, etc. These categories are fairly consistent with the categories of typical state departments, if not agencies. Therefore, the data set appears to be a good choice to test the main research question in this chapter. All dollar values are converted into year 2000 constant value, using the state and local government price deflator.

Budgetary incrementalism predicted that bounded rationality and political and institutional frictions will result in highly stabilized budget change patterns. Mostly, annual percentage changes will fall somewhere close to ± 5 to ± 10 percent ranges. Disproportionate information-processing theory assumed that there would be more frequent observations of sudden, dramatic budget changes due mainly to attention-driven choice or indicator lock of budget decision makers. Figure 6.1 strongly confirms the theoretical assertions: i.e., changes in state subfunctional expenditures show a leptokurtic distribution as discussed in Chapter 2. The actual observations with a leptokurtic distribution are starkly contrasted with those under their normal approximation curve. The mean value of *Increment* is about .35 percent; slightly smaller than annual budget changes reported in the budgeting literature, but still within the typical range for incremental changes. Standard deviation of *Increment* is about 22.4 percent with Kurtosis of 6.07, again denoting that the original data distribution is non-normal. For a visual purpose, observations of *Increment* were contained within ± 1 (i.e., 100 percent). When the range was extended to ± 5, however, the mean value of *Increment* was quite close to 5 percent changes which were the most frequently reported in the budgeting literature. Therefore, the state result introduced in Figure 6.1 is not substantial deviation from the findings in the budgeting literature. Figure 6.1 also includes a normal approximation curve over the histograms of actual frequency distributions of *Increment*.

Figure 6.1 Distributions of *Increment* in State Sub-functional Expenditures: 1993, 1996, 1998, and 2000

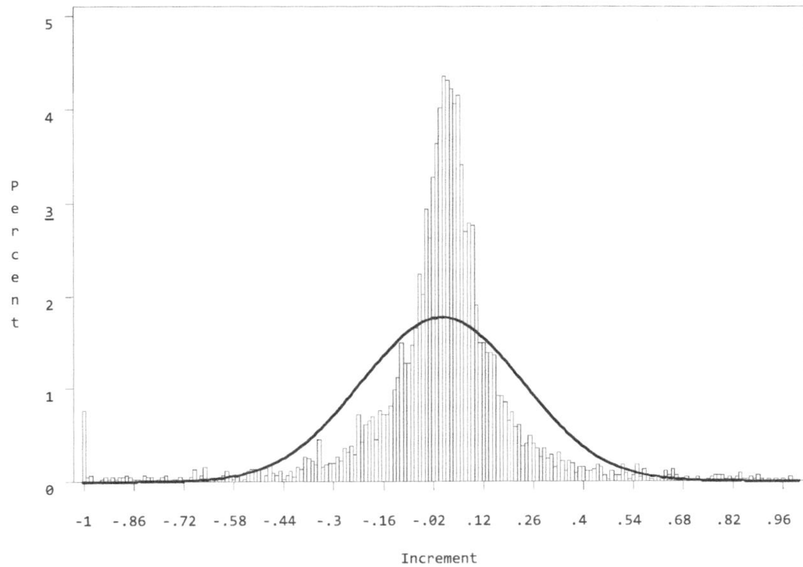

Notes: N: 4,453; Mean (.35 percent); Std. Dev. (22.4 percent); Kurtosis (6.07).

Compared to the normal approximation curve, actual frequency distributions of *Increment* have an abnormally high peak. The range of observations that belong to the area of high peak is between –.07 (i.e., –7 percent) and .1 (10 percent). The range was visually and statistically identified. Approximately 54 percent of all observations of *Increment* belong to this high peak area.[1] According to budgetary incrementalism, bounded rationality and political/institutional prescriptions make budget decision makers revert to some manageable and agreeable reference points or budget base. Given their capacity limits and potential conflicts, there is a tendency among budget actors not to touch the budget base. Instead, they tend to make marginal deviation from the budget base, often smaller than 5 percent. About 54 percent of observations of *Increment* falling within the zone of budget stability lend some support to the explanatory power of budgetary incrementalism.

Figure 6.1 also shows that approximately 39.3 percent of all observations of *Increment* fall within the range of moderate budget changes.

As noted in Chapter 4, moderate budget changes differ from budget moderation. Budget moderation has almost the same connotation as the budget stability where governmental budgets change annually by a small margin as shown in Figure 6.1. Due to capacity limits and institutional frictions, budget decision makers are cautious when making their agency budget requests. This is known as budget moderation. Thus, observations of *Increment* outside of the cutoff points for the budget stability but smaller than extreme values discussed shortly are defined as moderate budget changes, as opposed to budget moderation, in this book. Then, earlier critiques over budgetary incrementalism are also substantially supported. As much as about 39 percent of changes in state subfunctional expenditures reveal budget-change patterns much larger than those depicted in budgetary incrementalism. The frequency of moderate budget changes is much larger than that observed for U.S. budget authorities reported in Chapter 4, about 32 percent. Then, earlier critiques of budgetary incrementalism in the national government (LeLoup and Moreland 1978) also gain stronger credit for state budget outcomes.

Most importantly, about 6.5 percent of observations of *Increment* fall into the range of budget punctuations. This area is where disproportionate information-processing theory provided entirely new theoretical interpretations over budget choice under bounded rationality and institutional frictions. Since standard deviation of the distributions of *Increment* in Figure 6.1 is about 22.4 percent, most observations of *Increment* will taper off beyond ±.67 (67 percent) which is three standard deviations away from the mean value under normal distributions. Instead, the cutoff points for budget punctuations were −.59 and .51. Therefore, the frequency of budget punctuations will be slightly larger than that of the observations three standard deviations away from the mean value. As expected, still about 6.5 percent of observations fall within the area of budget punctuations. This observation also supports disproportionate information-processing theory well.

There is another very interesting point seen when comparing the findings for state budget outcomes with those for U.S. budget authorities. Compared with the findings in Figure 4.1, Figure 6.1 is closer to normal distributions (or less leptokurtic) although the distribution of *Increment* in Figure 6.1 is still highly leptokurtic. Although there are more similarities between state budget processes and the national budget process (Abney and Lauth 1985), there is no doubt that the national budget process is way more complicated in terms of size, program target population, political/institutional procedures, and computational burden thereof. Thus, it does not sound strange that the national budget process would be characterized by higher levels of bounded rationality and institutional frictions. If so, budget outcomes will be more leptokurtic as disproportionate information-processing theory suggested. Therefore, the comparison between state subfunctional budget outcomes and U.S. budget authority data support disproportionate information-processing theory.

Overall, empirical analysis of changes in state subfunctional expenditures for 1993, 1996, 1998, and 2000 evidences that budgetary incrementalism is still fairly alive and well but at the same time there are more frequent observations of budget changes larger than those depicted in incrementalism, especially budget punctuations. Then, the key question is whether adequate level of bureaucratic centralization can function as a tool to extend and augment budget decision makers' information-processing capacity and reduce institutional conflicts. Are there any additional contingencies that restrict the impact of bureaucratic centralization? For the purpose, one needs to investigate first the fundamental aspect of state budget processes, namely typical patterns in state executive budget systems, and roles and functions of state central budget offices.

State Executive Budgets

The rationale for state executive budgeting systems has been quite close to that for the national executive budgeting system. The main focus of the executive budgeting system is that central budget offices can coordinate and review agency budget requests pursuant to chief executives' policy preferences and forecast revenue. Through centralized budget coordination, the executive budgeting systems were supposed to improve efficiency and effectiveness of governmental decisions on resource allocations. One peculiar aspect of state executive budgeting systems is the diversity across the fifty states in budget processes. One way of observing such diversity would be exploring the executive budget processes of some selective states over the past several decades. Observations of selective states also show us that there is a typical pattern in state executive budgeting systems. In particular, common patterns emerge on how bureaucratic centralization might enhance the information-processing capacity of budget decision makers and reduce institutional frictions. Readers who are familiar with state executive budgeting systems might skip this section to the next section on state legislative budgeting systems.

The Idaho budget process exemplifies a typical state executive budgeting system. The Idaho Division of Financial Management (DFM) circulates budget guidelines for preparing agency budget requests at the beginning of the state budget process. Agency goals, objectives, line-item information, and even performance indicators are included in budget forms from each line agency. The DFM serves as the watchdog for gubernatorial policy preferences. Several budget analysts are split among four subdivisions, such as education, general government, human resources, and natural resources. The budget analysts focus on accuracy within each decision unit that decides upon the "maintenance of current operations" (MCO) level of appropriations. The MCO level plays an important role in coordinating agency budget requests along several budget targets. All increases in agency budget requests above the MCO level will be tightly reviewed pursuant to gubernatorial policy preferences, available funding sources, programmatic considerations, and general policy issues. The DFM makes recommendations to the governor who will make final decisions on agency budget requests. A key part of this central budget coordination is the revenue estimate that forecasts the available amount of funding for the upcoming fiscal years. Once finalized, the executive budget will be passed on to the legislature for approval (Duncombe and Kinney 1991, 63–70).

On the legislative side, the Joint Financial Appropriations Committee (JFAC) is made up of the House Appropriations Committee and the Senate Finance Committee. The presence of a joint budget committee is somewhat less common compared with other state legislatures. The JFAC holds hearings to listen to agency officials presenting their budget requests and sets appropriations for the upcoming fiscal year. The Legislative Budget Office (LBO) serves the JFAC in the way the DFM serves the governor in the executive budget process. The LBO reviews agency budget requests and develops the Legislative Budget Book. This document explains all programs of each agency, performance measures, and the cost and description of all departmental decision units. However, this document does not include LBO's budget recommendations for each agency unlike DFM's budget recommendations to the governor.

While the JFAC is holding hearings on agency budget requests, the Revenue Projection Committee works to determine the level of revenue intake for the upcoming fiscal year. The findings of this committee usually set the ceilings for appropriations given the current tax system. The JFAC introduces appropriations bills based on the budget hearings and the revenue estimate on the floor for final approval. The members of JFAC usually remain highly united on final appropriations bills once they are passed on to the floor. This is somewhat comparable to the role of the Senate Budget Committee in Congress during its floor action, as discussed in Chapter 5. In most cases, the appropriations bills pass without significant amendments or failures on the floor (Duncombe and Kinney 1991, 63–70). The Idaho legislative budget process also reveals typical aspirations and behaviors of legislative budget actors under the state executive budgeting systems although the Idaho legislative process has some peculiar aspects like the JFAC. In addition, in reaction to the strong executive budget power, especially information capacity rendered by the executive central budget offices, state legislatures have been professionalized. In typical states, state legislatures also have central budget offices. This is likened to the Congressional Budget Act of 1974. As discussed in the next section, however, the role of legislative central budget offices has been quite "reactive" to, rather than actively modifying, gubernatorial budget proposals. Additionally, there are only a few states where state legislatures retain preemptive authority to propose state budgets in the so-called legislative budget states.

California's budget system is also characterized by executive dominance over budget preparation. The legislature overviews executive budget proposals but mainly retains a capability of checking errors. California's executive budgeting system has been gradually developed since the early 1910s. Much similar to Idaho, the central budget office, the Department of Finance (DOF), develops the executive budget on behalf of the governor to be presented to the legislature. The executive budget document is presented by program categories organized around a line-item base. The base, approved by the legislature, reflects the costs of continuing current service levels, which is known as the base line budget in the national budget process. Once passed on to the legislature, nonpartisan legislative staffs in the Office of Legislative Analyst (OLA) review the executive budget proposals and summarize them for fiscal committees. Somewhat unlike the Idaho process, but more similar to other states, the California executive budget is introduced in two bills to the legislature: the Assembly Budget Committee and the Senate Budget and Fiscal Review Committee bills.

During the legislative hearings, representatives from departments and agencies, lobbyists, and the public are allowed to participate in budget discussions, supported by legislative staffs and OLA staffs. OLA staffs' works are very close to those of DOF budget analysts (McCaffery 1991, 7–16; 2007, 20).

Since the governmental reorganization in 1978, Connecticut has been relying on the executive budgeting system. The Office of Policy and Management (OPM) prepares governor's budget much like other typical executive budget states. The OPM reviews agency budget requests for accuracy, comprehensiveness, inclusion of legally required changes, and conformity to gubernatorial guidance. One subtle difference in Connecticut is the fact that the state legislature is also quite strong in terms of budget power. It retains the authority to increase or reduce expenditures and revenues. The Office of Fiscal Analysis (OFA) provides staff functions to the General Assembly. More interestingly, the General Assembly also receives agency budget requests. Therefore, agencies can actively participate in the appropriations phase. This aspect is a typical key function in state legislative budget systems as discussed in the following section. However, the General Assembly is allowed to only "respond" to governor's budget proposals, rather than develop its own legislative budget (Lewis 1991, 41–52; 2007, 84). In this sense, Connecticut can still be categorized as an executive budget state.

Georgia is also one of the states with the longest history of executive budgeting systems. From 1931 to 1961, the executive branch had been gradually moving away from the legislature when preparing governor's budget proposals. The Office of Planning and Budget (OPB), renamed through the 1972 Executive Reorganization, prepares the executive budgets. Despite the critiques that the OPB exerts too much influence over budget preparation, Georgia has maintained the basic executive budgeting system. As in other executive budget states, the Georgia state legislature created its staff agency, the LBO, in 1969 to support legislative committees over budget analysis (Lauth 2007, 35–36). As the Georgia executive budget system evidences, too strong central control would create institutional tensions. This indicates that excessive centralization might detract from its potential benefits especially of reducing institutional conflicts and frictions.

New York has maintained a budget system quite similar to Georgia's. The Division of Budget (DOB) mostly exerts its central budget power on behalf of the governor. The DOB initiates reviews of agency budget requests and takes the lead in negotiating with the state legislature. In consultation with the Tax Department and agency budget officers, the DOB analyzes agency budget requests and conducts revenue estimation. Originally, New York had a very strong executive budgeting system beginning in 1927. However, the legislature regained some budget control power, much like other executive budget states. New York was especially strongly influenced by the enactment of the 1974 Congressional Budget Act. At the same time, there has been rapid legislative professionalism and legislative sessions have been substantially extended. The Senate and Assembly have tripled their budgets from the 1970s to the 1990s in real dollar values and have been much more heavily involved in the state budget process. Despite the legislative professionalism, New York is still a state with stronger gubernatorial budget power, which is also evidenced by recent events. In 2004, the New York Court of Appeals ruled that the legislature can strike out or reduce items in budget bills only. If the legislature adds separate items in budget bills, they will be subject to gubernatorial item veto. In addition, the legislature is also prohibited from amending any provisions in appropriations bills submitted by the governor. This is equivalent to gubernatorial legislative power. In 2001, the governor already added substantive legislative provisions in school aid, Medicaid, and agency organization but the legislature could not amend them (Forsythe and Boyd 2007, 55–57, 70–71).

For some executive budget states, the state legislature obtained more budget control power such that they can be categorized as the states with legislative "independence." Kentucky exemplifies such a state. In 1972, the executive budgeting system was established through the creation of the OPM. In 1976, however, the House Appropriations and Revenue Committees also started their structured budget reviews, which were deemed as the beginning of the legislative budgeting system in Kentucky. In 1978, the state legislature created the Budget Review Office (BRO) that also prepared state budget instructions and drafted state budget memorandums. In sum, throughout the 1970s and the 1980s legislative role in the state budget process has been substantially enhanced. There were several causes for the augmented role of the legislature. First, the Kentucky Supreme Court ruling in 1989, based on the ground of efficiency and adequacy, enabled the General Assembly to more strongly intervene in state policy issues. It has also driven the governor to collaborate with the legislature. Second, the joint executive and legislative committee and task forces, represented by the executive branch and the legislature, intensified their collaboration over long-term broad-based public policy issues. Third, Kentucky has been under strong Democratic control in the state government, but in 1996, 1998, and 2002 Senate Republicans rapidly gained their majority power (Hackbart 1991, 83–91; Hackbart and Ramsey 2007, 170–71). Thus, Kentucky can be categorized as an executive budget state with legislative independence.

At the other end of the spectrum is Wisconsin. Wisconsin has had a strong executive budgeting system although the Legislative Audit Bureau (LAB) has also checked the executive agencies through its performance audits since the mid-1970s. However, unlike any other states Wisconsin governors have had the partial veto authority. Governors can strike out any part of line in budget bills, a whole line in budget bills, and a series of lines related to appropriations bills. This authority provides the governor with de facto legislative power. If the governor selectively deletes letters or words in the lines of appropriations bills, the revised provisos will be totally different from the original legislative intentions. The state legislature can override gubernatorial partial veto with the two-thirds majority, but almost always governors have been successful in finding a one-third minority to pass gubernatorial vetoes. By way of the so-called Vanna White amendment, the convention of selectively striking letters was prohibited because it will significantly distort original legislative intents (Conant 2007, 235–41). Despite the endeavor to reduce gubernatorial item veto power, the Wisconsin budget system has been featured by strong control by governor and the central budget office.

Observations of executive budgeting systems in selective states thus reveal that there are more commonalities than disparities in the executive budget processes. Another interesting observation is that central budget offices in many of executive budget states include some common budget reference in their budget instructions. Oregon is an executive budget state with a strong tradition of citizen participation through referendum and initiatives. The Budget and Management Division (BAM) circulates tentative budget estimates and instructions to agencies. Agencies prepare three budget packages by adjusting current budget levels based on service, personnel level changes, program increase/decrease, inflation, and mandates. A base budget is equal to previous year's appropriations. A baseline budget, which is called "essential budget," is the agency budget level that enables agencies to deliver the same level of service as in previous year. This is mostly the inflation-adjusted base budget. Policy packages account for program and policy changes, which will probably include service expansion (Simonsen 2007, 127–33).

Nevada shows a categorization much similar to Oregon's. The executive budget is composed of three alternatives. An adjusted base budget is an outlay in previous year. Almost 80 percent of agency budget requests fell in this category. A maintenance budget adjusts for demographic and caseload changes, inflation, fringe benefit rate, federal mandates, and court decisions. This is quite close to Oregon's baseline budget. Finally, an enhancement budget includes new programs or program expansions. The governor and legislators pay primary attention to the maintenance budget and the enhancement budget (Yeary 2007, 175). These different budget formats impose some extra work load onto line agencies when they are preparing their budgets. Central budget offices usually provide them with information relevant to the detailed budget levels. Therefore, bureaucratic centralization will be expediting information processing by budget decision makers.

Overall, state executive budgeting systems are characterized by tight central budget control by central budget offices. In Georgia, like most executive budget states, the central budget office controls agency budget requests so that it could stay within revenue limits. In some other states, like Illinois, bureaucratic centralization is very strong not just because of the executive budgeting process. In what is known as budgeting by negotiation, Snow and Rubin (2007, 109–15) show how politics, not just the executive budgeting system (although Illinois is an executive budget state), ultimately results in strong centralization in the state budget process. The budget process in Illinois has been featured by the frequent vetoes during the 1980s. From 1993 to 2003, however, it has been defined by "budgeting by negotiation" between the governor and legislative leaders. When there were more frequent negotiations, reduction and item vetoes were less likely. As legislative leaders met with each other more often in the negotiation process, the Bureau of the Budget (BOB) became pivotal in preparing main budget bills. As a result, appropriations committees became less important. Finally, while there were more than eighty bills in the 1980s, a few large appropriations bills were enacted during the more recent time period.

The emergence of budgeting by negotiation is originally ignited by the budget shortfalls in the early 1990s. The Republican governor, Jim Edgar, initiated negotiations with legislative leaders from the early stage of the state budget process to avoid confrontations, budget delays, and veto threats at the later budget stage. While the Republican majority after the 1992 election supported the Republican governor, House Democrats tried to get what they wanted through negotiation. At the same time, omnibus bills needed multiple votes for survival and this condition necessitated negotiation for budget decisions. To make budgeting by negotiation viable, the governor and legislative leaders took advantage of the so-called "Member Initiative Grants" with respect to the rank and file legislators. The Member Initiative Grants have traditionally allowed some pork-barrel benefits to legislators who were loyal to party leadership. One of the ramifications of budgeting by negotiation is that the power of executive agencies and appropriations committees has rapidly declined, further nullifying agency testimony in appropriations committees. Historically, each party caucus in Illinois has retained its own budget analysts who reported to party leadership. Then, the fiscal staff directors assign partisan staffs to various appropriations committees. The informal budgeting by negotiation ultimately deprived the committees and even party caucuses of their budget functions. Legislative leaders appointed a small group of political supporters who created the budget line by line. Under this situation, agency testimony before the appropriations committees was meaningless. Agencies felt more urgency in the budget process for securing their budget pies. This process overall strengthened the BOB. Therefore, even without referring to the executive budget structure, bureaucratic centralization was deeply embedded in the budget preparation process (Snow and Rubin 2007, 109–15).

Very similar to the national executive budget process, state budget processes can be featured by bureaucratic centralization. There are diverse applications of the executive budgeting systems in the fifty states. However, there are more commonalities in the core functions of the executive budgeting systems across states rather than deviant characteristics that defy comparison.

State Legislative Budgets

Observations of state executive budgeting systems reveal that common threads are found on how bureaucratic centralization can expedite information processing and lessen institutional frictions over budget choices in state governments. However, there are also several states that deviate from the typical pattern of state executive budget processes. In the states, state legislatures, not chief executives, are more dominating in almost entire phases of budget processes.

For instance, in Texas it is primarily the legislative budget that dominates final budget decisions although the executive budget is also prepared. In 1949, the Legislative Budget Board (LBB) was created to "prepare" budget estimates for the state legislature. Recently, the LBB is composed of the lieutenant governor, the speaker of the House, and eight other legislative members. It is this legislative budget prepared by the LBB that reflects current service levels. The executive budget reflects gubernatorial initiatives and policies only. It is less detailed than the legislative budget, and most of all, only the legislative budget functions as the financial working document because the governor does not have a formal budget power. In addition to the legislative dominance in the state budget process, the Texas budget system also has a very strong focus on rational budget approaches. Zero Base Budgeting (ZBB) was introduced but quickly repealed. Instead, planning and performance budgeting (PPB) was institutionalized into the Texas budget process.

The Texas PPB system consists of nine steps. The key part of the Texas PPB system is the development of statewide strategic planning. The strategic planning includes statewide vision, mission, and philosophy. The second step in the PPB system is to develop statewide goals and benchmarks. The LBB cooperates with the Governor's Office of Budget and Planning (GOBP) to develop the strategic planning and statewide goals during the first two stages of the Texas PPB process. Executive agencies take care of the remaining seven steps in the PPB process, such as agency mission, agency philosophy, external/internal assessment, agency goals, objectives and outcome measures, strategies and output, efficiency, and explanatory measures, and action plans. When the GOBP, on behalf of the governor, jointly develops the strategic plan with the LBB, there has been a high level of coordination and collaboration between the GOBP and the LBB. In particular, the GOBP and the LBB jointly review performance-related agency budget measures. The LBB receives agency budget requests and this aspect is typically found in legislative budgeting systems. The LBB and the GOBP also hold joint budget hearings and jointly develop the legislative budget. During these phases of the Texas budget process, however, the LBB virtually dominates the budget hearings and makes adjustments in budget opinions of the LBB and the GOBP. Although one might also expect a high level of institutional tensions between the two agencies, they have been collaborating over state budget preparation. Even in this highly legislature-dominating state, the executive budget office, the GOBP, is also strongly involved in the budget process (Bland and Clarke 2007, 277–84; Cope 1991, 115–24).

Much similar to the Texas budget process, the Mississippi budget process is another clear example of legislative budgeting systems. The fourteen-member Joint Legislative Budget Committee (JLBC), led by the lieutenant governor and the speaker of the House, prepares a unified state budget used in the legislative review stage. Gubernatorial budget power is not completely eliminated though. The governor and the JLBC jointly prepare revenue estimates. In addition, the governor and the JLBC jointly develop budget instructions circulated to executive agencies. The budget instructions do not provide any dollar ceilings. The only spending instructions are confined to new programs or program changes mandated in previous legislative sessions, court rulings, or changing federal requirements. Unlike what is typically found under executive budgeting systems, the LBO, which supports the JLBC, makes a detailed review of agency budget proposals. Then the JLBC holds budget hearings and marks up the agency budget requests, finally submitting a legislative budget to the full state legislature. Historically, the legislative budget is the starting point of appropriations subcommittee budget deliberations and legislators have tended to ignore the executive budgets. As in the case of Texas, however, budget analysts in the Governor's Budget Office (GBO) also review agency budget requests and assist the governor in developing the executive budget proposal for the state legislature (Clynch 2007, 258). For almost the same reasons highlighted so far, one can expect that bureaucratic centralization in the executive budget process can also enhance the information-processing capacity of budget actors and decrease institutional conflicts even under the legislative budgeting systems.

South Carolina's budget process stands out compared with the legislative budgeting systems and most of other executive budgeting systems. Since the early part of the twentieth century, South Carolina has had a statewide commission prepare state budgets in consultation with other state agencies. In 1919, the Budget Commission was created for tax issues but the governor was given relatively heavier budget power. The Budget Commission was composed of the governor, the Senate Finance Committee chair, and the House Ways and Means Committee chair. In 1950, the commission was expanded to the State Budget and Control Board (SBCB) and included further the state treasurer, and the comptroller general. The SBCB has been pretty much dominating the entire state budget process since then. The SBCB distributes revenue projections and technical budget instructions to department heads and agency budget officials. Agencies then submit their budget requests to the SBCB, not the governor. The SBCB then submits the final budget recommendations to the House Ways and Means Committee and the Senate Finance Committee. SBCB staffs have been mostly recruited from the education department that comprised the largest budget category in South Carolina. The SBCB staff's financial expertise has been highly visible especially on education finance (Graham 2007, 194–95; Whicker 1991, 137–48).

In 1972, one reform initiative authorized the office of executive director in the SBCB to oversee SBCB's entire budget operation. Although the measure did not enhance gubernatorial budget power, it obviously launched a more unified executive budget structures. In 1984, the Office of State Budget (OSB) was further created in the SBCB. The OSB has assisted the governor during executive budget hearings and coordinate agency budget requests pursuant to executive budget priorities. It has also assisted two legislative fiscal committees by maintaining the official database for various versions of appropriations bills and any provisos. Overall, the SBCB has been at the center of the South Carolina budget process, but OSB's central budget coordination role has also been heightened recently (Graham 2007, 196–204). Therefore, central budget coordination has been somewhat reinforced under this peculiar committee type budget system. In this sense, we can also expect that bureaucratic centralization in the South Carolina budget process might exert almost similar impacts on budget punctuations and stability.

Florida's budget process has been characterized by legislative dominance throughout the twentieth century. However, gubernatorial budget power has gradually increased during the recent decades. The 1968 Constitution stipulated governor's sole authority to propose the FY 1969 budget. Agencies were required to submit their budget requests to the governor. Like any other executive budget states the central budget office, the Division of Planning and Budgeting (DPB), has assisted the governor in the process of central budget coordination. DPB staffs have also assisted two appropriations committees in the state legislature until the mid-1970s when the committees recruited their own professional staffs. In 1978, the DPB was changed into the

OPB, now housed in the Executive Office of the Governor (Bradley 2007, 141–42).

However, from 1980 to 1990 the state legislature has somewhat regained its budget control power again. Beginning from the 1980 legislative session, the legislature required that agencies should submit their budget requests to the legislature at the same time when they submit the requests to the governor. The legislature also required agencies to base their budget proposals on their independent judgment of their programmatic needs, rather than gubernatorial direction. The period of legislative preeminence ended in 1990. The Democratic governor, Chiles, called for ending legislative micromanagement and allowing flexibility to the governor over budget preparation. The 1993 Government Performance and Accountability Act embraced various reform proposals, but the Republican-dominated legislature declined such gubernatorial flexibility over budget issues. In 1995, the Senate even required agencies to make budget recommendations that were not developed through the normal, legal budget process.

All these partisan contingencies changed with the advent of a Republican-unified government in 1998. The Republican-dominated state legislature has attempted to shift budgetary power to the Republican governor. Up to the mid-2000s, legislative influence on state budget preparation has greatly dwindled. Legislative budgets were nothing but rewriting of executive budgets. Agencies were allowed heightened flexibility over budget preparation. The state legislature did not receive agency budget requests any longer. Although the Legislative Budget Commission was authorized to review agency budgets every eight years based on ZBB, gubernatorial budget power is at its peak under the recent unified governments (Bradley 2007, 142–43). This aspect clearly evidences that partisan configurations can significantly affect the state budget process. Another issue worth noting in the Florida budget process is that OPB staffs are legally required to develop budget instructions jointly with legislative appropriations committee staffs (Grizzle 1991, 93–102). Even under the fluctuating partisan tensions, central budget office staffs have been collaborating over budget preparation.

Finally, budget scholars place Utah near legislative budget states. In Utah as in other executive budget states, the OPB, on behalf of the governor, prepares budget forms and instructions. Agency budget requests are developed per line item, which include problem definition, objectives, and two major alternative budgets, and justification for the budget chosen. The executive budget was adopted relatively recently in 1979. In 1966, however, the state legislature instituted the Office of Legislative Fiscal Analyst (OLFA). One aspect that places Utah near legislative budget states is that the OPB also submitted agency budget requests to the OLFA when it received them and before governor's hearings would be held. The OLFA conducted a tight review of the executive budget proposals and overall, OLFA staffs played the role of guardian to protect the public purse. Joint appropriations subcommittees typically received two budgets, one from the governor and the other from the OLFA. However, OLFA's budget has been given more weights (Hebert 1991, 103–14).

Utah has been a predominantly Republican-dominated state. As such, one might not expect intense political conflicts between state branches. However, Republicans from rural areas have been more conservative than their urban counterparts. In 1997, House Speaker Mel Brown demanded that the OLFA no longer use the governor's budget proposal as the starting point. Instead, he insisted that last year's appropriations be used as the reference point. This illustrates that subtle partisan disparity might arise even under unified party control, which can move the institutional power tension between the governor and the legislature slightly in the direction of enhancing the legislative budgeting system in Utah. However, despite the potential political frictions the OLFA and the OPB have sustained a high level of collaboration during budget preparation and review (Gosling 2007, 300–4).

As shown in this section, central budget offices in the executive branch even under the legislative budget state are substantially involved in reviewing agency budget requests and preparing gubernatorial budget recommendations. In general, the central budget offices in the legislative budget states tend to assist agencies with informational and analytic supports and to maintain good relationships with legislative budget staffs. Therefore, we can expect that bureaucratic centralization in the states with legislative budgeting systems might reveal fairly similar impacts on budget punctuations and stability.

State Budget Institutions: Item Veto and Balanced Budget Requirements

As noted earlier in this chapter, there are a couple of disparities between the national and state budget processes. One difference is that governors have the authority to veto items, reduce items, or delete narratives in appropriations bills. The other is that in most of states there are requirements for balanced budgets. The budgeting literature is more abundant in showing detailed procedures, mechanisms, and ramifications of gubernatorial veto power with respect to aspirations and behaviors of budget actors, as well as its fiscal impacts. Relatively less focus has been placed upon how balanced budget requirements do modify budget actors' strategies and behaviors and affect state budget outcomes. In this section, these two peculiar institutional features in the state budget processes are explored as the most potential sources for institutional frictions that might cause budget punctuations or reinforce the momentum of budget stability. Here again, readers who are familiar with state item vetoes or balanced budget requirements can skip this section. Alternatively, readers can read item veto issues in selective states.

Since the Confederate States of America, the line-item veto has been supported as a way to enhance fiscal responsibility for governments. The common belief regarding gubernatorial line-item veto power possessed by most of state governors is that it can mitigate logrolling or pork-barrel appropriations. The item veto is likely introduced as a fiscal constraint from governors to curb legislative logrolling, where legislators support a bill that might include pork-barrel spending. It has been thus supposed to make governments fiscally more responsible. Especially for the states that usually have appropriations bills covering the entire range of governmental spending, the line-item veto power is expected to control pork-barrel politics by state legislatures. As of 1998, one of the four study years in this chapter, most governors except for six states (Nevada, Indiana, New Hampshire, North Carolina, Rhode Island, and Vermont) had the line-item veto authority (Abney and Lauth 1985, 372; 1997, 882; Lee 2000, 265–66).

It should also be noted that there are wide variations in the line-item veto practices across states. Some governors further have the authority to reduce the amounts of appropriations items. This power relieves governors' burden of making all-or-nothing choices, and therefore is deemed as a useful opportunity to reduce pork-barrel spending. As of 1998, twelve state governors had such reduction veto power. In addition, twenty-three state governors had the power to strike the languages or provisos in appropriations items. The item veto authorities have frequently been regarded as a tool to control governmental budget totals and thereby reduce the size of governments, which in actuality has not been empirically supported (Lauth and Reese 2006, 1–2; Lee 2000, 266–67).

Wisconsin illustrates a state with the strongest gubernatorial item veto authority. The Wisconsin governor used to possess the constitutional and statutory authority to veto appropriations in a spending bill. The governor was also bestowed the authority to partially veto statutory or session law language within an appropriations bill. The governor may selectively strike any words or even letters in an appropriations bill. This power, as discussed in the earlier section, allows the governor de facto legislative power. In this manner, the Wisconsin governor could eliminate or modify legislative intentions in addition to striking appropriations (Gosling 1986, 293–95).

There have been even more diverse variations in how and why the gubernatorial item veto authority has been invoked across states and years. Exploring these issues will clarify whether or how gubernatorial item veto authority might invite institutional conflicts and frictions in the state budget processes. Opponents of the item veto have frequently contended that the item veto might lead to fiscal irresponsibility on the part of state legislatures. The item veto might transfer fiscal responsibility from the legislatures to governors, which would ultimately cause lack of legislative fiscal discipline. Some empirical observations suggest, however, that the legislatures facing item veto were not necessarily less fiscally responsible. In contrast, Abney and Lauth (1985, 373–74) found that some legislative strategies did affect the frequency of item vetoes. State legislatures were able to write appropriations bills in the way governors could not easily veto the bills. Surprisingly, fiscally *responsible* legislatures were more engaged in such strategic maneuvering. Item vetoes were also more frequently used under divided governments although Republican governors tended to use it more as fiscal restraint, rather than partisan tool (Abney and Lauth 1985, 375). These findings indicate that item veto is not necessarily related to fiscal austerity. Rather, it functions as a mechanism that makes the interbranch interaction more complex, probably in the way it augments institutional frictions in the state budget processes.

Reese (1997) conducted a comprehensive analysis of item vetoes over various dimensions, using data from 1973 to 1992 in ten southern states. This study suggests that the item veto power was used more against dollar amounts rather than languages or provisos in appropriations bills. This finding implies that the item veto power might be an effective tool as a fiscal constraint. However, the vetoed dollar amounts as annual percentages of state appropriations varied only from .01 to 1.15 percent. The variation is further mitigated because two states, Florida and Louisiana, drove the average up substantially. Overall, the findings are consistent with the earlier studies introduced above.

This study further investigated item vetoes in terms of the four dimensions (frequency of the use, dollar effects, reasons for use, and overrides by state legislatures) along another four dimensions (biennial vs. annual budgets, less itemized vs. more itemized budgets, large vs. small appropriations, and weak vs. strong executive budget power). Among the more detailed and comprehensive analysis of item vetoes, one aspect is relevant for this section. Most states with a higher degree of interbranch partisan disparity were more frequently using the item veto, albeit with low dollar effects (Reese 1997, 511–15). These empirical findings are quite consistent with the earlier studies, but additionally provide much more comprehensive and detailed information on state item vetoes. Overall, item vetoes were more likely to be used as partisan tools, and item vetoes are likely to cause institutional frictions especially under divided governments.

Recent studies deliver more elaborate and subtle discussions of how reduction and deletion vetoes affect budget outcomes and define interbranch partisan politics. When legislatures attempt to lump items of appropriations, which might nullify the item veto power, the reduction veto is a powerful fiscal control tool. As legislatures place conditions on how funds will be used in the appropriations bills, the power to delete provisos also help enhance gubernatorial item veto power. In addition, when governors have both the reduction and deletion veto power strengthens item veto power in terms of securing fiscal responsibility (Abney and Lauth 1997, 885–86). The deletion veto was generally not related with either mere spending control or efficiency (controlling pork-barrel). This was expected because narratives are typically linked to process rather than dollar amounts. As such, the deletion power is more a tool for policy agenda rather than budget issues. In addition, governors with the deletion and reduction veto are likely to use the item veto more often than other governors only with the ordinary veto power. Usage of the vetoes is also correlated with the presence of divided partisanship between the governor and the legislature. When there is divided partisanship, the states with the reduction veto reported more frequent usage of veto power. However, partisan division is not highly correlated with usage of the item veto in states without the reduction veto (Abney and Lauth 1997, 887–90). This study presents a more detailed story of item veto. Reduction and deletion veto power might engender higher interbranch partisan conflicts and institutional frictions. Abney and Lauth's (2002) study also shows that when governors have strong deletion veto power, item vetoes are more likely to be used. Furthermore, it implies that deletion vetoes are more frequently invoked under divided governments.

One interesting study shows that item vetoes might also be used as a tool to restore gubernatorial policy preferences (Lauth and Reese 2006). Georgia governors have used the item veto primarily for the purpose of eliminating "objectionable policy provisions from appropriations bills than to remove specific appropriations of money" (Lauth and Reese 2006, 9). Georgia governors have the initiative in reviewing agency budget requests and preparing a draft appropriations bill. The General Assembly meets only forty days each year, and subsequently is highly reliant on the gubernatorial budget agenda. Georgia has a balanced budget requirement and the governor's official revenue estimates form a constitutionally protected total ceiling for state budget. Because of this the legislative changes must occur within the total budget ceiling. Therefore, gubernatorial item vetoes boil down to restoring executive spending priorities, rather than controlling the size of the state budget. Under these environments, interbranch conflict is due to legislative initiatives that modified gubernatorial budget priorities (Lauth and Reese 2006, 8–15).

For instance, Governor Miller vetoed a 479,479 dollar item from the Department of Education section of the 1993 appropriations act even without the information provided by his staff of the OPB. He found that house members added the secret budget to fund special projects in local school districts. Miller also vetoed more than thirty-six million dollars in local projects. He believed that the General Assembly added the amount at the expense of his budgets for higher education initiatives. The veto was cast on eighty-nine community projects in the Department of Community Affairs section of the appropriations act of 1997. Miller argued that the General Assembly reduced his recommended appropriation for the University System and he tried to veto the same amount. "While this veto represents an executive check on pork barrel politics, it also reflects the differing policy preferences of Governor Miller for higher education spending compared with legislative preferences for community project spending" (Lauth and Reese 2006, 15). Therefore, the Georgia case further shows that item vetoes might augment institutional frictions.

Oftentimes, conflicts over item vetoes were not confined only within the executive and legislative branches. Courts frequently intervened in the political tensions between governors and state legislatures. Thus, legal dimensions further complicated the state budget process, ignited over item veto authorities. Lee (2000) succinctly summarizes various dimensions that were the main sources of confusion and caused institutional conflicts. A fundamental issue regarding lawsuits is that any party who files litigations must prove that an individual or organization is directly affected by a measure, which is known as standing. Additionally, anyone who is sued might use the standing concept as a tactic to avoid further legal actions. For example, when governors are sued for violating the veto power they can contend that the plaintiffs, who often are legislators, lack adequate standing. Similarly, labor union or would-be recipients such as local governments or nongovernmental agencies that expect grants from states might challenge governor's veto actions over the appropriations in favor of them. This issue of legal standing frequently heightened institutional frictions.

Although constitutional definitions of appropriations vary across states, there is some general agreement. That is, appropriations are not limited to what legislatures choose to name as appropriations in a bill. When specific dollar amounts are associated with a specific object or purpose, they tend to be defined as appropriations. However, there have been numerous court cases over such definitions of appropriations. Another controversial dimension of the item veto actions is how to define the item. Since most state constitutions did not provide accurate definition of items, state courts often have to fashion out the definition. For instance, in Washington State the legislature made appropriations in lump sums to agencies. The Supreme Court ruled that governor can veto provisos in each section for agencies in the lump sum appropriations. If the governor could not do this, then governor cannot help but veto the entire section in the lump sum appropriation for a certain agency. With some cautionary stance regarding the level of itemization, state courts have generally opted for the position that legislatures must itemize appropriations to avoid lump sum funding that might effectively nullify the governors' item veto powers (Lee 2000, 270–72).

State constitutions typically provide that "any substantive piece of legislation must have only one subject but that appropriation bills may have multiple subjects" (Lee 2000, 272). Since governors might not item veto general legislation, the constitutional single-subject rule is to prevent the legislature from forcing governor into a take-it-or-leave-it choice. Governor's item veto over appropriations will be especially effective because legislatures are constitutionally allowed to include multiple subjects in appropriations bills. For this reason legal actions arise when the single-subject provision is violated, or when a wrong provision is included into substantive provisions in appropriation bills (or more simply, the single-subject rule is mixed up with the multiple provision rule). In California, it was held that the legislature erroneously included multiple subjects in a substantive bill and consequently the various sections are subject to governor's veto. In Florida, the state court ruled that policy issues should not be included in an appropriation bill. The Okalahoma Supreme Court ruled that multiple general provisions cannot become law whether they were vetoed or not (Lee 2000, 272–73). These court litigations further imply that item vetoes are potential sources of institutional conflicts and frictions.

Another difference of the state budget process from the national budget process is that most states have balanced budget requirements. There are not as abundant studies on balanced budget requirements as on state item veto power. Briffault (1996) made one of the most comprehensive investigations over the status, nature, and fiscal impacts of balanced budget requirements. Balanced budget requirements usually mean the authority for the governor to submit, the legislature to pass, and the governor to sign balanced budgets. Throughout the 1980s and the 1990s, most states were reported to have some requirements to balance state budgets. If reviewed in detail, however, there were wide variations from various perspectives.

A close examination of state constitutions revealed that there were about thirty-six states that made any reference to balancing budgets. All but one state, Vermont, had *statutory* requirements for balancing state budgets. Only thirty-one state constitutions actually required the state legislatures to pass balanced budgets. Another close look at the state constitutions indicates that some balanced budget provisions did not strictly prohibit year-end deficits or a certain level of borrowing. Some states with balanced budget requirements were allowed to carry deficits over into the next fiscal year. In addition, balanced budget requirements were not applied to all funds. In many states special funds for such programs as capital projects were created. Those special funds were not subjected to balanced budget requirements. General funds that were constrained by balanced budget requirements constituted just about 50 percent of the total state budgets. Even when special funds were subjected to the requirements, bond proceeds were recorded only as revenues in most cases. Those conflicting legal procedures and budgetary structures fundamentally threatened the effectiveness of balanced budget requirements as fiscal constraint tool (Briffault 1996, 7–14).

Balanced budget requirements induce some states to achieve balanced budgets but at a cost. The New York state constitution requires the governor to submit, or the legislature to pass, a balanced budget. But it does not prohibit short-term borrowing, operating deficit carryover, or optimistic forecasts of economic conditions or federal grants. These allow state budget actors some room for bypassing the balanced budget requirements. Some states employed more sophisticated budget gimmickry. They applied the accrual basis of accounting when recording revenues but applied the cash basis to spending. This is highly likely to realize operating surplus but only on accounting books. A classic instance of such accounting gimmickry took place in 1976 when Michigan changed its fiscal year from July–June to October–September. This created an initial three months' worth of accrued revenue while school aid payment was supposed to be recorded later. Similarly, some states delayed payments to employees, vendors, or local governments. Some states intentionally overestimated trust fund investments to reduce the amounts that the states are required to fill into the fund for future payments to retirees (Briffault 1996, 15–22).

Some states achieve short-term surplus through state asset sales. The one-time cash obviously increases state cash flows, but most of such assets were sold at lower than market prices. Thus the state gave up potential future income flow from such assets, and in the longer-term such asset sales actually increased future deficits. Some states reduced annual interest payments for their bond obligations. However, if such refinancing was made by extending the bond maturity, then the total sum of the future interest payments might have increased in the long run. As noted above, in some states special funds were not subject to balanced budget requirements. The states transferred some funds from the special funds to make up for operating deficits. Of course, the interfund transfers would increase future operating deficits.

Some states took advantage of the intergovernmental aid system. Some states have not passed the full amount of federal aid to local governments. It is also well known that the rapid increase in state Medicaid costs around 1990 was partly attributable to states' fiscal manipulation. The national government paid matching grants covering somewhere between 50 and 83 percent of state Medicaid costs. In the late 1980s, state governments encouraged hospitals and other health care providers to make some donations to state Medicaid funds, which were known as Medicaid provider tax. The donation amounts could be eligible for the federal Medicaid matching grant. Later, the provider tax payments were paid back to the original sources. This technique, called states' raid over the federal coffer, was another widely employed technique around balanced budget requirements (Briffault 1996, 23–30).

The anecdotal evidence on the ineffectiveness of balanced budget requirements has been further confirmed by various empirical studies. Briffault (1996, 55–62) summarizes such empirical findings. Some studies show that whether states have the executive budget system was more influential on spending growth than balanced budget requirements. Other political, economic, cultural, and institutional factors were more important in affecting taxing, spending, and borrowing decisions in states. In other studies, gubernatorial term limits more affected state spending rather than balanced budget requirements. One study showed that balanced budget requirements can control state deficit, but the most important factor in the study was state wealth measured in terms of per capita income. Some studies indicated that no deficit carryover requirements exerted significant impacts on state deficit but only under unified governments, or when the governor's party is the same as the majority party of the lower chamber (Alt and Lowry 1994; Poterba 1994). A more recent study conducted by Ryu et al. (2008) used survey responses from 1,175 state agency heads in 1998. Their analysis found that having no carryover deficit significantly reduced annual percentage changes in legislative appropriations for agencies but balanced budget requirements did not have any significant impacts on the annual growth of agency budgets.

These studies overall suggest that balanced budget requirements might not have crucial impacts on state deficit control. Unfortunately, the studies do not suggest enough information on whether balanced budget requirements increase institutional frictions or not. One might expect, however, that the competition under balanced budget requirements might get intensified. Under the incrementalist perspective budget actors form their fair share of budget pies. For whatever reason when they feel their fair share is threatened, which is quite possible under balanced budget requirements, they might try to protect the share. Overall, balanced budget requirements are expected to increase institutional conflicts and frictions.

Bureaucratic Centralization and State Budget Punctuations

Bureaucratic centralization in the state budget process has some merits in that central budget offices can accumulate expertise with respect to agency budget review. In Nevada, the Budget Office (BO) staffs have maintained high levels of expertise and longevity in their positions. Almost all positions in the BO were classified and the turnover rate was very low. Since BO staffs have been working in the office for long time, they could maintain a kind of institutional memory that the federal OMB has retained throughout the recent decades, as discussed in Chapter 4. In addition, BO staffs have worked in various positions in the Nevada state government before they were recruited into their BO positions. In fact, the main reason for their promotion to the BO positions was due mainly to their accumulated technical skills and common senses, rather than political ties. Although BO staffs have been preparing the executive budget, BO's activities have been fairly nonpartisan in Nevada.

In particular, the role of budget analysts in the BO was crucial in fulfilling its central budget coordination. This has been possible in part because BO staffs have made adequate technical and maintenance decisions. Due to their apolitical stance, BO staffs could objectively check what agencies' long-term budget and personnel needs are. More importantly, each budget analyst in the BO has been reassigned to various state executive agencies. Thus, BO analysts could monitor whether the agencies achieve their programmatic goals and the agency leadership is effective or not. This will further facilitate communications between the agencies and the BO. In Nevada, there is one more elaborate organizational tool to relieve the risk from individual assessments of state agency programs. To avoid potentially inconsistent evaluation of agency programs, two supervisory positions were created to check such consistency in the agency evaluation. Of course, agencies with effective leadership, competent financial personnel, and a history of programmatic achievements are more likely to promote a successful and smoother budget process (Yeary 2007, 176–77). In actuality, the successful budget process is substantially attributable to bureaucratic centralization in the executive budget process. The accumulated expertise in the BO ultimately helped expedite information processing and reduce interagency conflicts by way of BO staffs' assignment to line agencies. Therefore, expedited information processing and reduced institutional conflicts are likely to decrease the frequency of budget punctuations.

The role of the California central budget office, DOF, more clearly shows how central budget offices can directly help line agencies over budget preparation with their superior information-processing capacity. The DOF circulates budget instructions that include information on population growth and the inflation forecast. The automated budget system in the DOF instantly provides departments and agencies with current budget base and subsequent legislative changes. It also provides them with budget changes that price and demographic changes might entail. Departments submit Budget Change Proposals (BCPs) to the DOF. BCPs include changes in workload/price, need for new technology, impact of court decisions, federal law changes, and new policy directions. During the 1980s, the DOF directed departments to consult with the DOF for a variety of technical assistance. Since then the DOF has checked: whether the quantification of program needs and benefits is accurate, there is sufficient documentation of cost justification, or if there are unreasonable assumptions in departmental and agency budget justifications. The DOF has also uploaded model versions of BCPs on its website (McCaffrey 2007, 16–17).

The enhanced information-processing capacity of central budget offices also tended to reduce potential institutional frictions between the executive branch and the legislatures, as well as among departments and agencies within the executive branch. The California budget process has been fairly open. In 1978, an open-access computer information system was already launched. Both the executive branch and the legislature have had access to agency budgets, revenue/spending levels, and even performance data. Thus, there was a high level of information sharing between budget actors, which was expedited by the centralized budget process in California (McCaffrey 1991, 7–16). During the legislative budget hearings, DOF and OLA budget analysts have been in a slightly competitive mood. However, such competition exposed budget issues to the surface and minimized errors. There have been various hearings between DOF staffs and departments/agencies. During such hearings, DOF budget analysts played substantial roles as an experienced information processor, which reduced potential tensions (McCaffrey 2007, 17, 20–21).

As discussed above, the New York DOB staffs take a lead role in negotiating with state legislative leaders. While reviewing agency budget request and revenue estimates, DOB staffs also consult with agency budget officers. The Nevada budget process was also discussed earlier. One of the reasons why BO staffs in the Nevada state government has accumulated expertise was because BO staffs worked in various state agency positions. This fact might enhance good relationship between BO staffs and agencies. In addition, there has been a certain level of collaboration between central budget office analysts from the executive branches and the legislatures for most of the states introduced above. In sum, bureaucratic centralization in the state executive budget process is expected to expedite information processing by budget actors and reduce potential institutional frictions over budget preparation.

In a legislative budget state like Texas, the executive central budget office served similar, albeit weaker than executive budget states, roles. Agency heads usually discuss over agency budget requests and performance achievements with the GOBP during the hearings. Agencies frequently face difficulties developing performance measurements required in the Texas PPB process. LBB staffs provide agencies with substantial levels of informational assistance when agencies prepare required documents and measures in the state budget process. For example, LBB staffs assist agencies to check whether performance measures of agency programs conform to legislative expectations, and if the level of current agency performance is acceptable. They also jointly develop agency strategic plans and agency-specific performance indicators. In addition, when agencies lack the technical capacity in developing new budget information and fulfilling budget requirements, LBB staffs offer them such technical and informational assistance. Overall, the Texas PPB system further reinforced the already strong influence of the LBB. One notable observation in Texas is that the GOBP also takes part in budget preparation and provides the agencies with similar technical, informational assistance to executive agencies (Bland and Clarke 2007, 284–89). This section shows the empirical results on whether and how bureaucratic centralization in state budget processes affects budget punctuations and stability under different political contexts.

The dependent variable is the same as that constructed in Chapters 4 and 5. *Punctuation* is coded one if *Increment* falls within the zone of budget punctuations. The cutoff points for the full sample model described below were –.59 and .51. Observations of *Increment* outside of the cutoff points were treated as budget punctuations. As noted earlier, some observations of *Increment* with nonzero values for current year's expenditures but zero values for previous year's expenditures were counted back into *Punctuation* because they are clear examples of positive budget punctuations.

To test the impacts of bureaucratic centralization on budget punctuations, four measures tapping bureaucratic centralization were developed in almost the same way the measures were constructed for bureaucratic centralization in the national budget process. *Centralization* was measured as the number of budget analysts in state executive central budget offices, divided by total full time equivalent (FTE) executive employees. One difference in this variable from the equivalent measure in the national budget process is that the specific number of budget analysts is used. As discussed above, budget analysts are at the center of budget preparation under the executive budgeting systems. As such, they will be more relevant to tap bureaucratic centralization on budget preparation. All control variables, unless specified otherwise, are standardized for easier comparison between them. In addition, all control variables are one-year lagged variables. This is because budget preparations usually take place more than a year before the final approval of state budgets. Table 6A.2 presents descriptions of variable definition, its hypothesized influence on budget punctuations, and data source.

Multiple cases of state executive budget processes indicate that *Centralization* will enhance the information-processing capacity of budget actors, especially executive agencies, and reduce institutional frictions through expedited interbranch and interdepartmental communications and collaboration. However, excessive bureaucratic centralization beyond a certain threshold point might detract from such merits, especially expedited communications and collaboration. Thus, the squared measure of centralization, *Centralization*^{2}, is expected to hamper such information-processing capacity and augment institutional conflicts and frictions. Therefore, *Centralization* will reduce the frequency of budget punctuations while *Centralization*^{2} will increase it.

Like any other members in bureaucratic organizations, the staffs in central budget offices will perform best with an adequate level of workload. *Central Capacity Load* is developed as the state subfunctional expenditures for each agency divided by the number of budget analysts in central budget offices. In similar reasons discussed in previous chapters, *Central Capacity Load* is expected to reduce the probability of budget punctuations while *Central Capacity Load*^{2} is likely to increase the probability.

In addition to these measures of bureaucratic centralization, several more control variables were constructed. In the literature of state budget process, the role of lobbyists is quite salient. When lobbyists are representing two opposing group interests, they might increase institutional frictions. However, in the process of legislation, legislators obtain both substantive and political information on public programs. Hundreds of lobbyists are found in state capitols during legislative sessions (Rosenthal 2004, 86–88). Thus, one of the most important roles of lobbyists might be to provide budget actors with program-specific budget information. Therefore, *Per Capita Lobbyist* is expected to enhance the information-processing capacity of budget decision makers and will reduce the probability of budget punctuations.

As Robinson et al. (2007) contended, the number of employees in bureaucratic organizations might be a good measure of organizational size. As organizational size grows, it is increasingly likely that more veto points are created; therefore, institutional frictions might get heightened. *FTE* is constructed as a standardized measure of FTE executive employees, instead of per capita FTE. When per capita FTE was used in regression models, explanatory power of all models was substantially lessened. This is another difference between state models and national government models. *FTE* is expected to increase institutional frictions and the frequency of budget punctuations. However, *FTE* can also measure the information-processing capacity of bureaucratic organizations as a whole. In that case, it is expected to negatively correlate with budget punctuations. In actuality, Robinson et al. (2007) found a negative relationship between the number of employees and budget punctuations.

As dominant political majority is shifting, one might observe intensified political tension and institutional frictions. *Political Change* is constructed as the absolute value of partisan shift. The total number of Democratic legislators, minus that for Republican legislators, divided by state population, was first computed. Then, the absolute value of annual percentage changes in this variable was developed as *Political Change. Political Change* is expected to positively correlate with budget punctuations. Gubernatorial item veto authority, as discussed above, might generally intensify institutional frictions. However, its expected influence on budget punctuation is still somewhat open. *Veto* is the sum of three dummies for governor's item veto, reduction veto, and deletion veto. This variable is not standardized because it just ranged between one and three. One caveat is that the actual number of item veto invoked will be a more accurate measure for institutional tensions associated with gubernatorial item veto. However, the threat of using the item veto is frequently regarded as an important part of the item veto authority (Lauth and Reese 2006, 18). Thus, *Veto* will be a good measure tapping gubernatorial item veto power. In a similar manner, *Balanced Budget Requirements* is the sum of three dummies of the requirements for governors to submit, legislatures to pass, and governors to sign balanced budgets. This is not standardized because it ranged between one and three. *Balance Budget Requirements* are, in general, expected to increase the frequency of budget punctuations. Another important aspect of balanced budget requirements is no carryover deficit requirement. Some states require that there should be year-end budget balance. However, due to the difficulty obtaining no deficit carryover data, this measure was not developed for the study period.

Earlier studies reported that whenever agencies had extra fund sources like federal grants, budget decision makers, especially legislators, tended to exert tighter budget review over agency budget requests (Sharkansky 1968; Thompson 1987). In that case, institutional frictions might increase. *Per Capita IGR Revenue* is the per capita value of: federal and local aids to states minus intergovernmental expenditures by states. *Per Capita IGR Revenue* is expected to augment institutional frictions, thus positively correlating with budget punctuations. As discussed in Chapter 4, budgetary incrementalism indicates that more assertive agencies are more likely to get more budgets from appropriators. Upon finding a possibility of more resources, competition for claiming over public money would be enhanced, thus increasing institutional frictions. In that case, a measure of economic condition, *Per Capita Income*, will be positively correlated with budget punctuations. Finally, three year dummies were controlled for unobservable fixed effects across the four study years.

Table 6.1 reports empirical findings from multilevel logit regression models. In terms of generalized χ^2/DF, inclusion of control variables in the full model increases explanatory power compared with the unconditional model. Most of the variables, when statistically significant, show expected direction of influence on budget punctuations.

Table 6.1 Multilevel Logit Regression Results Explaining State Budget Punctuations: Executive Models (1993, 1996, 1998, and 2000)

Variable	Unconditional means model		Full model (Cutoff: –.59, .51)	
	Coefficient	Pr > |*t*|	Coefficient	Pr > |*t*|
Intercept	–3.0484	< .0001	–3.0071	< .0001
Centralization			–.4321	.1201
Centralization^2			.0768	.7435
Central capacity load			–1.9594	< .0001
Central capacity load^2			1.0317	.0009
Per capita lobbyist			.0066	.9388
FTE			–.1921	.0609
Political change			–.0271	.6896
Veto			–.1463	.0643
Balanced budget requirements			–.0377	.6268
Per capita IGR revenue			.1382	.0576
Per capita income			.1354	.1070
Year 1996 dummy			–.1227	.5339
Year 1998 dummy			–.1500	.5825
Year 2000 dummy			.1738	.3905
Number of observations	4,545		4,545	
Number of punctuations	297		297	
–2 Res log pseudo-likelihood	28,114.62		29,674.19	
Generalized χ^2	3,723.27		4,408.24	
Generalized χ^2/DF	.82		.97	

Notes: Class variables (sub-functional expenditures). All regressions are based on a random intercept model.

However, when partisan configurations are further accounted for the findings were much more consistent with hypothesized directions, especially for the measures of bureaucratic centralization. In fact, there were sufficient enough reasons for why such partisan configurations moderate the impact of these variables. Thus, we need a bit more explanation on how state budget processes are moderated by partisan configurations.

Of course, there are some state cases that show observations different from the expectation. As introduced above, there has been strong collaboration between the executive branch and the legislature in Kentucky even under divided governments. As in the Illinois case described earlier, the minority party, even under unified governments, can exert legislative influence through skillful negotiation. The case of New York is much more complicated and subtle. Since 1974 up to the early 2000s, the New York state government has been under divided governments where legislators were resistant to the governor. In each chamber, partisan leadership exerted strong influence on the rank and file through assignments of committees, chairmanships, extra stipend, and staff. Moreover, due to the high national profile of the New York governor, national party leaders have tried to induce New York legislators to rough up the governor from other party and the politics in DC repeated itself in New York. In addition to the intense political conflicts in New York, there is another layer of subtle complexity. Republicans in New York differ from those in other states. They have been more flexible with spending and borrowing. They have also been in fairly good relationships with Democrats in the state legislature especially when there has been fiscal crisis. Ironically, New York's partisan politics has been characterized by both competition/conflict and conformity/cooperation. If divided governments can also be associated with cooperation, bureaucratic centralization might exert its hypothesized (or closer to the hypothesized) influence on budget punctuations even under divided governments.

The Connecticut budget process has been decidedly formed along partisan lines and characterized by divided governments. Under such divided government conditions, conflicts over budget issues were resolved through negotiations between the governor and legislative leadership on the one hand, and the leadership and fiscal committee chairs on the other. The party leadership gathers votes needed to pass appropriations bills submitted by the governor and modified by the legislature. The groundwork for passing the bills is laid in party caucus, selective electoral supports, and allegiance secured through pork-barrel projects. During the entire budget process, fairly smooth and delicate budget processes have been maintained, even under divided governments, due mainly to the informal practices of budget negotiations between main budget actors (Lewis 2007, 81–84). If this is the case, one might expect that bureaucratic centralization might exert hypothesized influence on budget punctuations much similar to the New York case.

Despite some deviant state cases, the Florida case introduced earlier illustrates well that partisan configurations moderate the impact of bureaucratic centralization as expected. As briefly implied earlier, there was a potential for institutional frictions that might be augmented by contingent partisan configurations. Like other typical executive budget states, Georgia established the LBO in 1969. Originally, the LBO provided legislative committees with budget information that would be as good as the information provided by the OPB in the executive branch. The House Appropriations Committee utilized the budget information provided by the LBO. However, the Senate Appropriations Committee has had preference toward the OPB budget information. In 2002, the state legislature was split into House Democrats and Senate Republicans. Under this split legislature government condition, the relationship between the Senate committee and the LBO deteriorated and ultimately the Senate created its own staff office, the Senate Budget Office (Lauth 2007, 36). This shows how bureaucratic centralization induces different behaviors of budget actors under different partisan configurations. In other words, the creation of central budget staff office in one institution invited institutional tensions rather than cooperation under divided partisan control.

As shown above, Republicans gradually regained some political control in the Kentucky state legislature that had long been controlled by the Democratic majority. In the 2000 legislative session, Senate Republican majorities "were in a position to stop or significantly alter executive branch budgetary and revenue initiatives that were proposed by the Governor and supported by the Democratically controlled House" (Hackbart and Ramsey 2007, 163). A gubernatorial tax reform initiative failed due mainly to the partisan disparities between Senate Republican majorities and House Democrat majorities. Despite some deviant state examples, divided governments are most likely to invite institutional frictions. Table 6.2 confirms most of the expectation.

Under unified governments, the four measures of bureaucratic centralization exert all expected influence on budget punctuations. *Centralization* is significantly negatively related to the frequency of budget punctuations ($p = .0274$). However, excessive centralization increases budget punctuations ($p = .0683$). Thus, bureaucratic centralization is

Table 6.2 Multilevel Logit Regression Results Explaining State Budget Punctuations across Different Partisan Configurations: Executive Models (1993, 1996, 1998, and 2000)

Variable	Unified governments (Cutoff: –.53, .55)		Split branch governments (Cutoff: –.53, .57)		Split legislature governments (Cutoff:–.48, .48)	
	Coefficient	Pr > |*t*|	Coefficient	Pr > |*t*|	Coefficient	Pr > |*t*|
Intercept	–2.2863	< .0001	–4.4253	< .0001	–3.6069	< .0001
Centralization	–1.1175	.0274	–.9828	.0924	.4915	.5396
Centralization^2	.9601	.0683	.1860	.6784	–.9920	.1898
Central capacity load	–1.6833	.0030	–3.1429	.0001	–3.5004	.0041
Central capacity load^2	1.0229	.0253	1.6124	.0065	1.9170	.0427
Per capita lobbyist	–.0695	.5293	.0495	.8572	–.4027	.3324
FTE	–.4842	.1015	.1203	.3410	–.3942	.1147
Political change	.8709	.0253	–1.5852	.1780	–.0412	.5912
Veto	–.1305	.3268	–.2242	.2047	–.4668	.0081
Balanced budget requirements	–.0874	.4901	.2224	.2264	.1806	.4330
Per capita IGR revenue	.2370	.0453	.1421	.3821	–.0610	.7437
Per capita income	–.0090	.9528	.2989	.0138	.4568	.1181
Year 1996 dummy	–.7966	.0063	.4865	.3073	.3535	.4689
Year 1998 dummy	–.2899	.4475	–.3817	.5577	–.2391	.7496
Year 2000 dummy	–.0525	.8685	.8274	.0851	–.2383	.6657
Number of observations	1,959		1,441		926	
Number of punctuations	146		94		53	
–2 Res log pseudo-likelihood	11,913.34		10,193.09		6,213.15	
Generalized χ^2	1,591.67		1,777.28		700.52	
Generalized χ^2/DF	.82		1.25		.77	

Notes: Class variables (sub-functional expenditures). All regressions are based on a random intercept model.

observed to enhance the information-processing capacity of budget decision makers and reduce institutional frictions. However, excessive centralization detracts from such gains. This is also what was found from the national budget process. Unified governments might nourish budget environments that are highly compatible with the conditions under which hierarchical bureaucracy can function the most efficiently. The findings are starkly contrasted with those under split legislature governments, which confirm hypothesized influence of bureaucratic centralization on budget punctuations, as discussed in Chapter 3. Under split legislature governments, the measures of centralization and its squared value do not attain statistical significance.

Under split branch governments, Alt and Lowry's (1994, 2000) hypotheses also gain strong empirical support. As also discussed in Chapter 3, following unified governments, split branch governments are the second fastest style of government at making fiscal adjustments. *Centralization* significantly reduces budget punctuations ($p = .0924$). However, its squared value does not attain statistical significance. This finding needs more detailed further empirical investigation. One possible clue at this moment is that under unified governments, excessive bureaucratic centralization might consume all benefits from centralization because unified governments provide already fairly uniform control. Then, under split branch governments that are observed to be closer to unified governments, uniform control is not that tight, so as to detract from the benefits from centralization. *Central Capacity Load* and *Central Capacity Load*^{2} show all expected impacts on budget punctuations under the three partisan configurations. An adequate level of work load for central budget analysts significantly improves information-processing capacity of budget decision makers under any partisan contingencies. An answer to this deviation from the original expectation can be obtained from the comparison between state budget processes and the national budget process. Divided governments might not impose extra computational burden although they might invite extra institutional frictions. In addition, divided governments in states might not invite as strong institutional frictions as those in the national government.

Oftentimes, it is very hard to interpret the coefficients of logit models. Figure 6.2 shows how the probability of budget punctuations changes as the measures of bureaucratic centralization changes by unit of the standardized variables under unified governments. When *Centralization* is three standard deviations below the mean value of zero

Figure 6.2 Bureaucratic Centralization and Probability of State Budget Punctuations: Unified Governments

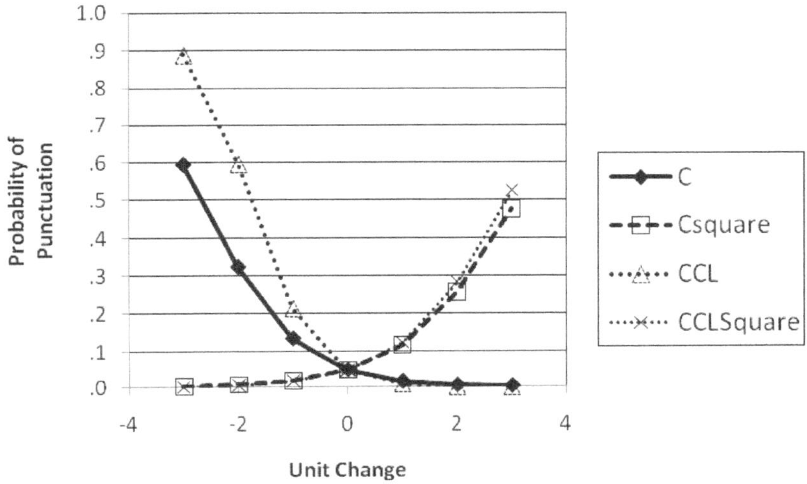

Notes: C (Centralization); CSquare (Centralization^2); CCL (Central capacity load); CCLSquare (Central capacity load^2)

while holding all other variables at their mean values, the probability of budget punctuations is about 59.4 percent. The probability rapidly drops to about 4.9 percent around the mean value of zero. However, the probability rapidly increases as there is excessive centralization. Beginning from the mean value of zero, the probability increases to about 47.7 percent when *Centralization*^{2} increases up to the unit value of three (i.e., three standard deviations above the mean value of zero). When *Central Capacity Load* is three standard deviations below the mean value of zero, the probability of budget punctuations is about 88.9 percent. When it is at the mean value of zero, the probability is about 4.9 percent. When the capacity load is squared, the reversed patterns are observed.

Figure 6.3 reports the visual relationship between the measures of bureaucratic centralization and budget punctuations under divided governments. Two measures of capacity load visually confirm their expected impacts on budget punctuations. These patterns were also confirmed when the cutoff points were gradually increased from ±.3 to ±.9 by ±.1. The results were virtually the same as the findings reported earlier. Thus, although defining the cutoff points has been a

Figure 6.3 Bureaucratic Centralization and Probability of State Budget Punctuations: Split Branch and Legislature Governments

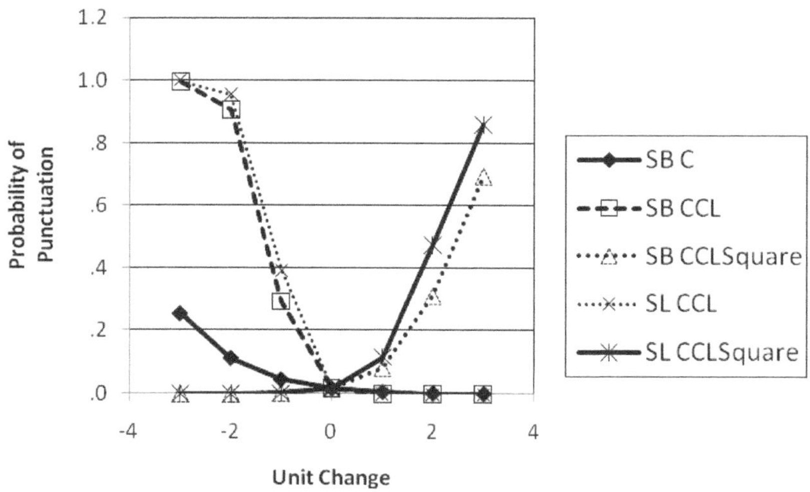

Notes: SB (Split Branch Governments); SL (Split Legislature Governments); C (Centralization); CCL (Central capacity load); CCLSquare (Central capacity load^2).

controversial issue, the results in this chapter are pretty solid (readers are referred to Chapter 4 for details of this discussion).

Under unified governments only, *Political Change* significantly increases the probability of budget punctuations ($p = .0253$). Although this variable exerts expected influence on budget punctuations, it is quite difficult to interpret why it is significant only under unified governments. Perhaps under divided governments political majority shift might cause political turbulence, but the system is already in political turbulence. Under unified governments, however, political changes might shake the previous political equilibrium and cause institutional frictions. Earlier, we have observed such a possibility from the Utah case. Even under Republican unified governments, there was new tension between urban vs. rural Republicans.

Another hard-to-interpret variable under unified governments is *Per Capita IGR Revenue*. It is significant and positively correlated with budget punctuations ($p = .0453$). Probably, we can apply almost the same reason for *Political Change* to interpreting this unexpected finding. Federal grants are usually distributed with strings attached. Under divided governments the strings might function as good excuses for opposing parties' watchdog roles. Then, federal statutory mandates will be used as a tool to silence partisan competition over the external resources under divided governments. Under unified governments, however, the collusion between the single dominating political powers is so strong that even federal mandates might be bypassed, if not directly challenged. This might invite political frictions even within the same party because now the dominant party might use the funds at its discretion but its members might vie for the funds.

In contrast, *Per Capita Income* is significant and positively related to budget punctuations only under split branch governments ($p = .0138$). State personal income is quite different from IGR revenue in that state legislators have discretion over how much fiscal share, as defined in Alt and Lowry (1994, 2000), can be obtained for tax revenues. In that case, the governor's party and the opposition party in the legislatures might confront each other because there are no statutory provisions that can be used as excuses to control the opposing party. They will rely more on their typical partisan lines for public spending, which will increase political frictions. Alt and Lowry (1994, 2000) reported that fiscal adjustment with respect to external revenue shocks under split branch governments is somewhat closer to that under unified governments. However, they also contended that even when the legislature is less powerful it can impose its preferences by virtue of its appropriation power subject to previous year's budget conditions, which will be potential sources for institutional frictions. The potential institutional conflicts might materialize when the legislature retains some budget power (Alt and Lowry 1994, 2000; Clarke 1998). Discussions of control variables are beyond the scope of this book. Readers are referred to note 5 in Chapter 4.

Clarke (1998) offers more plausible explanations on the negative sign of *Veto* under split legislature governments, as discussed in Chapter 3. Under split legislature governments, governors usually have one partisan chamber ally in state legislatures. During conference committee sessions, governor's partisans might support that governor's positions. This will result in weaker conflict between the executive and legislative branches by driving the both sides to adopt gubernatorial policy positions. In addition, governors notify legislative leaders and legislators that they might invoke item vetoes over specific projects in legislators' districts in case of changes in governor's budget recommendations. The threats of item veto powers therefore serve as a tool to contain potential conflict over problematic pork projects in advance. Therefore, governors might exert a stronger leveraging influence on budget decisions under split legislature government. In particular, item veto powers, which are supposed to control pork spending added by legislators for their districts, might function as fiscal restraints. Therefore, *Veto* likely reduces institutional frictions under split legislature governments as shown in Table 6.2 (p = .0081).

The negative sign of *Veto* needs some further discussion. Some earlier observations of item vetoes in Wisconsin also evidence that item veto might not necessarily create interbranch conflicts and institutional frictions. As noted above, Wisconsin governors were conferred the authority to veto items, reduce items, and delete narratives in appropriations bills. As in other item veto states; however, item vetoes were more frequently invoked for policy reasons rather than fiscal reasons. One interesting point in Wisconsin is that the Wisconsin budget process could aptly be described as a typical policy-making process. Governors traditionally included many heavily policy-laden initiatives in their budget proposals. This convention had multiple merits for governors. Governors could veto items that they initiated but were not accompanied by appropriations. It was also much easier for governors to work with legislative leadership in managing more contained budget processes, rather than to deal with more fragmented authorization processes.

Furthermore, gubernatorial deletion veto power is also likely to induce interbranch compromise or collaboration over budget choices. Recently, more states have been adding riders in appropriations bills. Potential threats from the trend are that they might deter authorization committees from allowing full policy consideration to policy proposals and appropriation committees from giving careful review of budget dollars. Legislators especially favor these measures; adding riders. Attaching conditions on dollars will be more powerful control over agencies. Additionally, appropriations bills are generally more veto resistant and less subject to control by the legislative leadership. Finally, when legislation is handled by narratives, policy making might be expedited because the legislative leadership may have more control over the legislative contents. Chief executive officers might also feel that narratives in appropriations bills might expedite the policy-making process (Abney and Lauth 2002, 492–94). These cases signify that item vetoes might be used as a tool to expedite policy negotiations between governors and legislatures.

The empirical findings in this section are very similar to what was found for the national budget process. Bureaucratic centralization improves the information-processing capacity of budget decision makers and reduces institutional frictions. However, excessive centralization tends to increase budget punctuations. This aspect implies that excessive centralization might expose the inherent malfunctions of bureaucratic organizations. Excessive centralization might hamper effective communications and collaboration within the organizations and might even slow down their interactions with external organizations. Furthermore, whether bureaucratic centralization reduces budget punctuations or not significantly hinges on political partisan configurations surrounding the bureaucratic decision premises.

Bureaucratic Centralization and State Budget Stability

As detailed in Chapter 4, bureaucratic centralization is hard to shake loose the steadfast budget inertia. In other words, the main budget actors have formed strong consensus on how they can share their budget pies based on the so-called concept of fair share. Even increased information-processing or friction-reducing capacity from bureaucratic centralization might remain mute faced with the invincible consensus on the fair share. This implies that the second part of the right-hand side in equation (2.5) will be zero: i.e., $M.B.A. * (\beta_1 \cdot Z_{1t} + \beta_2 \cdot Z_{2t} + \cdots + \beta_m \cdot Z_{mt}) = 0$. Budget decision makers, even with the help of bureaucratic centralization, cannot process budget information cues more efficiently when their decision procedures are closer to the programmed decision procedures discussed in Chapter 3. They might be even dominated by the budget consensus formed between the main budget actors. Findings in Table 6.3 partially confirm these expectations. Bureaucratic centralization accelerates budget inertia under unified governments. A similar finding is obtained under split branch government that is closer to unified governments in terms of fiscal adjustment.

Under all three partisan contingencies, *Central Capacity Load* increases budget stability. This implies that information-processing or friction-reducing capacity of bureaucratic centralization is nullified in the face of the steadfast budget inertia. The capacity serves the steadfast budget consensus. This finding is fairly strong supporting evidence for budgetary incrementalism. Only when central budget analysts are assigned exceptionally heavy workload, budget stability is somewhat mitigated as shown in the negative sign of *Central Capacity Load*^{2}. As implied in Chapter 3 in terms of governor's budget power,

Table 6.3 Multilevel Logit Regression Results Explaining State Budget Stability across Different Partisan Configurations: Executive Models (1993, 1996, 1998, and 2000)

Variable	Full model (Cutoff: –.07, .1)		Unified governments (Cutoff: –.09, .11)		Split branch governments (Cutoff: –.07, .13)		Split legislature governments (Cutoff:–.08, .1)	
	Coefficient	Pr > |t|	Coefficient	Pr > |t|	Coefficient	Pr > |t|	Coefficient	Pr > |t|
Intercept	.1261	.5688	.0386	.8983	.6470	.0688	.2363	.4825
Centralization	.2215	.1291	.5066	.0767	.5287	.0705	.1363	.6956
Centralization^2	–.0173	.8842	–.4641	.1201	–.1371	.5107	.0116	.9661
Central capacity load	.3655	.0011	.5807	.0020	.5993	.0037	.4528	.0486
Central capacity load^2	–.2167	.0062	–.4009	.0050	–.1883	.3823	–.3547	.0231
Per capita lobbyist	–.1177	.0029	–.1225	.0228	–.3154	.0013	.1101	.4633
FTE	–.0090	.8316	–.3066	.0378	–.1410	.0399	.1741	.0501
Political change	–.0367	.2890	.0395	.8681	.6857	.2569	–.0125	.7612
Veto	.0130	.7546	.0328	.6708	–.0744	.3869	.0919	.2723
Balanced budget requirements	–.0801	.0471	.0092	.8941	–.0745	.4015	–.0897	.3963
Per capita IGR revenue	–.1278	.0005	–.2164	.0006	–.1892	.0239	–.1220	.1917
Per capita income	–.0034	.9394	–.0589	.4567	–.0690	.3009	.1439	.3251
Year 1996 dummy	–.0103	.9141	–.0211	.8874	–.2008	.3550	–.0910	.6959
Year 1998 dummy	.3586	.0116	.6456	.0039	.7835	.0104	–.1099	.7592
Year 2000 dummy	.2679	.0098	.0569	.7488	.3649	.1150	.0157	.9545
Number of observations	4,545		1,959		1,441		926	
Number of budget stability	2,462		1,130		873		526	
–2 Res log pseudo-likelihood	20,270.91		8,782.19		6,579.15		446.11	
Generalized χ^2	4,466.64		1,872.59		1,394.39		887.11	
Generalized χ^2/DF	.99		.96		.98		.97	

Notes: Class variables (sub-functional expenditures). All regressions are based on a random intercept model.

split legislature government is closer to unified governments. Lopsided influence within the main budget actors by governors clearly explains the common patterns between unified and split legislature governments. In other words, the dominating budget power of governors might accelerate budget inertia under unified and split legislature governments. However, there is one point worth further attention. Under split branch governments *Central Capacity Load*^{2} is not statistically significant, but its impact on budget inertia is still negative. Overall, the findings on central capacity load imply that the increased workload of central budget offices merely reinforces the continuing momentum for budget stability.

In terms of fiscal adjustment or reflecting external budget cues into decision making, split branch governments are closer to unified governments. In contrast to bureaucratic centralization; however, lobbyists function as information processor under the two partisan configurations. *Per Capita Lobbyist* significantly reduces budget stability. Lobbyists might bring politically meaningful budget information to the main budget actors, thus helping expedite some scrutiny over the budget base. Lobbyists are different from central budget offices that are under direct control of the main budget actors, especially governors. Thus, they might be freer from such dominance and more efficiently process budget information such that even budget inertia is scrutinized. In a very similar vein, *FTE* reduces budget stability under the two partisan configurations. If *FTE* measures the overall information capacity of bureaucratic organizations, it is expected to expedite some information processing. In terms of fiscal adjustment, the two partisan configurations are similar and *FTE* seems to trigger such responsiveness under the two conditions. Under split legislature governments that are slower in responding to external fiscal shocks; however, *FTE* seems to function as additional veto points as Robinson et al. (2007) suggested. *Per Capita IGR Revenue* reduces budget inertia under unified and split branch governments. Although the findings are difficult to interpret, the reasons might be related to a possibility that the main budget actors are now moving toward new budget pies under unified and split branch governments that are relatively faster in fiscal adjustment to external revenue shocks. This mobility might shake the steadfast budget inertia or stability. Here again, readers are referred to note 5 in Chapter 4 for more detailed discussions of the control variables.

In sum, bureaucratic centralization does not shake loose budget stability. It even accelerates the budget inertia especially under unified governments. Once again, the utility of bureaucratic centralization is somewhat *bounded* by budget inertia in the state budget processes.

Conclusion

Many critiques of bureaucracy have asserted that bureaucracy is one of main reasons for bounded rationality. The stories found in this chapter suggest otherwise. In actuality, bureaucracy has been invented to augment and supplement the limited cognitive capacity of individual human beings. The fact is not that bureaucracy detracts from the information-processing capacity of human beings, but that bureaucracy under *limited* conditions augments the information-processing capacity. It also functions as friction-reducing mechanisms.

Bureaucratic centralization reduces budget punctuations in the state budget process. This implies that bureaucratic centralization might expedite information processing, or reduce institutional frictions. However, excessive centralization consumes the benefits gained by bureaucratic centralization. Second, bureaucratic centralization is highly tangential on its surrounding political environments. Unified governments proffer the conditions that are fairly similar to the uniform hierarchical structures found in typical bureaucratic organizations. Bureaucratic centralization reveals its expected functions under unified governments. Unfortunately, bureaucratic centralization even accelerates the already steadfast budget inertia. Quite similar to what was found from the national executive budget process and the Congressional budget process, the strengths of bureaucratic centralization are bounded by the three contingencies. However, all in all the *bounded bureaucracy* is a potential solution to bounded rationality.

Note

1. As detailed later in this chapter, observations of previous year's subfunctional expenditures with zero values but current year's expenditures with *non*zero values are clear examples of positive budget punctuations. These observations are added back into the final regression models. The percentage here is computed with the full sample including such budget punctuations. One difference of state budget data from U.S. budget authorities is that the minimum value of the former is zero (i.e., no expenditures). This is starkly contrasted with U.S. budget authorities, especially those with offsetting receipts. This also denotes that the minimum value of *Increment* is −1. If B_t $\frac{B_t - B_{t-1}}{B_{t-1}}$ in is zero (i.e., current year expenditures are zero) and B_{t-1} is nonzero, *Increment* will be −1.

Appendix: Legislative Professionalization and State Budget Punctuations and Stability

At the state level, there are not many states that have the legislative budget process similar to Congressional resolution or reconciliation procedures. There are not many states that have central budget offices, comparable to the CBO. For this reason, models were not run to test how bureaucratic centralization affects budget punctuations and stability in the state budget processes. Instead, state legislatures have been recently highly professionalized (Rosenthal 2004). Tables 6A.3 and 6A.4 show how legislative professionalism influences budget punctuations and stability. State subfunctional expenditure data that are consistent and the control variables for the test were available from 1989 to 2004, with 18,296 observations over 31 subfunctional categories. Related papers on the findings are available upon requests to the author.

Table 6A.1 Subfunctional Categories of State Government Expenditures

Number	Name
1	Elementary and secondary education
2	Higher education
3	Other education
4	Employment security administration
5	Financial administration and general control
6	General public building
7	Health
8	Own hospitals
9	Other hospitals
10	Regular highways
11	Toll highways
12	Housing and community development
13	Libraries
14	Natural resources
15	Parks and recreation
16	Police protection
17	Public welfare

continued on next page

Table 6A.1 (*continued*)

Number	Name
18	Sanitation
19	Sewerage
20	Solid waste management
21	Water transport and terminals
22	Interest on general debt
23	General expenditure, NEC
24	Liquor stores
25	Water utilities
26	Electric utilities
27	Gas utilities
28	Transit utilities
29	Employee retirement
30	Unemployment compensation
31	Other insurance trusts

Notes: NEC denotes *Not Elsewhere Categorized.* All expenditures are direct (excluding intergovernmental) expenditures. Total denotes summing various, miscellaneous expenditure categories.

Table 6A.2 Descriptions of the Explanatory Variables in State Executive Models

Variable	Definition	Hypothesized effects on budget punctuations	Data source
Centralization	Budget analysts in State Executive Central Budget Offices / FTE (Full Time Equivalent) executive employees	–	NASBO
$Centralization^2$	*Centralization* squared	+	NASBO
Central capacity load	State subfunctional expenditures / Budget analysts in State Executive Central Budget Offices	–	NASBO
Central capacity $load^2$	*Central capacity load* Squared	+	NASBO

continued on next page

Table 6A.2 (*continued*)

Variable	Definition	Hypothesized effects on budget punctuations	Data source
Per capita lobbyist	State lobbyists / State population	–	CSG
FTE	Full time equivalent executive employees	+/–	NASBO/ *Statistical Abstract of United States*
Political change	Absolute value of annual changes in the variable: (Democratic House members + Democratic senators – Republican House members – Republican senators) / State population	+	*Statistical Abstract of United States*
Veto	Item Veto + Reduction Veto + Deletion Veto (Sum of three dummies)	+/–	CSG
Balanced budget requirements	Requirements for governors to submit, legislatures to pass, and state governments to achieve at the end of fiscal year, balanced budgets (Sum of three dummies)	+	CSG
Per capita IGR revenue	(Federal aids to states + Local aids to States – Intergovernmental expenditures) / State population	+	Obtained from the U.S. Census Bureau
Per capita income	State personal income / State population	+	*Statistical Abstract of United States*

Source: NASBO: National Association of State Budget Officers. *Budget Processes in the States* (various versions). CSG: Council of State Governments. *Book of the States* (various versions).

Table 6A.3 Multilevel Logit Regression Results Explaining State Budget Punctuations across Different Partisan Configurations: Legislative Models (1989–2004)

Variable	Full sample (Cutoff:–.57, .57)		Unified government (Cutoff: –.60, .55)		Split branch government (Cutoff: –.51, .54)		Split legislature government (Cutoff:–.46, .52)	
	Coefficient	Pr > |*t*|	Coefficient	Pr > |*t*|	Coefficient	Pr > |*t*|	Coefficient	Pr > |*t*|
Intercept	–2.8973	< .0001	–1.9041	.0002	–3.0457	< .0001	–3.3540	< .0001
Senator staff	.0886	.0545	.0444	.5670	.1784	.0146	–.0719	.5417
House representative Staff	–.1199	.0086	–.0464	.5639	–.1708	.0112	.0486	.6680
Senate committee staff	–.0401	.5357	–.0335	.7207	–.0221	.8857	.1933	.2217
House committee staff	.0020	.9739	–.1918	.0493	.0444	.7514	–.1103	.4029
Per capita lobbyist	.0599	.0878	.1024	.0570	.0317	.6334	.0928	.1364
Political change	–.0094	.7770	.0614	.7079	–.4143	.1319	.0269	.4473
Veto	–.0994	.0189	–.1024	.1414	–.1365	.0627	.0208	.8129
Balanced budget requirements	.0403	.2990	–.0293	.5479	.0392	.6534	.0052	.9442
Per capita IGR revenue	–.0343	.3138	.0120	.8165	–.0321	.6042	–.3042	.0007
Per capita income	.0222	.4990	.0325	.5762	.0487	.3192	–.0490	.6229
Number of observations	18,296		7,455		5,954		3,959	
Number of punctuations	649		274		207		128	
–2 Res log pseudo-likelihood	116,985.5		46,043.1		36,622.2		24,250.8	
Generalized χ^2	17,045.13		6,561.16		4,885.74		3,192.42	
Generalized χ^2/DF	.93		.88		.82		.81	

Notes: Class variables (subfunctional expenditures). All regressions are based on a random intercept model.

All four staff variables are constructed from *The Book of the States.* When individual legislators have session-only staff assistance in state capitols or their individual districts, *Senator Staff* and *House Representative Staff* are assigned the value of one. For year-round staff assistance, the value of two is assigned. The two indices are the sum of all these values. When a legislative chamber has professional or clerical staff support for some committees, then *Senate Committee Staff* and *House Committee Staff* are assigned the value of one and when it has the support for all committees, then the value of two was assigned. Finally, the two indices are the sum of all these values. All indices range from zero to four.

Table 6A.4 Multilevel Logit Regression Results Explaining State Budget Stability across Different Partisan Configurations: Legislative Models (1989–2004)

Variable	Full sample (Cutoff:–.09, .13)		Unified government (Cutoff: –.09, .12)		Split branch government (Cutoff: –.08, .13)		Split legislature government (Cutoff:–.09, .12)	
	Coefficient	Pr > |t|	Coefficient	Pr > |t|	Coefficient	Pr > |t|	Coefficient	Pr > |t|
Intercept	.3324	.1245	–.0222	.9330	.4449	.0846	.4467	.1345
Senator staff	.0360	.1467	.0185	.6620	.0317	.4347	.0421	.4929
House representative staff	–.0274	.2546	–.0128	.7630	–.0529	.1453	.0194	.7486
Senate committee staff	.0054	.8806	–.0055	.9189	–.0693	.4115	–.0604	.8988
House committee staff	.0148	.6588	.0850	.1350	.0783	.3203	.0091	.0106
Per capita lobbyist	–.0830	< .0001	–.0693	.0168	–.1185	.0006	–.0945	.7163
Political change	–.0166	.3151	–.0174	.8488	.0877	.5056	–.0072	.8538
Veto	–.0076	.7295	–.0028	.9399	–.0591	.1322	–.0086	.3492
Balanced budget requirements	–.0090	.6565	–.0062	.8600	.0173	.7084	–.0364	.2519
Per capita IGR revenue	–.0407	.0226	–.0767	.0054	–.0548	.1056	.5302	.0175
Per capita income	.0010	.9570	–.0532	.0869	–.0042	.8799	.1222	
Number of observations	18,296		7,455		5,954		3,959	
Number of budget stability	11,132		4,349		3,645		2,337	
–2 Res log pseudo-likelihood	82,066.75		33,182.97		26,665.80		17,734.23	
Generalized χ^2	18,184.06		7,374.06		5,881.96		3,894.36	
Generalized χ^2/DF	.99		.99		.99		.99	

Notes: Class variables (subfunctional expenditures). All regressions are based on a random intercept model.

All four staff variables are constructed from *The Book of the States.* When individual legislators have session-only staff assistance in state capitols or their individual districts, *Senator Staff* and *House Representative Staff* are assigned the value of one. For year-round staff assistance, the value of two is assigned. The two indices are the sum of all these valucs. When a legislative chamber has professional or clerical staff support for some committees, then *Senate Committee Staff* and *House Committee Staff* are assigned the value of one and when it has the support for all committees, then the value of two was assigned. Finally, the two indices are the sum of all these values. All indices range from zero to four.

7

Conclusion: Bounded Bureaucracy to Bounded Rationality

Despite continued critiques over bureaucracy, this book finds that some aspects of bureaucratic organizations merit further scrutiny. Bureaucratic centralization in the national and state budget processes expedite information processing and reduce organizational conflicts. The benefits from bureaucratic centralization are highly contingent on its surrounding political environments. These observations raise important questions against one of the latest critiques over bureaucratic inefficiency, which plagues all levels of governments nationwide. As discussed throughout this book, performance budgeting systems have recently been suggested as a way to reform the inefficiency and ineffectiveness of bureaucratic organizations. It is very ironic, however, that such bureaucratic reform initiatives are not likely to achieve their intended goals without utilizing a certain aspect of bureaucracy itself. Two recent studies warrant our intensive discussions to clarify why this is the case.

The first study conducted by West, Lindquist, and Mosher-Howe (2009) evidences how important clarification of agency goals and facilitated communications across organizational divisions are for the success of bureaucratic reform efforts. Housed within the U.S. Department of Commerce, the National Oceanic and Atmospheric Administration (NOAA) is a scientific and regulatory agency over weather and ocean conditions. The NOAA has six line units and their heads (assistant administrators) report to the undersecretary of commerce for oceans and atmosphere. NOAA's goals and institutional means to achieve them have accumulated incrementally to the level of overlapping in organizational autonomy to further their units' agendas. Thus, there was a high necessity for reforming NOAA's organizational structures through coordination. As briefly discussed in Chapter 1, almost all levels of governments have been strongly called on for reforming bureaucratic inefficiencies through performance-budgeting systems. The NOAA was no exception to the call. NOAA's challenges of coordination were also underscored by external pressures for fiscal and administrative reforms such as the Government Performance Results Act of 1993 or the Program Assessment Rating Tool (PART) implemented in the national government during the Bush administration. There have also been specific concerns about the redundancy in NOAA's organizational structures and the lack of clearly defined organizational objectives.

Previous efforts of NOAA to reorganize through coordination were limited by the infeasibility of disrupting ongoing operations and the political influence of constituencies attached to programs and particular agency officials. As an alternative to restructuring, the NOAA attempted to improve its management practices. The NOAA elaborated the planning process by creating an Office of Program Planning and Integration for this purpose. The NOAA has also adopted a new management system designed to rationalize performance across its organizational units. The NOAA instituted a planning, programming, budgeting, and execution systems (PPBES) in 2002.

The planning stage is initiated three years before the beginning of the fiscal year. It is based on inputs from stakeholders within and outside the NOAA and accounts for any changes in its operating environment. The programming stage emphasizes the use of performance measures and evaluates NOAA's forty-four programs, also called subgoals, in terms of their contributions to one of the five goals in NOAA's strategic plan. Programs are in turn composed of activities that are also evaluated in terms of their contribution to programmatic goals. This process is orchestrated by the Office of Program Analysis and Evaluation. One aspect of PPBES is, as noted in Chapter 1, is cross-walking across different line units. When certain activities of line units contribute to a certain program, line managers from the line units build up a program team. In addition, "the contributions that programs make to their respective goals are, in turn, evaluated by goal teams. These are also composed of implementing officials, and their leaders are upper-level line managers" (West, Lindquist, and Mosher-Howe 2009, 438). The budgeting phase is managed by NOAA's chief financial officer and distributes actual budget in light of agency goals and priorities. The execution stage disburses funds and maintains oversight to ensure accountability and effectiveness.

One peculiar aspect of NOAA's implementation of PPBES was the introduction of more enhanced cross-walking procedures during the above "programming" stage. The NOAA has further initiated a matrix program to facilitate communication and coordination among line units. For instance, extensive bottom-up inputs in evaluation of programs and resource needs were reflected into decision making but the inputs were supposed to be orchestrated by central coordination in the matrix system. The matrix programs combine activities to which two or more of NOAA's five line offices contribute. Key individual staffs from the five offices report to the matrix program manager in addition to their line office supervisors. The matrix program manager then reports to higher-level line managers and to the Office of Program Planning and Integration mentioned earlier. Thus, NOAA's attempts to implement PPBES were well designed and supported by organizational reengineering. Then, what are the impacts of PPBES on organizational performance?

West, Lindquist, and Mosher-Howe (2009) present an overall evaluation of NOAA's reform initiatives. The coordinative goal of PPBES implemented by the NOAA and a matrix organization "has been undermined by conflicting line loyalties, by the separation of planning and analysis from managerial authority, by the political realities of budgeting, and by the simplicity of the assumptions about means-ends relationships that define NOAA's program structure" (West, Lindquist, and Mosher-Howe 2009, 439). The authors more specifically list practical and conceptual limits on coordination.

First, although PPBES improved communications across organizational units, it could not improve cooperation in the pursuit of efficiency. Conflicting loyalties to line units prohibited organizational units from making dispassionate analysis. Analysis, in actuality, was used as program advocacy. For this reason, there were even proposals for new or expanded activities as opposed to redistributing resources across existing activities. Second, programming only results in recommendations and authority with line units still prevails. Even headquarter officials noted about the presence of two budgets: a program budget and a line-item budget. The practical effects of NOAA's PPBES were constrained by the existence of two budgets, two separate submissions, and two separate narratives. Third, legislators and legislatures that are the ultimate decision makers of final spending might have policy goals and constituent interests different from NOAA's spending priorities (e.g., environmentalists, fishermen, or universities). In addition, some senior scientists have established personal relationships with Congress, which reinforces their influence on their favorite programs beyond the priorities suggested in PPBES reforms. Fourth, the assumptions of hierarchically ordered goals and means-ends chains do not make realistic senses and thus do not accurately reflect what the NOAA has been actually doing.

West, Lindquist, and Mosher-Howe (2009) cautiously contend that the invisible hand of the political market place, in lieu of centralized coordination through PPBES, is better for a more efficient resource allocation. The messy fragmentation of bureaucratic powers might be pretty much a part of the American political system. However, the main findings in this book suggest slightly different lessons. Particularly in the state budget processes, numerous anecdotal stories indicate that central budget offices can orchestrate inter-unit conflicts that cannot be easily coordinated by the central offices within line units. Some cases further show that the central budget offices even coordinate potential conflicts between executive line agencies and legislatures. In addition, the offices provided line agencies with significant levels of assistance to relieve agencies' computational burden over agency budgets and programs, which is lacking in the NOAA experience. As observed in this book, an adequate level of bureaucratic centralization can enhance information-processing capacity of bureaucratic organizations and help reduce inter-organizational conflicts. Ironically, such reforms of bureaucratic organizations as performance budgeting systems can better be achieved by utilizing a certain aspect of bureaucracy itself.

Another recent study shows that success of performance budgeting systems is largely driven by political environments surrounding bureaucratic organizations that are implementing such reforms. In the last decade, performance-based budgeting has been adopted by various levels of governments. Beginning from FY 2004, the OMB has been implementing PART for evaluating federal programs. Gilmour and Lewis (2006) explored how merit evaluation and politics formed OMB recommendations for the 234 federal programs in the 2004 president's budget proposal to the U.S. Congress.

The authors investigated two major questions. First, to what extent were budget allocations in the FY 2004 budget proposal influenced by PART scores? Second, to what extent was the relationship between performance measures and budgets a function of politics? In other words, the authors tested whether performance measures are used in an impartial manner. Many empirical studies indicated that there has been very weak connection between budget allocations and performance evaluation results. In some senses, the weak linkage is self-evident from the nature of public programs. If a certain program performs poorly, should the fund be cut or increased to enhance public programs that might be important for the public? Due partly to this contradiction, the OMB was cautious in claiming a direct link between PART scores and budget allocation. Performance measures still need to be evaluated in terms of the programs, their missions, and their historical backgrounds. If it is the case, there is a risk that its implementation is likely to involve subjective judgments and thereby politicize its use. Thus, there is a possibility that the party in power might bias the implementation of performance budgeting systems. It might insulate its favorite programs from negative performance evaluations but cut the budgets of programs they do not favor especially when they are unable to demonstrate results. Therefore, the risk is that performance measurement itself might reflect political favoritism. In a previous study conducted by the authors, programs initiated under Democratic presidents received systematically lower PART scores compared with those under Republican presidents. The authors investigate this potential risk with more detailed budget allocation data.

The Bush administration graded the management quality of 234 federal programs in its 2004 budget. The grading scheme was developed by the OMB in consultation with the President's Management Council. It includes a total weighted numerical management grade of four categories with each of them ranging from 0 to 100 over four categories of performance evaluation: e.g., program purpose and design (20 percent weight), annual and long-term strategic planning (10 percent), program management (20 percent), and program results (50 percent). Grades were determined in each category based on survey responses adjusted for program type. Decisions are jointly made by the agency and an OMB examiner. Cases of disagreement were resolved through arbitration between the OMB and program associate director. PART scores are the sum of each of answers from line agencies. In addition to numerical scores, the OMB also assigns management and performance grades ranging from *effective, moderately effective, adequate, results not demonstrated,* and *ineffective.*

The first round of empirical results partially support that performance evaluation results might have been reflected into the president's (OMB's) budget recommendations for agency programs. The target variable is the change in the OMB's budget recommendations from FY 2003 to FY 2004. The mean budget change was 3.6 percent. One key finding is that the coefficients of PART scores are all positively and significantly correlated with the dependent variable. However, authors' preliminary analysis indicated that only Democratic programs were significantly correlated with the recommendation changes. Programs established under unified Democratic control received systematically lower budget recommendations. The authors investigate this second finding in much more details.

Programs housed in the Departments of Commerce, Education, Energy, Housing and Urban Development (HUD), Labor, Health and Human Services (HHS), and EPA were categorized as Democrat-preferred programs to which the Republican Party has been somewhat hostile. Some Republicans might support programs in these Democratic department programs. President Bush showed great support for education. However, core Democratic departments generally include HUD, HHS, Labor, and EPA that have missions generally matching Democratic Party platform. Education, Energy, and Commerce have been opposed by Republicans because their missions are generally inconsistent with markets or federalism. When the authors further controlled for the party preference over agency programs, strong partisan impacts over budget allocations were evidenced. The authors ran regressions over two separate samples, one sample with Democratic programs and the other with non-Democratic programs. Strikingly, the PART scores were significantly and positively correlated with only Democrat programs. This means that their budget recommendations were cut when their PART scores were low and vice versa. "This indicates that evaluations of management quality matter for programs traditionally supported by Democrats but less so for Republican programs" (Gilmour and Lewis 2006, 750). So, if Democratic programs perform poorly they are likely to be punished but they are rewarded for good performance. This also means that Republican programs are fairly free from performance results. In other words, none of PART scores was reflected into Republican programs. This is the evidence that the PART scores might be used in an impartial way.

In the 108th Congress from 2003 to 2005 compatible with the study period in Gilmour and Lewis (2006), there was a Republican majority (R—229 vs. D—204) in the House. In the Senate, there was also a Republican majority (R—51 vs. D—48). President Bush was also a Republican.[1] The partisan political configurations in the national government can be labeled as a Republican-unified government. However, in terms of the number of Congressmen the two parties were neck in neck. In some sense, the partisan configurations were closer to divided governments rather than unified governments. Furthermore, the executive budget preparation and submission phase begins almost eighteen months prior to the beginning of new fiscal years (Mikesell 2011, 103–7). This implies that OMB's centralized budget coordination over agency budget requests might have started a couple of years before the final president's budget proposals. Therefore, we also need to pay attention to the partisan configurations during the 107th Congress from 2001 to 2003. In the House, there was a slim Republican majority (R—221 vs. D—212). In the Senate, however, there was divided partisan control (R—50 vs. D—50). Overall, the partisan configurations surrounding bureaucratic centralization were much closer to divided partisan control. As findings in Chapter 4 for the national budget process and those in Chapter 6 for the state budget processes clarify, the politicization of PART scores might be partly attributable to divided governments. In particular, central budget offices in the executive branch are observed to expedite information processing and reduce organizational conflicts. This is especially true when their surrounding partisan environments are conducive to their operations. For instance, unified governments are characterized by unitary partisan control and this is fairly compatible with the hierarchical control found in bureaucratic hierarchies.

In Chapter 5, the Congressional Budget Office (CBO) was observed to expedite information processing and reducing organizational conflicts under "divided" partisan control. This is also strong evidence showing that whether the partisan environments surrounding bureaucratic centralization are conducive to the nature of the latter. In other words, as clarified in Chapter 5 the CBO has been viewed as Congressional bureaucracy. More importantly, the CBO was originally expected to be a bipartisan, politically neutral information-processing agency. As such, we can easily expect that the CBO can function best when there are two parties pitted against each other. That was exactly what we found in Chapter 5.

While the findings in this book strongly support that bureaucratic centralization expedites information processing and reduce institutional conflicts, one might also raise a question: i.e., how can we be sure that budget punctuations are the signals of bounded rationality and institutional conflicts. If budget punctuations are not their signals, then the findings in this book might not be evidence for the functions of bureaucratic centralization because we cannot be sure whether budget punctuations are the results of bounded rationality and institutional frictions. In their seminal studies, Davis, Dempster, and Wildavsky (1966, 1974) asserted that sudden budget lurches or budget punctuations are likely to be results of random errors. For instance, emergency budgets in response to the hurricane Katrina might show a sudden increase. In this case, sudden budget increases are not necessarily the results of bounded rationality or institutional frictions.

However, sudden increases in the homeland security budgets in the national budgets after the 9-11 terrorist attack are a totally different story. Throughout the 1990s, there have been tensions over whether to increase budgets for potential terrorist attacks within the U.S. territory. The 9-11 attack was just a triggering mechanism for budget punctuations. Political scientists and budget scholars have long been criticizing budgetary incrementalism in that it did not clearly explain why sudden budget punctuations take place except for treating them as random errors. As detailed in Chapters 2 and 3, disproportionate information-processing theory nicely explained the "why." Bounded rationality and institutional conflicts are the main reasons also for budget punctuations. Furthermore, Mortensen (2009) clearly shows how a triggering external event can result in budget punctuations. U.S. national spending was partially characterized by budget punctuations. However, the punctuations were mostly preceded by heightened public attention on the specific programs, after a long period of no attention to the program issues, before they were accompanied by sudden budget increases. Mortensen's study strongly implies that the sudden budget increase is not simply a random error.

During the early 1950s, Social Security program budgets made sudden and rapid increases after long years of small, incremental changes (Jones, Sulkin, and Larsen 2003). Natchez and Bupp's (1973) study is a very early example of such budget punctuations. Natchez and Bupp used twenty-three programs administered by the Atomic Energy Commission (AEC) from FY 1958 to FY 1972 to test whether budget choices at the program level are featured by fluctuation or regularity. One contribution by the study, compared with incrementalism, is that

Natchez and Bupp showed that there are more frequent observations of fluctuations at the program level below agencies (i.e., subagency level programs) that were the main target of studies on incrementalism. Some programs administered by the AEC experienced fairly large budget increases beginning from the mid-1960s. The programs were related to the thermonuclear bombs. But the sudden increase in the budgets was the result of strong external political support that was ignited by the so-called "great thermonuclear debate" in the 1950s (Natchez and Bupp 1973, 960–61). How can we explain all these delayed reflection of external budget inputs into budget choices? This has long been a controversial issue in the literature of policy and budget processes. In this sense, disproportionate information-processing theory detailed in Chapters 2 and 3 is a breakthrough in the literature. Overall, sudden budget lurches are highly likely the results of bounded rationality and institutional conflicts.

Chapter 3 explains how a bureaucratic organization, especially bureaucratic centralization, reduces the bounded rationality and organizational conflicts (see also Figure 3.1). In sum, the findings in this book strongly suggest that bureaucratic centralization can help expedite information processing and reduce institutional conflicts to a certain degree. The functions of bureaucratic centralization are also highly tangential on its surrounding partisan configurations.

According to incrementalism, marginal changes in budgets or policies are also symptomatic of bounded rationality or institutional conflicts. One might thus argue that bureaucratic centralization cannot realize the expected benefits when budget changes are marginal as reported in Chapters 4–6. Hammond and Knott (1966), in their elaborate study of who controls bureaucracy, reveal that bureaucracy is a function of the president and Congress. In particular, they showed that a strong status quo, which they define as "institutional core," cannot be changed easily. Bureaucratic agencies, Congressional committees, or even partisan majorities cannot easily break the status quo. Of course, the status quo is very similar to the budget stability that is frequently found under programmed decision-making settings detailed in Chapter 3. Hammond and Knott's study strongly implies that bureaucracy cannot be singularly criticized for its incapacity to break the budget stability.

The conclusion of this book is that the merits of bureaucratic centralization are worth our further attention. This is especially the case given the fact that numerous attempts including performance budgeting systems have been made to reform bureaucratic malfunctions. Ironically, however, even such reform initiatives are doomed to failure without utilizing a certain aspect of bureaucracy itself, bureaucratic centralization. In this book, the somewhat limited function of the bureaucratic centralization is defined as bounded bureaucracy. If well managed, bounded bureaucracy can substantially improve bounded rationality and institutional frictions.

Note

1. Data are obtained from *Statistical Abstract of the United States.*

Bibliography

Abney, Glenn, and Thomas P. Lauth. "Gubernatorial Use of the Item Veto for Narrative Deletion." *Public Administration Review* 62, no. 4 (2002): 492–501.

_____. "The End of Executive Dominance in State Appropriations." *Public Administration Review* 58, no. 5 (1998): 388–94.

_____. "The Item Veto and Fiscal Responsibility." *The Journal of Politics* 59 (August 1997): 882–92.

_____. "The Line Item Veto in the States: An Instrument of Fiscal-Control or an Instrument of Partisanship?" *Public Administration Review* 45, no. 3 (1985): 372–77.

Agranoff, Robert. *Managing within Networks: Adding Value to Public Organizations.* Washington, DC: Georgetown University Press, 2007.

Alt, James E., and Robert C. Lowry. "Divided Government, Fiscal Institutions, and Budget Deficits: Evidence from the States." *American Political Science Review* 88, no 4 (1994): 811–28.

_____. "A Dynamic Model of State Budget Outcomes under Divided Partisan Government." *The Journal of Politics* 62, no. 4 (2000): 1035–69.

Andrews, Rhys, George A. Boyne, Jennifer Law, and Richard M. Walker. "Centralization, Organizational Strategy, and Public Service Performance." *Journal of Public Administration Research and Theory* 19, no. 1 (2009): 57–80.

Baumgartner, Frank R., and Bryan D. Jones. *Agendas and Instability in American Politics.* Chicago, IL: The University of Chicago Press, 1993.

Berry, William D. "The Confusing Case of Budgetary Incrementalism: Too Many Meanings for a Single Concept." *The Journal of Politics* 52 (1990): 167–96.

Bingham, Lisa Blomgren, and Rosemary O'Leary, eds. *Big Ideas in Collaborative Public Management.* Armonk, NY: M. E. Sharpe, 2008.

Bland, Robert L., and Wes Clarke. "Texas: The Use of Performance Data in Budgeting and Management." In *Budgeting in the States: Institutions, Processes, and Politics,* edited by Edward J. Clynch and Thomas P. Lauth, 277–92. Westport, CT: Praeger, 2007.

Bradley, Robert B. "Florida: Ebb and Flow in Executive-Legislative Relations." In *Budgeting in the States: Institutions, Processes, and Politics,* edited by Edward J. Clynch, and Thomas P. Lauth, 137–54. Westport, CT: Praeger, 2007.

Briffault, Richard. *Balancing Acts: The Reality behind State Balanced Budget Requirements.* New York, NY: the Twentieth Century Fund Press, 1996.

Clarke, Wes. "Divided Government and Budget Conflict in the U. S. States." *Legislative Studies Quarterly* 23, no. 1 (1998): 5–22.

Clynch, Edward J. "Mississippi: Changing Gubernatorial-Legislative Dynamics in Budget Decision Making." In *Budgeting in the States: Institutions, Processes, and Politics,* edited by Edward J. Clynch, and Thomas P. Lauth, 257–76. Westport, CT: Praeger, 2007.

Cogan, John F., Timothy J. Murris, and Allen Schick. *The Budget Puzzle: Understanding Federal Spending.* Stanford, CA: Stanford University Press, 1994.

Coleman, John J. "Unified Government, Divided Government, and Party Responsiveness." *The American Political Science Review* 93, no. 4 (1999): 821–35.

Conant, James K. "Virginia: Expenditure Increases, Tax Cuts, and Budget Deficits." In *Budgeting in the States: Institutions, Processes, and Politics,* edited by Edward J. Clynch, and Thomas P. Lauth, 213–34. Westport, CT: Praeger, 2007.

Cope, Glen Hahn. "Texas: Legislative Budgeting in a Post-Oil-Boom Economy." In *Governors, Legislatures, and Budgets: Diversity across the American States,* edited by Edward J. Clynch, and Thomas P. Lauth, 115–24. New York: Greenwood Press, 1991.

Davis, Otto A., M. A. Dempster, and Aaron Wildavsky. "A Theory of the Budgetary Process." *The American Political Science Review* 60, no. 3 (1966): 529–47.

_____. "Towards a Predictive Theory of Government Expenditure: US Domestic Appropriations." *British Journal of Political Science* 4 (1974): 419–52.

Duncombe, Sydney H., and Richard Kinney. "Idaho: Process and Politics in Gem State Budgeting." In *Governors, Legislatures, and Budgets: Diversity across the American States,* edited by Edward J. Clynch, and Thomas P. Lauth, 63–70. New York: Greenwood Press, 1991.

Egger, Rowland. "The Period of Crisis: 1933 to 1945." In *American Public Administration: Past, Present, Future,* edited by Frederick C. Mosher, 49–96. Tuscaloosa, AL: The University of Alabama Press, 1990.

Fenno, Richard Jr. *The Power of the Purse.* Boston: Little, Brown, 1966.

Forsythe, Dall W., and Donald J. Boyd. "New York: The Growth, Waning, and Resurgence of Executive Power." In *Budgeting in the States: Institutions, Processes, and Politics,* edited by Edward J. Clynch, and Thomas P. Lauth, 55–78. Westport, CT: Praeger, 2007.

Fry, Brian R., and Jos C. N. Raadschelders. *Mastering Public Administration: From Max Weber to Dwight Waldo.* 2nd ed. Washington, DC: CQ Press, 2008.

Gilmour, J. B., and D. E. Lewis. "Does Performance Budgeting Work? An Examination of the Office of Management and Budget's PART Scores." *Public Administration Review* 66, no. 5 (2006): 742–52.

Glisson, Charles A., and Patricia Yancey Martin. "Productivity and Efficiency in Human Service Organizations as Related to Structure, Size and Age." *Academy of Management Journal* 23, no. 1 (1980): 21–37.

Goodsell, Charles T. *The Case For Bureaucracy: A Public Administration Polemic.* 4th ed. Washington DC: CQ Press, 2004.

Gosling, James J. *Budgetary Politics in American Governments.* 5th ed. New York, NY: Taylor & Francis, 2009.

_____. "Utah: Economics, Political Culture, and Priority Setting." In *Budgeting in the States: Institutions, Processes, and Politics,* edited by Edward J. Clynch, and Thomas P. Lauth, 293–308. Westport, CT: Praeger, 2007.

_____. "Wisconsin Item-Veto Lessons." *Public Administration Review* 46, no. 4 (1986): 292–99.

Graham, Cole Blease Jr. "South Carolina: Executive Budgeting Brings a Stronger Gubernatorial Voice to the Table." In *Budgeting in the States: Institutions,*

Processes, and Politics, edited by Edward J. Clynch, and Thomas P. Lauth, 189–212. Westport, CT: Praeger, 2007.

Grizzle, Gloria. "Florida: Miles to Go and Promises to Keep." In *Governors, Legislatures, and Budgets: Diversity across the American States*, edited by Edward J. Clynch, and Thomas P. Lauth, 93–102. New York: Greenwood Press, 1991.

Hackbart, Meril M. "Kentucky: Transitions, Adjustments, and Innovations." In *Governors, Legislatures, and Budgets: Diversity across the American States*, edited by Edward J. Clynch, and Thomas P. Lauth, 83–91. New York: Greenwood Press, 1991.

Hackbart, Merl M., and James R. Ramsey. "Kentucky: The Executive/Legislative Budget Role Transition Continues." In *Budgeting in the States: Institutions, Processes, and Politics*, edited by Edward J. Clynch, and Thomas P. Lauth, 155–72. Westport, CT: Praeger, 2007.

Hammond, Thomas H., and Jack H. Knott. "Who Controls the Bureaucracy?: Presidential Power, Congressional Dominance, Legal Constraints, and Bureaucratic Autonomy in a Model of Multi-Institutional Policy-Making." *Journal of Law, Economics, and Organization* 12, no. 1 (1996): 119–66.

Hebert, Ted F. "Utah: Legislative Budgeting in an Executive Budget State." In *Governors, Legislatures, and Budgets: Diversity across the American States*, edited by Edward J. Clynch, and Thomas P. Lauth, 103–14. New York: Greenwood Press, 1991.

Ingraham, Patricia W., and Laurence Lynn, eds. *The Art of Governance: Analyzing Management and Administration*. Washington DC: Georgetown University Press, 2004.

Jones, Bryan D. "Bounded Rationality and Political Science: Lessons from Public Administration and Public Policy." *Journal of Public Administration Research and Theory* 13, no. 4 (2003): 395–412.

Jones, Bryan D., and Frank R. Baumgartner. "A Model of Choice for Public Policy." *Journal of Public Administration Research and Theory* 15, no. 3 (2005a): 325–51.

_____. *The Politics of Attention*. Chicago, IL: The University of Chicago Press, 2005b.

Jones, Bryan D., Frank R. Baumgartner, and James L. True. "Policy Punctuations: U.S. Budget Authority." *The Journal of Politics* 60, no. 1 (1998): 1–33.

Jones, Bryan D., Tracy Sulkin, and Heather A. Larsen. "Policy Punctuations in American Political Institutions." *American Political Science Review* 97, no. 1 (2003): 151–69.

Jordan, Meagan M. "Punctuations and Agendas: A New Look at Local Government Budget Expenditures." *Journal of Policy Analysis and Management* 22, no. 3 (2003): 345–60.

Kamensky, John M. "GPRA Modernization Act of 2010 Explained: Part I. IBM Center for The Business of Government," 2011. http://www.businessofgovernment.org/blog/business-government/gpra-modernization-act-2010-explained-part-1 (accessed January 11, 2011).

Kamlet, Mark S., and David C. Mowery. "The Budgetary Base in Federal Resource Allocation." *American Journal of Political Science* 24, no. 4 (1980): 804–21.

Lauth, Thomas P. "Georgia: Shared Power and Fiscal Conservatism." In *Budgeting in the States: Institutions, Processes, and Politics*, edited by Edward J. Clynch, and Thomas P. Lauth, 33–54. Westport, CT: Praeger, 2007.

Lauth, Thomas P., and Catherine C. Reese. "The Line-Item Veto in Georgia: Fiscal Restraint or Inter-Branch Politics?" *Public Budgeting and Finance* 26, no. 2 (2006): 1–19.
Lee, Robert D., Jr. "The Line Item Veto Legal Issues in the 1990s." *Public Budgeting and Finance* 20, no. 2 (2000): 49–73.
LeLoup, Lance T. *Budgetary Politics: Dollars, Deficits, Decisions.* Brunswick, OH: King's Court Communications, 1977.
_____. *The Fiscal Congress: Legislative Control of the Budget.* Westport, CT: Greenwood Press, 1980.
_____. "The Myth of Incrementalism: Analytical Choices in Budgetary Theory." *Polity* 10, no. 4 (1978): 488–509.
LeLoup, Lance T., and William B. Moreland. "Agency Strategies and Executive Review: The Hidden Politics of Budgeting." *Public Administration Review* 38, no. 3 (1978): 232–39.
Lewis, Carol. "Connecticut: Prosperity, Frugality, and Stability." In *Governors, Legislatures, and Budgets: Diversity across the American States,* edited by Edward J. Clynch, and Thomas P. Lauth, 41–52. New York: Greenwood Press, 1991.
_____. "Connecticut: Public Scarcity and Private Wealth." In *Budgeting in the States: Institutions, Processes, and Politics,* edited by Edward J. Clynch, and Thomas P. Lauth, 79–102. Westport, CT: Praeger, 2007.
Lindblom, Charles E. "The Science of 'Muddling Through.'" *Public Administration Review* 19 (1959): 79–88.
_____. "Still Muddling Not Yet Through." *Public Administration Review* 39, no. 6 (1979): 517–26.
Mansfield, Roger. "Bureaucracy and Centralization: An Examination of Organizational Structure." *Administrative Science Quarterly* 18, no. 4 (1973): 477–88.
Maynard-Moody, Steven, and Michael Musheno. *Cops, Teachers and Counsellors: Stories from the Front Lines of Public Service.* Ann Arbor, MI: Univ. of Michigan Press, 2003.
Maynard-Moody, Steven, Michael Musheno, and Dennis Palumbo. "Streetwise Social Policy: Resolving the Dilemma of Street-level Influence and Successful Implementation." *Western Political Quarterly* 43, no. 4 (1990): 833–48.
McCaffery, Jerry L. "California: Changing Demographics and Executive Dominance." In *Governors, Legislatures, and Budgets: Diversity across the American States,* edited by Edward J. Clynch, and Thomas P. Lauth, 7–16. New York: Greenwood Press, 1991.
_____. "California: Revenues Scarcity, Incremental Solutions, the Rise of Citizen Initiatives, and the Decline of Trust." In *Budgeting in the States: Institutions, Processes, and Politics,* edited by Edward J. Clynch, and Thomas P. Lauth, 9–32. Westport, CT: Praeger, 2007.
Meier, Kenneth J., and John Bohte. "ODE TO LUTHER GULICK: Span of Control and Organizational Performance." *Administration and Society* 32, no. 2 (2000): 115–37.
Merton, Robert K. "Bureaucratic Structure and Personality." *Social Forces* 18 (1940): 560–68.
_____. *Social Theory and Social Structure.* New York: Free Press, 1957.

Mikesell, John L. *Fiscal Administration: Analysis and Applications for the Public Sector.* 7th ed. Boston, MA: Wadsworth, 2011.

Miles, Raymond E., and Charles C. Snow. *Organizational Strategy, Structure and Process.* New York, NY: McGraw-Hill, 1978.

Mortensen, Peter B. "Political Attention and Public Spending in the United States." *Policy Studies Journal* 37, no. 3 (2009): 435–55.

Mosher, Frederick C., and Max O. Stephenson Jr. "The Office of Management and Budget in a Changing Scene." *Public Budgeting and Finance* 2, no. 4 (1982): 23–41.

Moynihan, Donald P., and Sanjay K. Pandey. "Testing How Management Matters in an Era Of Government by Performance Management." *Journal of Public Administration Research and Theory* 15, no. 3 (2005): 421–39.

Natchez, Peter B., and Irwin C. Bupp. "Policy and Priority in the Budgetary Process." *The American Political Science Review* 67, no. 3 (1973): 951–63.

Niskanen, William A. Jr. *Bureaucracy and Representative Government.* Chicago, IL: Aldine Atherton, 1971.

O'Leary, Rosemary, and Lisa Blomgren Bingham, eds. *The Collaborative Public Manager.* Washington, DC: Georgetown University Press, 2009.

Osborne, David, and Ted Gaebler. *Reinventing Government: How the Entrepreneurial Spirit is Transforming the Public Sector.* Reading, MA: Addison Wesley, 1992.

Padgett, John F. "Bounded Rationality in Budgetary Research." *American Political Science Review* 74, no. 2 (1980): 354–72.

Peltzman, Sam. "Toward a More General Theory of Regulation." *The Journal of Law and Economics* 19, no. 1 (1976): 211–40.

Poterba, James M. "State Responses to Fiscal Crises: The Effects of Budgetary Institutions and Politics." *Journal of Political Economy* 102, no. 4 (1994): 799–821.

Provan, Keith G., and Brinton H. Milward. "A Preliminary Theory of Interorganizational Network Effectiveness: A Comprehensive Study of Four Community Mental Health Systems." *Administrative Science Quarterly* 40, no. 1 (1995): 1–33.

Provan, Keith G., and Patrick Kenis. "Modes of Network Governance: Structure, Management, and Effectiveness." *Journal of Public Administration Research and Theory* 18, no. 2 (2008): 229–52.

Rainey, Hal G. Understanding and Managing Public Organizations., 4th ed. San Francisco, CA: Jossey-Bass, 2009.

Rainey, Hal G., and Jay E. Ryu. "Framing High Performance and Innovativeness in Government: A Review and Assessment of Research." In *The Art of Governance: Analyzing Management and Administration,* edited by Patricia W. Ingraham and Laurence Lynn, 20–45. Washington DC: Georgetown University Press, 2004.

Rainey, Hal G., and Paula Steinbauer. "Galloping Elephants: Developing Elements of a Theory of Effective Government Organizations." *Journal of Public Administration Research and Theory* 10, no. 2 (1999): 1–32.

Raudenbush, Stephen W., and Anthony S. Bryk. *Hierarchical Linear Models: Applications and Data Analysis Methods.* 2nd ed. Thousand Oaks, CA: Sage Publications, 2002.

Reese, Catherine C. "The Line-Item Veto in Practice in Ten Southern States." *Public Administration Review* 57, no. 6 (1997): 510–16.
Robinson, Marc, and Jim Brumby. *Does Performance Budgeting Work? An Analytical Review of the Empirical Literature.* IMF Working Paper WP/05/210. Washington, DC: International Monetary Fund, 2005.
Robinson, Scott E., Floun'say Caver, Kenneth J. Meier, and Lawrence J. O'Toole. "Explaining Policy Punctuations: Bureaucratization and Budget Change." *American Journal of Political Science* 51, no. 1 (2007): 140–50.
Rosenbloom, David H., Robert S. Kravchuk, and Richard M. Clerkin. *Public Administration: Understanding Management, Politics, and Law in the Public Sector.* 7th ed. Boston, MA: McGraw Hill, 2009.
Rosenthal, Alan. *Heavy Lifting: The Job of the American Legislature.* Washington, DC: CQ Press, 2004.
Rubin, Irene. "Aaron Wildavsky and the Demise of Incrementalism." *Public Administration Review* 49, no. 1 (1989): 78–81.
_____. *Balancing the Federal Budget: Trimming the Herds or Eating the Seed Corn?* Washington, DC: CQ Press, 2003.
_____. "Early Budgetary Reformers: Democracy, Efficiency, and Budge Reforms." *American Review of Public Administration* 24, no. 3 (1994): 22951.
_____. *The Politics of Public Budgeting: Getting and Spending, Borrowing and Balancing.* 6th ed. Washington, DC: CQ Press, 2010.
Ryu, Jay E. "Exploring the Factors for Budget Stability and Punctuations: A Preliminary Analysis of State Government Sub-Functional Expenditures." *Policy Studies Journal* 37, no. 3 (2009): 457–73.
Ryu, Jay E., Cynthia J. Bowling, Chunglae Cho, and Deil S. Wright. "Effects of Administrators' Aspirations, Political Principals' Priorities, and Interest Groups' Influence on State Agency Budget Requests." *Public Budgeting and Finance* 27, no. 2 (2007): 22–49.
_____. "Exploring Explanations of State Agency Budgets: Institutional Budget Actors or Exogenous Environment?" *Public Budgeting and Finance* 28, no. 3 (2008): 23–47.
SAS Institute Inc. *The GLIMMIX Procedure.* Cary, NC: SAS Institute Inc, 2005.
Schick, Allen. *Congress and Money: Budgeting, Spending and Taxing.* Washington, DC: The Urban Institute, 1980.
_____. *The Federal Budget: Politics, Policy, Process.* 3rd ed. Washington, DC: Brookings Institution Press, 2007.
_____. "Incremental Budgeting in a Decremental Age." *Policy Sciences* 16 (1983): 1–25.
Shafritz, Jay M., E. W. Russell, and Christopher P. Borick. *Introducing Public Administration.* 7th ed. Boston, MA: Longman, 2011.
Sharkansky, I. "Agency Requests, Gubernatorial Support and Budget Success in State Legislature." *The American Political Science Review* 62, no. 4 (1968): 1220–31.
Shepsle, Kenneth A., Robert P. Van Houweling, Samuel J. Abrams, and Peter C. Hanson. The Senate Electoral Cycle and Bicameral Appropriations Politics. *American Journal of Political Science* 53, no. 2 (2009): 343–59.
Simonsen, Bill. "Oregon: The Influence of Direct Democracy on Budget Outcomes." In *Budgeting in the States: Institutions, Processes, and Politics,* edited

by Edward J. Clynch, and Thomas P. Lauth, 119–36. Westport, CT: Praeger, 2007.

Snow, Douglas R., and Irene S. Rubin. "Illinois: Constitutional versus Negotiated Powers." In *Budgeting in the States: Institutions, Processes, and Politics*, edited by Edward J. Clynch, and Thomas P. Lauth, 103–18. Westport, CT: Praeger, 2007.

Thompson, Joel A. "Agency Request, Gubernatorial Support, and Budget Success in State Legislature Revisited." *The Journal of Politics* 49, no. 3 (1987): 756–79.

Thompson, Victor A. *Modern Organization.* New York: Knopf, 1961.

True, James L. *Historical Budget Records Converted to the Present Functional Categorization with Actual Results for FY 1947–2006.* Policy Agendas Project: Center for American Politics and Public Policy, 2007. http://www. policyagendas.org/codebooks/index.html (accessed March 19, 2008).

United States General Accounting Office. *Performance Budgeting: Past Initiatives Offer Insights for GPRA Implementation.* Washington, DC: U. S. GAO, 1997.

Wanat, John. "Bases of Budgetary Incrementalism." *The American Political Science Review* 68, no. 3 (1974): 1221–28.

West, William F. *Controlling the Bureaucracy: Institutional Constraints in Theory and Practice.* Armonk, NY: M.E. Sharpe, 1995.

West, William F., Eric Lindquist, and Katrina N. Mosher-Howe. NOAA's Resurrection of Program Budgeting: Déjà Vu All Over Again? *Public Administration Review* 69, no. 3 (2009): 435–47.

Whetten, David A. "Coping with Incompatible Expectations: An Integrated View of Role Conflict." *Administrative Science Quarterly* 23, no. 2 (1978): 254–71.

Whicker, Marcia Lynn. "South Carolina: The Demise of Legislative Dominance?" In *Governors, Legislatures, and Budgets: Diversity across the American States*, edited by Edward J. Clynch, and Thomas P. Lauth, 137–48. New York: Greenwood Press, 1991.

Wildavsky, Aaron. *Budgeting: A Comparative Theory of Budgetary Processes.* 2nd ed. New Brunswick, NJ: Transaction Publishers, 1997.

Wildavsky, Aaron, and Naomi Caiden. *The New Politics of the Budgetary Process.* 5th ed. New York: Pearson-Longman, 2004.

Yeary, Paula D. "Nevada: Budgeting at the Crossroads." In *Budgeting in the States: Institutions, Processes, and Politics*, edited by Edward J. Clynch, and Thomas P. Lauth, 173–88. Westport, CT: Praeger, 2007.

Index

Abney, Glenn, 155, 157–58
accountability, 51
agency acquisitiveness, 20–21
agency budget proposals, 65–66, 72, 94
Alt, James E., 56, 57, 58, 92, 97, 172, 175
analyzers, 51–52
Andrews, Rhys, 50, 54
appropriations, 82, 158–59, 176
Appropriations Committees, 94, 105–6, 107, 108, 110, 111, 113, 114, 145, 170
Assembly Budget Committee, 143
Atomic Energy Commission (AEC), 194–95
attention-driven choice, 3–4, 12, 29, 31, 71, 79, 96, 138
Authorization Committees, 105–6, 109, 110

Balanced Budget Act (1997), 124
balanced budget agreement (1998), 116
balanced budget requirements, 157, 159–62, 167
BAM (Budget and Management Division), 146
Barnard, Chester, 37–38, 39–40, 42
base line budget, 143
Baumgartner, Frank R., 24–25, 27, 28–29, 40–41, 69, 82
BCPs (Budget Change Proposals), 163
BEA (Budget Enforcement Act; 1990), 116, 117, 124, 134n1
bicameralism, 77
  see also partisan configurations
bipartisan confrontations, 8
  see also partisan configurations; partisan environments
BO (Budget Office), 162–63, 164
BOB (Bureau of Budget), 48, 72, 73, 147
Bohte, John, 55, 123
bonds
  obligations, 160
  proceeds from, 160
Briffault, Richard, 159, 161
BRO (Budget Review Office), 145
Brown, Jesse, 87
Brown, Mel, 153
Brownlow, Louis, 48
Brownlow Committee, 48–49
Budget and Accounting Act (1921), 72, 73
Budget and Management Division (BAM), 146
budget authorities, 66, 68–71, 73, 106, 125–26, 137
budget base, 18, 70, 93, 96, 104, 129, 131, 133, 136, 139
Budget Change Proposals (BCPs), 163
Budget Commission, 150–51
Budget Committees, 114
Budget Enforcement Act (BEA; 1990), 116, 117, 124, 134n1
budget environments, 71, 108, 129, 131
budget inertia
  budget authorities and, 121–22
  budgetary incrementalism and, 133
  centralization and, 59, 97, 99, 104, 177, 179
  incrementalism and, 60
  main budget actors and, 96
  programmed decision making and, 54
  unified governments and, 132
budget moderation, 70, 140
Budget of the United States Government, 66
Budget Office (BO), 162–63, 164

budget outcomes, 31
budget processes
  centralization of, 49. *see also* executive budgets
  national, 140–41
  state vs. national, 8–9
budget punctuations
  budget authorities and, 121–22, 125–26
  categorization and, 66–67
  causes of, 194
  CBO and, 133
  central capacity load and, 75
  centralization and, 6–7, 75, 93, 98, 103–4, 119–28, 127–28, 136
  cutoff points and, 82–83, 134n4
  decision makers and, 135–36
  definition of, 4
  disproportionate information-processing theory and, 98–99, 140
  divided governments and, 173–74
  elections and, 78
  environmental factors and, 45
  indicator lock and, 59
  partisan configurations and, 8, 79–80, 88–91, 96–97, 177
  probability of, 6
  reasons for, 31
  state, 162–77, 181–85, 184
  unified governments and, 173
  zone of, 71–72
budget reconciliation, 110, 117, 124
budget resolutions, 110, 112, 124
Budget Review Office (BRO), 145
budget stability
  budget authorities and, 121–22
  central capacity load and, 131, 177
  centralization and, 7, 75, 93–98, 99, 103, 129, 133–34, 136, 177–80
  characteristics of, 5–6
  cutoff points and, 83
  decision makers and, 30
  definition of, 3
  FTE and, 179
  incrementalism and, 60
  indicator lock and, 59
  partisan configurations and, 8, 79–80
  state, 181–85, 185
  unemployment rate and, 132
  zone of, 70
budgetary incrementalism, 71, 131, 133, 136, 138, 141, 177
budgeting by negotiation, 147–48, 169–70
Bupp, Irwin C., 194–95
Bureau of Budget (BOB), 48, 72, 73, 147
bureaucracies
  characteristics of, 36
  creation of, 33
  dysfunctions of, 54
  human capacities and, 36–39
bureaupathology, 33–34, 60
Bush, George W., 188, 191, 192, 193
Byrd rule, 124

California, 143–44, 159, 163
capacity load, 85–86, 96, 97
  see also central capacity load
carryover deficit, 161
categorization, 34, 66–67, 75
CBA. *see* Congressional Budget Act (CBA; 1974)
CBO. *see* Congressional Budget Office (CBO)
Census Bureau, 137
  central budget offices
  central capacity load and, 179
  collaboration and, 164
  executive budgets and, 72–73, 141
  information network and, 81
  institutional frictions and, 170
  main budget actors and, 94
  overview of, 6–9
  PART and, 193
  staffs of, 73–74, 75
  state, 135, 143, 151, 152, 153, 162, 163, 181, 190
central capacity load, 91–92, 123, 131–32, 165–66, 172–73, 177, 179
  see also capacity load
Central Limit Theorem, 25
centralization
  benefits from, 42, 64
  of budget processes, 49
  Gulick and, 48–49
  impact of, 2, 4–5
  information-processing capacity and, 74–75
  meanings of, 50–51
  partisan configurations and, 55–59
  prominence of, 47–48
  purpose of, 2, 4

centralization index, 6
Chiles, Lawton, 152
Clarke, Wes, 175
Clinton, Bill, 87, 115–17, 118
cognitive costs, 29
COLA (cost of living adjustment), 47
Coleman, John J., 58
collaboration, 2, 64
Committee on Administrative Management, 48
committee systems, 40–41, 77
  see also individual committees
complex formal organizations, 39–40
comprehensive review, 11, 16
computational rationality, 65
conformance, 33
Congressional Budget Act (CBA; 1974), 7, 106, 111, 112–13, 117, 122, 123–24, 143, 145
Congressional Budget and Impoundment Control Act (1974), 49, 105
Congressional Budget Office (CBO)
  budget punctuations and, 133
  centralization and, 136
  Congressional budget committees and, 109
  creation of, 7, 41, 122
  function of, 125–26
  main budget actors and, 131
  organization of, 120
  partisan configurations and, 58, 193
  role of, 113–19
  staffs of, 122–23, 126
  unified governments and, 131
congressional committee system, 40–41, 77
  see also individual committees
Connecticut, 144, 169
constitutions, state, 158–59
cooperation, 37–39
cost of living adjustment (COLA), 47
Council of Economic Advisers (CEA), 81
court cases, 158–59
cross-walking procedures, 189
cumulative pressure theory, 22

Davis, Otto, 18, 19, 22, 44, 194
"decision maker" models, 13–14
decision-making processes, individual, 14–15
defenders, 51–53, 54, 98, 104, 119, 123
deficit controls, 161, 167
Dempster, M.A., 18, 19, 22, 44, 194
Department of Commerce, 187, 192
Department of Education, 192
Department of Energy, 192
Department of Finance (DOF), 143–44, 163
Department of Health and Human Services (HHS), 192
Department of Housing and Urban Development (HUD), 192
Department of Labor, 192
DFM (Idaho Division of Financial Management), 142
disjointed incrementalism, 16–17
disproportionate information-processing theory
  attention-driven choice and, 12
  budget punctuations and, 98–99, 140–41, 194
  concepts of, 6, 59
  critiques of, 41–42
  decision makers and, 3–4, 43, 129, 135, 138
  dramatic budget changes and, 71, 133
  environmental factors and, 20, 45
  incrementalism and, 19
  information-processing capacity and, 93
  institutional frictions and, 31
  main budget actors and, 21
  as model, 9
  overview of, 24–30
  selective attention and, 15
divided governments
  budget environments and, 129, 131
  budget punctuations and, 173–74
  CBO and, 136
  central capacity load and, 131
  centralization and, 133
  federal grants and, 174–75
  institutional frictions and, 170
  PART and, 193
  political change and, 132
  state, 156–57, 169
  see also split branch governments; split legislature governments
Division of Budget (DOB), 144–45, 164
division of labor, 40–41, 49

Division of Planning and Budgeting (DPB), 151–52
DOB (Division of Budget), 144–45, 164
DOF (Department of Finance), 143–44, 163
domestic discretionary subfunctions, 67
DPB (Division of Planning and Budgeting), 151–52
dramatic budget changes, 71, 82–83, 133, 138
dynamic scoring, 116–17, 119, 127
see also scoring

economic model, 13–14
Edgar, Jim, 147–48
elections, 76–78, 79, 98, 100
emergency budgets, 27–28, 194
entitlement programs, 92–93, 106
environmental factors, 20, 21, 22, 27, 28, 44, 45
Environmental Protection Agency (EPA), 192
EPA (Environmental Protection Agency), 192
episodic policy adjustments, 29
executive branch, 120
see also divided governments; partisan configurations; unified governments
executive budgets, 65, 72–75, 103–4, 105, 113–14, 115, 118–19, 136–37, 138, 141–48, 165
Executive Reorganization (1972), 144
executives, decision-making processes and, 40

Fenno, Richard, Jr., 107
filibuster, 111
Finance Committees, 114
financial subfunctions, 67
fiscal balance, 56
Florida, 151–52, 156, 159, 170
fragmentation, 105
fragmentation of analysis, 17
functional budget classification, 67–68

Gaebler, Ted, 35
GBO (Governor's Budget Office), 150
Georgia, 144, 147, 157–58, 170
Gilmour, J.B., 190–91, 192
goal displacement, 60, 63
GOBP (Governor's Office of Budget and Planning), 149–50, 164
Goldin, Dan, 87
Government Performance and Results Act (GPRA; 1993), 10, 152, 188
governors, partisan configurations and, 56–58
see also divided governments; partisan configurations; unified governments
Governor's Budget Office (GBO), 150
Governor's Office of Budget and Planning (GOBP), 149–50, 164
GPRA (Government Performance and Results Act; 1993), 10, 152, 188
GPRA Modernization Act of 2010, 10
Gramm-Rudman-Hollings (GRH), 87, 124
GRH (Gramm-Rudman-Hollings), 87, 124
Gulick, Luther, 36, 48–49, 55, 75, 123

Hammond, Thomas H., 195
healthcare reform, 115, 118
heuristic problem solving, 46
HHS (Department of Health and Human Services), 192
hierarchical systems/authority, 38–39, 50–51, 52, 136
homeland security budgets, 194
horizontal specialization, 38–39
House Appropriations Committee, 114, 145, 170
see also appropriations; Appropriations Committees
House Budget Committee (HBC), 107–10, 111–12, 114, 123–24
House Revenue Committee, 145
House Ways and Means Committee, 105, 150–51
HUD (Department of Housing and Urban Development), 192
human decision-making process, overview of, 11

Idaho, 142–43
Idaho Division of Financial Management (DFM), 142
Illinois, 147–48, 169
impersonality, 34

income security programs, 79, 80, 92
incremental perspectives, 18
incrementalism
  assertions of, 31
  budget inertia and, 60
  budget stability and, 59, 93
  critiques of, 15, 18–19, 27
  decision makers and, 3, 129
  disproportionate information-processing theory and, 24
  environmental factors and, 44
  main budget actors and, 43
  overview of, 11–12, 16–21
  predictions of, 29–30
  summary of, 19–21
indicator lock, 3–4, 12, 30, 31, 59, 79, 86, 138
individual decision makers, 40
inducements-contributions exchange model, 38
information costs, 29, 42
information-processing systems, human beings and, 14
institutional frictions
  attention-driven choice and, 12, 71
  balanced budget requirements and, 161–62
  budget inertia and, 31
  budget punctuations and, 31, 75, 84–85, 93
  CBO and, 133–34
  centralization and, 54–55, 96–97, 103–4, 135–36, 137, 172, 180
  divided governments and, 170
  executive budgets and, 73
  FTE and, 166
  indicator lock and, 59, 86
  information processing and, 29–30
  macrobudgeting and, 110, 124
  national budget process and, 141
  nonprogrammed decision making and, 60
  overview of, 75–80
  partisan configurations and, 58, 99
  politics-induced, 78
  split legislature governments and, 92
  staffs and, 132
  state budgets and, 148, 163, 165, 170
  studies and, 64–65
  unified governments and, 174
  vetoes and, 155–56, 158, 159
institutional memory, 81, 85, 94, 162
interchamber politics, 77–78
intergovernmental aid system, 160–61

JFAC (Joint Financial Appropriations Committee), 142–43
JLBC (Joint Legislative Budget Committee), 150
Joint Financial Appropriations Committee (JFAC), 142–43
Joint Legislative Budget Committee (JLBC), 150
Jones, Bryan D., 24–25, 27, 28–29, 40–41, 69, 79, 82

Kentucky, 145–46, 169, 170
Knott, Jack H., 195

LAB (Legislative Audit Bureau), 146
Larsen, Heather A., 29, 79
Lauth, Thomas P., 155, 157–58
LBB (Legislative Budget Board), 149–50, 164
LBO (Legislative Budget Office), 142, 144, 170
Lee, Robert D., Jr., 158
Legislative Audit Bureau (LAB), 146
Legislative Budget Board (LBB), 149–50, 164
Legislative Budget Book, 142
Legislative Budget Commission, 152
Legislative Budget Office (LBO), 142, 144, 170
legislative budgets, state, 148–53
legislative professionalization, 181–85
legislatures, partisan configurations and, 56–58
  see also divided governments; partisan configurations; unified governments
LeLoup, Lance T., 107, 114, 122
Lewis, D.E., 190–91, 192
Lindblom, Charles, 16–18, 23, 25, 54, 93
Lindquist, Eric, 187, 189, 190
line agencies, 135
Line Item Veto Act (1996), 124
  see also vetoes
lobbyists, 166, 179
Louisiana, 156
Lowry, Robert C., 56, 57, 58, 92, 97, 172, 175

macrobudgeting, 105–14, 117, 120, 124
macrofunctions, 67–68, 120
main budget actors
  aspirations of, 44
  budget authorities and, 137
  budget base and, 129, 133
  budget choices and, 131
  centralization and, 177
  conflict and, 43
  environmental factors and, 21, 27, 45
  governors and, 179
  influence of, 97
  relationships between, 94, 96
  search activities of, 24
  search strategies and, 54
  Social Security and, 47
  unified governments and, 132
maintenance of current operations (MCO), 142
mandatory subfunctions, 67
market crisis, 9–10
MCO (maintenance of current operations), 142
Medicaid, 161
Medicare, 118
Meier, Kenneth J., 55, 123
Member Initiative Grants, 148
memory, 14–16
  see also institutional memory
Merriam, Charles, 48
Merton, Robert K., 33
Michigan, 160
Miles, Raymond E., 50, 51
Miller, Zell, 157
Mississippi, 150
moderate budget changes, 70–71, 121, 122, 140
monopolistic control, 63
Mortensen, Peter B., 194
Mosher-Howe, Katrina N., 187, 189, 190
Moynihan, Donald P., 51

NASA, 87
Natchez, Peter B., 194–95
National Oceanic and Atmospheric Administration (NOAA), 187–90
National Performance Review (NPR), 82
national security subfunctions, 68
negotiation. *see* budgeting by negotiation
neutrality, 115–17, 118–19
Nevada, 147, 162–63, 164
New Public Management (NPM) movements, 34–35
New York, 144–45, 160, 164, 169
Nixon, Richard, 106
NOAA (National Oceanic and Atmospheric Administration), 187–90
nonprogrammed decision making, 45–46, 47, 54, 60
NPM (New Public Management) movements, 34–35
NPR (National Performance Review), 82

OFA (Office of Fiscal Analysis), 144
Office of Fiscal Analysis (OFA), 144
Office of Legislative Analyst (OLA), 143–44, 163
Office of Legislative Fiscal Analyst (OLFA), 153
Office of Management and Budget (OMB)
  budget authorities and, 73, 78
  budget punctuations and, 103
  budget stability and, 96
  centralization and, 82
  centralization index and, 6
  committees and, 41
  functional budget classification and, 67–68
  information network and, 81
  institutional frictions and, 131
  institutional memory and, 162
  neutrality of, 7–8
  PART and, 190–93
  politicization of, 86–88, 90, 104
  renaming of, 72, 73
  scoring and, 118–19
  staffs of, 74, 85–86, 97, 100
  subfunctional authorities and, 85, 100, 120
  subfunctions of, 80
  US budget and, 66
Office of Planning and Budget (OPB), 144, 152, 157, 170
Office of Policy and Management (OPM), 144, 145
Office of Program Analysis and Evaluation, 188
Office of Program Planning and Integration, 188, 189

Office of State Budget (OSB), 151
Oklahoma, 159
OLA (Office of Legislative Analyst), 143–44, 163
Old Age and Survivors Insurance, 28
OLFA (Office of Legislative Fiscal Analyst), 153
OMB. *see* Office of Management and Budget (OMB)
OMB 2000, 82
OPB (Office of Planning and Budget), 144, 152, 157, 170
OPM (Office of Policy and Management), 144, 145
optimizing, 43
orderly thinking, 46
Oregon, 146–47
organizational arrangements, 40
organizational decision-making process, 42–43
organizational growth, 39
organizational performance, 50
organizational size, 76
OSB (Office of State Budget), 151
Osborne, David, 35
outcome incrementalism, 18, 22, 28

Padgett, John F., 22–23
Pandey, Sanjay K., 51
PART. *see* Program Assessment Rating Tool (PART)
participation in decision making, 50, 52–53
partisan analysis, 17, 54–55
partisan configurations
  108th Congress and, 193
  budget inertia and, 129
  budget punctuations and, 126–28, 171, 177–78
  budget stability and, 130
  capacity load and, 97
  centralization and, 59, 60, 104, 133, 195
  committee systems and, 111–12
  congressional budget process and, 119
  impact of, 131
  interbranch disparity and, 156
  legislative models and, 184–85
  lobbyists and, 179
  macrobudget process and, 123
partisan configurations (*continued*)
  OMB and, 88
  overview of, 55–59
  state governments and, 136, 152–53, 166, 168–69, 170
partisan environments
  centralization and, 5, 7–8, 103
  HBC and, 108–9
  mutual adjustment and, 17
  performance budgeting systems and, 10
  see also partisan configurations; politics
partisan fragmentation, 112–13
Pay-as-you-go (PAYGO), 115, 116, 117, 124
PAYGO (Pay-as-you-go), 115, 116, 117, 124
per capita employee, 132
per capita IGR revenue, 167, 174–75, 179
per capita income, 78–79, 98, 100, 132, 167, 175
perceptions of effectiveness, 51
performance budgeting systems, 9–10, 187, 190, 191
performance evaluation, 192
performance gap, 45–46
planning, programming, budgeting, and execution systems (PPBES), 188–90
planning and performance budgeting (PPB), 149, 164
points of order, 111
policy gridlock, 58
political environments, 2, 187, 190, 192
political neutrality, 115–17, 118–19
politics
  centralization and, 147
  incrementalism and, 17
  see also partisan configurations; partisan environments
pork-barrel appropriations, 154, 157, 169
PPB (planning and performance budgeting), 149, 164
PPBES (planning, programming, budgeting, and execution systems), 188–90
prescription drug benefits, 118
Presidents' budgets. *see* executive budgets
President's Management Council, 191

private market system, 79
problem space, defining, 16
problem-solving processes, 14–15
process incrementalism, 18, 22, 23
productivity, 55
Program Assessment Rating Tool (PART), 73, 188, 190–92, 193
program shift parameters, 22
programmed decision making, 43–44, 47, 54, 60, 96
Progressive reformers, 72
proportionate information processing, 25–26, 29
prospectors, 51–53
psychological model, 13
public administration, principles of, 39
punctuated equilibrium theory, 19

rational updating, 24–25
reactors, 52–54, 96
Reagan, Ronald, 34, 116
Reese, Catherine C., 155–56
reform initiatives, 196
REGO (reinventing government) movement, 35
Reinventing Government (Osborne and Gaebler), 35
Reischauer, Robert, 118
Reorganization Act (1939), 48
representation, 105, 120
Revenue Projection Committee, 142–43
Robinson, Scott E., 74, 75, 76, 83, 91, 97, 121, 166, 179
Roosevelt, Franklin D., 48
Rosenthal, Alan, 58
Rubin, Irene, 72, 87, 117, 119, 147
Ryu, Jay E., 44, 80, 161

satisficing, 12–16, 17, 43
SBC. *see* Senate Budget Committee (SBC)
SBCB (State Budget and Control Board), 151
Schick, Allen, 112, 113, 118
scoring, 115, 116–17, 118, 119, 125–26, 127
search costs, 42
selective attention, 15, 29, 41, 47
Senate Appropriations Committee, 107, 108, 170
  see also appropriations; Appropriations Committees
Senate Budget and Fiscal Review Committee, 143
Senate Budget Committee (SBC), 107–10, 111–12, 114, 116, 123–24, 143
Senate Budget Office, 170
Senate Finance Committee, 105, 150–51
sequential searches, 11, 16, 23
serial judgment, 21–24
Sharkansky, I., 20–21
Shepsle, Kenneth A., 76–77
shift points, 22
Simon, Herbert, 12–13, 14, 16, 17, 37–39, 42–43, 45, 46–47, 49, 60
simple formal organizations, 39–40
simple incremental analysis, 16–17
simulations, 46
Snow, Charles C., 50, 51, 147
Social Security Act (1933), 28
Social Security benefits, 47, 54, 194
sociological model, 13
South Carolina, 150–51
span of control, 55, 75, 123
special funds, 159–60
split branch governments
  budget punctuations and, 88–90, 96–97
  budget stability and, 95, 98
  CBO and, 119, 127
  central capacity load and, 92
  centralization and, 172, 177, 179
  description of, 56–57
  fiscal adjustment and, 58
  per capita income and, 175
split legislature governments
  budget punctuations and, 88–90
  budget stability and, 95
  centralization and, 172, 179
  description of, 57–58
  institutional frictions and, 92
  OMB staffs and, 97
  vetoes and, 175–76
standing, concept of, 158
state asset sales, 160
State Budget and Control Board (SBCB), 151
state budget outcomes, 137–41

state budget processes, 8–9
  see also individual states
state subfunctional expenditures, 137, 138, 139, 140, 165–66, 181–82
stimuli, 14–15, 38
strategic analysis, 18, 23, 25
strategic stance of organizations, types of, 51–53
sudden budget increases, emergencies and, 27–28, 194
sudden dramatic changes, 29, 31
Sulkin, Tracy, 29, 79

Taft conservatives, 72, 136
tax cuts, 116
term limits, 161
Texas, 149–50, 164
Thompson, Joel A., 20–21
Thompson, Victor A., 33
transaction costs, 29, 42, 58, 91
True, James L., 28, 66
Truman, Harry S., 28

unemployment rate, 79, 80, 86, 92–93, 100, 132
unified governments
  budget inertia and, 179–80
  budget punctuations and, 88–90, 96–97, 170, 173
  budget stability and, 95, 98, 129, 134
  CBO and, 127
  centralization and, 60, 104, 131, 172, 177
  entitlement programs and, 93
  federal grants and, 175
unified governments (*continued*)
  fiscal adjustment and, 58, 91
  information-processing capacity and, 99
  main budget actors and, 98
  political change and, 132, 174
  state governments and, 136
Utah, 152–53, 174

Vanna White amendment, 146
variables, description of, 100, 182–83
Vermont, 159
Veterans Affairs, 87
vetoes
  gubernatorial, 145
  imbalances induced by, 56
  institutional frictions and, 158, 159
  item-veto, 57–58, 153–59, 166–67
  Line Item Veto Act (1996), 124
  line-item veto power, 137
  partial veto authority, 146
  points, 110, 131, 132
  split legislature governments and, 175–76

Washington (state), 158
Ways and Means Committees, 105, 107, 114, 150–51
West, William F., 187, 189, 190
Wildavsky, Aaron, 18, 19, 22, 44, 194
Wisconsin, 146, 155
workload, 55, 104, 126

ZBB (Zero Base Budgeting), 149, 152
Zero Base Budgeting (ZBB), 149, 152

For Product Safety Concerns and Information please contact our EU representative GPSR@taylorandfrancis.com Taylor & Francis Verlag GmbH, Kaufingerstraße 24, 80331 München, Germany